SALAH

SALAH

A Believer's Ascension to the Heavens

M. FETHULLAH GÜLEN

قَدْ أَفْلَحَ الْمُؤْمِنُونَ ۝ الَّذِينَ هُمْ فِي صَلَاتِهِمْ خَاشِعُونَ

*Certainly, the faithful have attained salvation,
those who are humble in their prayers...*

al-Mu'minun (23:1-2)

Copyright © 2025 by Tughra Books
28 27 26 25   1 2 3 4

All rights reserved. No part of this book may be reproduced or transmitted in any form or by any means, electronic or mechanical, including photocopying, recording or by any information storage and retrieval system without permission in writing from the Publisher.

Published by Tughra Books
335 Clifton Ave.
Clifton, NJ, 07011, USA
www.tughrabooks.com

ISBN
Paperback: 979-8-89729-000-0
Ebook: 979-8-89729-001-7

Library of Congress Cataloging-in-Publication Data

Names: Gülen, Fethullah, author. | Altay, Korkut, translator. | Çetin, Muhammed, editor. | Khan, Sana Imtiaz, editor. | Ekşili, Lyndsey, editor.
Title: Salah : a believer's ascension to the heavens / M. Fethullah Gülen ; translated and edited by Korkut Altay, Muhammed Çetin, Sana Khan, Lyndsey Ekşili.
Other titles: Miraç Enginlikli Ibadet Namaz. English
Description: Clifton, NJ, USA : Tughra Books, [2025] | Includes index. | Text in English. Translation from Turkish.
Identifiers: LCCN 2025001979 (print) | LCCN 2025001980 (ebook) | ISBN 9798897290000 (paperback) | ISBN 9798897290017 (ebook)
Subjects: LCSH: Prayer--Islam. | Islam--Customs and practices.
Classification: LCC BP184.3 .G85513 2025 (print) | LCC BP184.3 (ebook) | DDC 297.3/82--dc23/eng/20250207
LC record available at https://lccn.loc.gov/2025001979
LC ebook record available at https://lccn.loc.gov/2025001980

Printed in Canada

Contents

Introduction xiii

THE ESSENCE OF ISLAM 1

SALAH 25

PREPARATION FOR SALAH 121

THE COMPONENTS OF SALAH AND THEIR WISDOM 151

PRAYER TIMES 183

THE FRUITS OF SALAH 205

THE FRIDAY PRAYER 231

NAFILA PRAYERS 249

SOME SUPPLICATIONS TO BE OFFERED DURING SALAH 273

REFLECTIONS ON SALAH 283

Index 293

Extended Contents

Chapter 1
The Essence of Islam 1

1. The definition of Islam 1
2. The *shahadah* and Islam 4
3. The essence and meaning of "*la ilaha illa'llah*" 5
   When faith enters the heart 7
4. Islam – what all the Prophets taught 9
5. Obedience to the Prophetic message 12
6. The last Prophet 15
7. Faith, actions, and worship 17
   a. Faith and actions 17
   b. Reflections on worship 20

Chapter 2
Salah 25

1. The importance of salah 25
   a. The first worship to be questioned about 29
   b. The identical sibling of *iman* 32
   c. The index of all acts of worship 32
   d. Preparation for salah 37
   e. The reward of prayer 39
2. Salah as a form of worship 44
   a. *Ta'abbudi* worship 44
   b. Worshipping without expecting anything in return 47
   c. *Shirk* and *riya* in worship 49
   Minor shirk: Riya (affectation) 51
   Doing unusual actions in salah 54
   d. The consciousness of servitude in worship 55
3. Observing salah mindfully 56
   a. The true meaning of salah 59
   b. Feeling salah profoundly 62
   c. Performing salah with awe (*hashyat*) and reverence ... 66

    d. Some crucial points to consider about salah 71
    e. Concentration in salah... 72
    f. As if your last prayer 75
    g. The three levels of salah 76
    h. Salah lovers... 77
    i. One hundred *rak'ahs* of salah everyday 79
4. The seeds of salah 82
    Tafakkur in salah.. 84
5. *Dhikr* and *tawbah* 88
6. Salah and refinement of the heart 91
7. The salah of the Messenger of God 96
8. Diseases that inflict salah 101
    a. The *waswasa* (evil suggestions) of Satan 101
    b. Satan's stealing from salah 103
    c. Laziness for salah... 104
    d. Weariness of worship 108
    Salah that yields nothing but tiredness............................ 109
    A memory and the importance of being careful in salah. 111
9. Salah and communicating the message of God 112
    Salah's influence and a person's relationship with God 114
    The three conditions for being a paragon of salah 115
10. The function of mosques... 118

Chapter 3
PREPARATION FOR SALAH 121

1. Ablution (*wudu*) 121
    The first exhortation on the way to salah......................... 122
    Observing salah mindfully.. 124
    Detaching oneself from other engagements..................... 127
    a. Cleaning of the teeth during ablution......................... 128
    b. The prayers recited during ablution 130
    Taking ablution properly despite difficulties.................... 132
    Worship: too much or too little?...................................... 135
    c. Blessings completed with ablution 138
    d. Degrees of purification in salah................................... 140

2. The *adhan* – The call to payer 143
3. *Sunnah* prayers 146
4. *Iqamah* 148

Chapter 4
THE COMPONENTS OF SALAH AND THEIR WISDOM 151

1. Conditions of prayer 152
    a. Elimination of *hadath* 152
    b. Purification from *najasah* 153
    c. *Satr al-awrah* – covering the body 153
    d. *Istiqbal al-qiblah* – turning to the *qiblah* 154
    e. Prayer times 156
    f. Intention 156
    Intention is the spirit of our deeds 158
2. The pillars of salah 161
    a. The opening *takbir* 161
    b. *Qiyam* – standing 162
    c. *Qiraat* — Qur'an recitation 163
    d. *Ruku'* 167
    e. Prostration 168
    f. Sitting in *tashahhud* and *tahiyyat* 171
3. Complementary components for salah 174
    a. *Ta'dil al-arkan* inwardly and outwardly 174
    b. Salah in congregation 179

Chapter 5
PRAYER TIMES 183

1. Salah observed at five different times 185
    a. The five daily prayers in the Qur'an 185
    b. The five daily prayers in hadith 189
2. The time of daily prayers, the Qur'an, and the universe 192
    a. The time of *fajr* 196
    b. The time of *dhuhr* 197
    c. The time of *asr* 198

d. The time of *maghrib* 199
e. The time of *isha* 200
f. The darkness of the night and *tahajjud* 202

Chapter 6
THE FRUITS OF SALAH 205

1. The fruits of salah regarding the individual 205
   a. Giving peace and relief to the heart 205
   Inner peace and presence of heart 209
   b. Attaining integrity with feelings 212
   c. Accepting the Divine call 214
   d. Speaking with the Lord 216
   e. Preventing illicit behaviors 217
   f. A reminder of the essentials of faith 219
   g. Expiating sins 222
   h. Coming closer to God 222
2. The fruits of salah for society 226
   a. Maintaining equality among people 227
   b. Discipline in both individual and societal levels 228
   c. Generosity 229

Chapter 7
THE FRIDAY PRAYER 231

1. Significance of the Friday Prayer 231
2. The Friday Prayer encompasses comprehensive worship . 238
3. Conditions of the Friday prayer 239
4. The first Friday Prayer ever 243
5. The time when prayers are responded to on Fridays 245

Chapter 8
NAFILA PRAYERS 249

1. The virtue of *nafila* prayers 249
   a. Making up for the obligatory prayers 249

    b. A means to gain closeness to God..................................250
    c. A means to rise spiritually..251
2. Two important *nafila* prayers: *tahajjud* and *hajah*............256
    a. *Tahajjud* 256
    b. The salah of *hajah* (need) and its supplication 265

Chapter 9
SOME SUPPLICATIONS TO BE OFFERED DURING SALAH   273

1. Supplications during *ruku'* (bowing)..............................273
2. While rising from *ruku'*..274
3. During *sajdah* (prostration)..275
4. When sitting between two prostrations 277
5. During sitting (*tashahhud*)..277
6. Verses of the Qur'an which can be recited as supplication at any phase of salah...279
7. Some prayers from the Prophet ﷺ 280

REFLECTIONS ON SALAH   283

Index   293

Introduction

Prayer is an essential part of a Muslim's life. While a believer can pray and offer their devotions any time and any where they like, Islamic tradition prescribes a specific form of prayer to be performed at five different times of the day. It is a celebratory act of submission in which believers align themselves with all other creation by offering their praise and gratitude to God, the Merciful, the Compassionate, as they stand, bow, and prostrate in propriety. These daily prayers are called salah, and the book in your hands is an all-comprehensive exploration of this spiritual act by one of the leading Muslim scholars of our time. The focus in this book is more on the spiritual aspect of salah, rather than its formulaic details which can be easily found in many other manuals.

Salah can be offered in any clean space, whether at home or at work or in a mosque. It is performed either individually or collectively in congregation. Congregational worship, especially in the mosque, has special merit and is much rewarded.

Salah is one of the five pillars of Islam. It is the main pole that holds the religion, and the essence of worship. It is not only a means of bringing the person closer to God; salah per se is an act of coming closer to God. Bearing utmost importance for believers, it is therefore not a task to be remiss about as we run from one worldly pursuit to another. One is expected to regulate one's daily life so as not to neglect salah for the sake of mundane matters. It is therefore not proper to perform salah hurriedly, either.

Salah is considered to be a person's own ascension into heavenly realms (*mi'raj*). It is the most effective way to meet and converse with the Creator directly, without any need for intercession. Moreover, it grants access to the company and blessings of all the Prophets. Depending on the depth of one's consciousness and sincerity, the practice of performing the five daily prayers elevates and uplifts the individual even further.

During salah, worshippers may experience a profound sense of humility, love, enthusiasm, and fervor in the presence of God. At times, one may feel as if they are standing in prayer alongside the entire Muslim ummah behind the Messenger of God, Muhammad, peace be upon him ﷺ. Other times, they may feel among the ranks of angels or in prostration beneath the Sublime Throne (*Arsh*). The prerequisite for such experiences is to recognize salah as one's personal ascent to God and the Heavenly realms, akin to a personal emulation of the *Mi'raj* (ascension) of Prophet Muhammad ﷺ.

Muslims believe that each salah is an occasion or a means of *mi'raj*. Therefore, they are expected to go the extra mile with each salah and fulfill their *mi'raj*, even though the experience they have might feel different each time. Each believer should try to be in full resonance with the salah so much so that every "cord" of their heart must sound like a "heartstring" during the prayer, and the prayer of each is seen exemplary by others. A salah in which prostration (*sujud*) transforms into an exhilarating experience believers crave endlessly, and supplications become a nourishment they never tire of. Their bowing (*ruku'*) turns into a full prayer by itself, and recitations evolve into a harmonious flow of articulate and living words. The verse "He sees you when you rise (in the prayer) as well as your strenuous efforts in prostration among those who prostrate," (ash-Shuara 26:218-219) describes how the Messenger of God Muhammad ﷺ observed salah, but also exemplifies and teaches us the way and manner in which we should observe it.

Surely, it is not possible for our salah to equate with that of a Prophet in terms of form or meaning – we cannot feel exactly as he did. However, this does not mean that we should not pursue his path in this matter. In one Prophetic saying, what is known as Hadith Jibril, Prophet Muhammad ﷺ explains the concept of *ihsan* (perfect goodness) as "to worship as if you see Allah," and adds that "even though you do not see

Him, indeed He sees you."¹ When salah is observed with such profound consciousness, it will yield the expected and desired effects.

Likewise, the Messenger of God ﷺ stated, إِذَا قُمْتَ فِي صَلَاتِكَ فَصَلِّ صَلَاةَ مُوَدِّعٍ "Pray as if you are saying farewell."² This means salah is to be observed as if it were the last prayer in this life. Consider the scenario of a person nearing the end of their life, with only enough time to perform salah once more. Surely, they would strive to observe it meticulously, with utmost care and concentration. Indeed, this should be the way we all approach our prayers.

Proper observance of salah should not be understood narrowly as meeting the minimum requirements of validity mentioned in reference books of *fiqh*. Salah's meaning should be taken in a much wider sense and include all of its material and spiritual aspects. If salah is thoroughly observed, it wipes away and cleanses sins, as is stated in many hadiths. Because, during salah, asking for forgiveness and *tawbah* (turning to God; repentance) happen to be what a beliver must be conscious of. Repentance permeates all components of salah so much that one cannot help but think of them as one single entity. Surely, salah does not mean only repentance. However, when a believer stands before God in full devotion, then that salah can fertilize some consciousness of *tawbah* in his or her soul, given that they observe it properly.

> Surely, the Prayer restrains from all that is indecent and shameful, and all that is evil. (al-Ankabut 29:45)

For salah to have an impact as described in the verse, believers must first and foremost feel the burden of their sins deep in their soul – such a remorse might serve as an initial appeal for forgiveness. Moreover, if the person performs the principles (*rukn – arkan*, plural) of salah properly, with ease, accurately, not in haste, but in full concentration and devotion, with proper recitation as extended as it can be, spending enough time during standing (*qiyam*), bowing (*ruku'*) and prostration (*sujud*), they will definitely experience far more distinct dimensions in each and every stage of salah.

---

1   Bukhari, Iman 37, Tafsir al-Surah (31)2; Muslim, Iman 5, 7.

2   Ibn Majah, Zuhd 15; Ibn Hanbal, *Musnad* 5/412.

Any deviation in one of these principles may lead a person to perform salah unmindfully.[3] Accordingly, salah is meant to call the person to become *insan al-kamil* (perfected soul, or universal human, who offers the worship of the entire creation to God). Believers should review their salah from this perspective and endeavor to feel the true meaning of the standing, bowing, and prostration deep in their soul.

In addition to a having sense of awe and obedience, observing salah in accordance with its conditions and requirements is of paramount importance. One should not regard this as a trivial matter, as there exists a profound connection between the outward form of salah and its essence. However, it is erroneous to solely focus on the external aspects. Salah must be observed not only with the correct form but also in alignment with its intrinsic meaning and essence.

In short, the salah holds a significant place in worship. Considering the meanings it embodies, salah can rightly be termed, "the essence of worship." Therefore, the Companions of the Prophet regarded those who did not observe salah as *munafiqun* (hypocrites) and scholars commonly cited abandoning the salah as an example of hypocrisy in deeds.

Dismissing, neglecting, and delaying salah as unimportant can lead the person to do the same for their faith one day. Failing to observe salah signifies experiencing one of the greatest losses in life. Therefore, it is never enough to insist on salah.

---

[3] Some hadiths make comparisons of people observing salah unmindfully to animals: "Does he who raises up his head before the imam at bowing and prostration not fear that Allah will make his head like that of a donkey or make his appearance similar to that of donkey (in the Day of Judgment)" Regarding hurried prostration, the Prophet advised believers against resembling a crow pecking at food. Similarly, concerning improper sitting positions, he cautioned against imitating mares and sitting like dogs on the ground. (Bukhari, Adhan 53; Muslim, Siyam 114, 115; Abu Dawud, Salah 147; Nasai, Adhan 55; Ibn Hanbal, Musnad, 2/311; at-Tayalisi, Musnad, p.338)

Chapter 1

The Essence of Islam

1. The definition of Islam

Derived from the Arabic root "*s–l–m*," the word "Islam" has meanings like submission, obedience, leading to deliverance, and rendering sound and stainless. In the definitions he made in different instances, the Messenger of God ﷺ, peace be upon him, rather focused on the comprehensive meaning of Islam and brought to the fore what it has come to mean in religious scholarship.

The hadith Jibril (also known as the Hadith of Gabriel) is found in almost all the essential books of hadith. In that hadith, in the words of Umar, the second Caliph, the Messenger of God ﷺ gives a concise definition of Islam:

> I was sitting near the Messenger of God ﷺ. Suddenly a man emerged; his clothes were pure white and his hair was dark. There were no signs of traveling on him. Moreover, none of us knew him. He came and sat before the Messenger of God ﷺ, his knees against the Prophet's knees. He respectfully placed his hands on his knees and said, "O Muhammad, tell me about Islam."

> The Prophet ﷺ explained Islam thus: "Islam is to testify there is no God but Allah and Muhammad is the Messenger of Allah, to establish *salah* (prayer), to give *zakat* (charity), to fast the month of Ramadan, and to perform pilgrimage to the House if you can make the journey."

The stranger confirmed: "You have spoken the truth." (Umar whose attention was caught by this point adds that they were surprised by the fact that the stranger both asked a question and then confirmed the answer). Then he said, "Tell me about *iman* [belief]?"

The Prophet replied: "It is to believe in Allah, His angels, His Scriptures, His Prophets, the Day of Judgment, and the Divine Destiny—that both good and evil are from Allah."

The stranger confirmed again: "You have spoken the truth." Then he said, "Tell me about *ihsan* [perfect goodness]?"

The Prophet said: "*Ihsan* is to worship as if you see Him; even though you cannot see Him, He does see you."

Stranger: "Then inform me about the Hour (Doomsday)?"

The Prophet said, "The one asked does not know more than the one asking."

Stranger: "What are the signs of the Hour?"

The Prophet replied: "You see that slave-girl gives birth to her master and that barefoot, (half-)naked, poor camel shepherds compete at constructing higher buildings."

After these words the stranger left. I remained there for quite some time. The Prophet ﷺ said, "O Umar! Do you know who he was?" I said, "Allah and His Messenger know better." Upon this, the Messenger of God stated: "He was Jibril (Gabriel), peace be upon him. He came to teach you your religion."[1]

As evident from this hadith, three significant matters are highlighted. These include the six articles of *iman*/faith, the five pillars of Islam, and the consciousness of *ihsan*, which entails observing the aforementioned with mindfulness and inner illumination. It is incumbent upon every responsible Muslim to adhere to these principles to the best of their ability.

---

1 Muslim, Iman 5, 7; Bukhari, Iman 37, Tafsir al-Surah (31) 2.

Another description of "Islam" is in the following hadith reported by Talha ibn Ubaydullah, a Companion of the Messenger of God:

> One day, a person from the people of Najid came. His hair was untidy. We did hear his voice but could not understand what he was saying. When he came very close, we understood that he was asking questions about Islam. The Prophet told him to observe the five Daily Prayers night and day, then the man asked again: "Do I have any liabilities (of salah) other than these five?"
>
> Prophet: "No, but you observe *nawafil*/voluntary prayers if you wish," and added: "There is also the Ramadan fasting."
>
> Man: "Is there fasting other than that?"
>
> Prophet: "No, but you observe *nawafil*/voluntary fasting if you wish."
>
> Prophet also mentioned *zakat* to him. The man asked: "Do I have liability other than *zakat*?"
>
> Prophet: "No, but you can give *nawafil* alms."
>
> The man raised to leave and said the following: "By Allah! I will neither do less nor more than this."
>
> The Prophet stated, "If he keeps his promise, he will go to Paradise."[2]

Once more, in this and similar hadiths, the Messenger of God provided a concise overview of Islam by mentioning its fundamental pillars, such as the *shahadah, salah, zakat, sawm* (fasting), and Hajj (the Pilgrimage to Mecca). Looking at the Qur'an as a whole and considering them in the light of these hadiths, one can see Islam with all of its aspects – from belief to good character – described in them. All along, scholars dealt with these matters separately and they grouped topics related to Islam under the headings of *itiqad* (belief), *ibadah* (worship), *muamalat* (dealings), and *uqubat* (penal code). For this reason, with the word "Islam" we see a whole that encapsulates life with its entirety from belief to character development, from mannerliness to administration and politics. All of these aspects of Islam were taught to us by the Messenger of God, Muhammad ﷺ, and we aspire nothing but loyalty to his path.

---

2   Bukhari, Iman 34; Shahadat 26; Muslim, Iman 8.

2. The *shahadah* and Islam

The *shahadah* (the Muslim profession of faith) is one of the five essential pillars of Islam. In other words, the first condition of Islam is the word of testimony expressed as, "*Ash-hadu an la ilaha illa'llah, wa ash-hadu anna Muhammadan Abduhu wa Rasuluhu*," (I bear witness that there is no god but God, and I bear witness that Muhammad is His servant and messenger) or the proclamation of faith expressed as "*La ilaha illa'llah Muhammadun Rasulullah*" (there is no god but God; Muhammad is the messenger of God). In either of these conceptualizations, there are two meanings that bear the essence and spirit of Islam. One of them is testifying that the Almighty God is the Absolute One to be worshipped (*al-Ma'bud al-Mutlaq*) and the Eternally Besought of all (*al-Maqsud b'il-Istihqak*); these testimonials are an act of expressing the heart's conviction by taking all atoms in the universe as your witness. The second meaning is that we are declaring our faith in all of the Prophets when we testify to Prophet Muhammad's ﷺ messengership by saying, "*Muhammadun Rasulullah*" or "*ash-hadu anna Muhammadan Abduhu wa Rasuluhu*." Because Muhammad ﷺ, as the last in the line of the Prophets, is the representative and affirmer of the untainted essentials, and he is also the corrector of the values corrupted by the previous communities as a consequence of deviations. All words found their final destination in him; he is the one to certify them with his seal. And the progress of humanity was completed only with him. Therefore, he came to humanity with a perfect religion and as a perfect Prophet and bore witness to the Prophethood of all the Messengers from Adam to Jesus, peace be upon them all, which is expressed in this second part of the *shahadah*—"I bear witness that Muhammad is His servant and messenger."

These two statements of declaration of faith are such blessed clauses that in God's sight their weight and value are more than any other words. The Messenger of God expressed this in a hadith as:

The most meritorious of supplication is the one made in Mount Arafat; and the most meritorious phrase I and the Prophets before me stated is "*La ilaha illa'llah*."[3]

3 Mostly translated as "There is none worthy of worship but Allah" or simply "There is no god but Allah." Al-Muwatta, Qur'an 32, Hajj 246; Abdurrazzaq, al-Musannaf

Another hadith narrated by Abu Dharr is as follows:

One day, I went near the Prophet ﷺ. He was sleeping then. When he woke up I sat near him and we started talking. During our conversation, he stated that every servant who says, "*La ilaha illa'llah*" and then dies upon this word enters Paradise. In astonishment I asked, "Even if he commits adultery and theft?" He affirmed that it would be so even if he committed adultery and theft. I could not help but ask again, "Even if he commits adultery and theft?" The Messenger of God affirmed once more that it would be so even if he committed adultery and theft. He had repeated this statement three times. At the fourth time he stated, "(it will be so) in defiance of Abu Dharr."[4]

3. The essence and meaning of "*la ilaha illa'llah*"

Everything that belongs to the compilation of worship and servitude to God can be deduced from the comprehensive meaning of the proclamation of faith. By saying "*la ilaha illa'llah*" believers express their acknowledgement of Allah as the One and Only Lord (Rab), and that they will not find true inner contentment if they do otherwise. The following verse of the Qur'an states:

أَلَا بِذِكْرِ اللّٰهِ تَطْمَئِنُّ الْقُلُوبُ

> Be aware that it is in the remembrance of (and whole-hearted devotion to) God, that hearts find rest and contentment. (ar-Ra'd 13:28)

This can be expounded as, "Only observe servanthood for God, do not acknowledge anyone other than Him as your true refuge and support; because except for Allah, there is no power whatsoever to be relied on and trusted. And thus, you will have found contentment." The word "Allah" contains all these meanings.

In truth, my heart does not consent to accept the honorable word "Allah" as derived from any particular lexicon or to attempt to attribute it to a root word. While some may endeavor to find a root for it based on certain words, I humbly assert that just as the Almighty God has eternally existed, His name has always been "Allah" in the same pre-eternal sense. It is not fitting to seek a root word for the term "Allah."

4/378. Also, see Tirmidhi, Daawat 123.
4   Bukhari, Libas 24; Muslim, Iman 154.

The existence of everything hinges on Allah, and everything persists through Him. The radiance illuminating the face of the universe is encapsulated in the word "Allah." Without this word, all sciences and knowledge become mere conjectures and illusions, remaining as a jumble of inexplicable ideas whose ends cannot be properly grasped.

As'ha was one of the Jahiliyya (pre-Islamic) poets. When he heard about Prophet Muhammad ﷺ, he came to learn about his message. He was captivated by the meanings and truths expressed in the Qur'an. However, he felt unprepared to grasp the deeper beliefs and meanings encapsulated in *"la ilaha illa'llah."* Thus, he asked for additional time from the Prophet to contemplate these profound concepts and returned to his hometown. It was as though he was saying the following to the Prophet: "You ask for a declaration from me—a declaration with vast significance. I need time to internalize these immense meanings, to feel them resonate within my conscience, and to imbue every atom of my being with their essence." As in the case of As'ha, the proclamation of faith is not merely a statement to be uttered casually. Rather, when declared, it signifies the speaker's acceptance of a comprehensive system that encompasses all aspects of life—a life order that demands and deserves unwavering loyalty until the end.

God Almighty created the universe because He willed to be known and He put that universe in an order because He willed His Divine Attributes to be "read." Therefore, the order we see around us speaks of Him, the harmony reminds and makes remembrance (*dhikr*) of Him, and the universe continually echoes His presence anew. Conscious or not, each being in the universe becomes a tongue that calls out His name in constant recitation. Blessed with the ability of speech, the humankind serves as interpreters to these calls and recitations in the universe using their consciousness, cognition, and willpower. With their tongues, they put these truths into words.

When the appointed time arrives, everything joins in the chorus of those tongues that already proclaim the existence of Allah; gradually, their tongues awaken and become the voice of truth. It is akin to the arrival of spring, where ice melts, tongues are unshackled, and nightingales begin their melody. Seeds sown previously burgeon and thrive during this season of renewal. Today, *"la ilaha illa'llah"* resounds from all corners, as if ushering in a new era akin to the Age of Bliss (*Asr al-Saadat*)– the time of the Prophet ﷺ.

The original Age of Bliss was born in the bosom of those who stood against troubles and sufferings, who steadfastly confronted numerous challenges faithfully, and who remained steadfast in practicing Islam. In the valleys of Mecca, which had witnessed the darkest kind of life with idolatry, the declaration of *"la ilaha illa'llah"* sounded out and echoed throughout the world thanks to those early Muslims, who endured the severe difficulties and hardships of that time.

When faith enters the heart – an example from the Age of Bliss

God Almighty had opened the doors of Medina for Muslims after a difficult period of thirteen years in Mecca. With every passing day, believers were gaining strength and beginning to stand on their own feet.

They were unshaken even when opponents to the new faith came in big numbers to erase them off the earth. In the Battle of Badr, they were able to fend off the Meccan polytheists' offensive and gain a great victory. With that victory, the polytheists' resistance was broken, and it was proven that Islam was able to persist and flourish with efficiency. The polytheists had a lingering grudge as they could in no way stomach being defeated by a group of three hundred people, and they sought revenge at every opportunity.

Umayr ibn Wahb and Safwan ibn Umayya, both from the Meccan polytheists, were two cousins whose every breath seemed to be filled with grudge and rancor against Prophet Muhammad ﷺ. They held a shared grudge, for Umayr's son had been captured and Safwan's father had been killed at the Battle of Badr. Soon after the battle, they started to maliciously scheme against the Prophet. Eventually, they reached a decision: Umayr would travel to Medina under the guise of visiting his son, and would approach the Messenger of God ﷺ under another pretext. He planned to martyr him using a sword coated with poison, thus exacting revenge for both himself and the entire tribe of Quraysh, which was consumed by resentment. So, Umayr went to Medina, full of such thoughts. However, Umar ibn al-Khattab noticed the man in front of the mosque.

Umar said, "This is Umayr ibn Wahb, the enemy of God."[5] Before the man dismounted his camel Umar warned people: "Watch this man! There seems to be a sword under his garment; do not let him do any evil against the Messenger of God." Afterwards, Umar went to the Prophet and said, "O Messenger of God! Umayr is coming, do not let him do any evil to you." The Messenger of God smiled and said: "O Umar, let him come!" When Umayr came in, the Messenger of God asked, "Why have you come, O Umayr?" Umayr said that he had come to save his son by paying the due ransom. Then the Messenger of God said that he would reveal the real reason for Umayr's coming and started sharing the details of the plot Umayr made with Safwan. This man, nicknamed "the devil of the Quraysh," was utterly astonished upon hearing the Prophet's words and accepted faith by proclaiming, *"la ilaha illa'llah Muhammadun Rasulullah."*

When Providence decrees, even a person called a devil by others can become a disciple to the Messenger of God ﷺ. During the time he spent near the Messenger of God, Umayr was filled with love and enthusiasm for faith, becoming a fervent Companion. He asked permission from the Messenger to return to Mecca. The Messenger thought that the Meccans would do no harm to Umayr because Umayr was as brave as Umar ibn al-Khattab. For this reason, he allowed Umayr to return. In Mecca, Safwan eagerly awaited news of the success of their plot. He questioned every passing caravan about updates from Medina, as such news would bring great joy to him and the entire community of Mecca. Contrary to what he was expecting, he heard the shocking news of Umayr's becoming a Muslim.

Umayr spent most of his days in Mecca by telling people about the truth. During this time he really gave his faith its due, because on his next return to Medina almost two years after, there was a large group of people who accepted Islam along with him. Despite his cousin Umayr's insistence, Safwan remained stubborn and refused to join the ranks of the blessed ones. After the Muslims conquered Mecca, he gathered whatever belongings he could and fled to foreign lands overseas.

5 Ibn Hisham, *al-Sirah al-Nabawiyya*, 3/213.

Deeply saddened by this turn of events, Umayr pleaded with the Prophet to grant assurance of protection for Safwan. As proof of the authenticity of this assurance, he requested the turban the Prophet ﷺ wore when entering Mecca, a moment witnessed by all. Umayr firmly believed that Safwan would eventually serve Islam with dedication.

Eventually Umayr succeeded in bringing Safwan before the Prophet. In the presence of the Prophet, Safwan was too ashamed to look at him in the face. He asked, "O Messenger of God! Umayr told me you have given assurance of protection for me. Is that true?" The Messenger, the paragon of leniency and tolerance, replied in the affirmative, in a manner that suits him. Safwan thereupon said, "O Rasulullah! I accept that the teachings you brought are true, however I am asking about a respite of two months, so that I can think it over." As if he were beholding the future scenes of Safwan's heroism at Yarmuk against the Roman army, the Messenger of God smiled and gave him not just two but four months' respite. Within a few weeks, Safwan returned to the Prophet's presence and sincerely proclaimed his belief in the oneness of God and acceptance of Muhammad as His Prophet, reciting the *shahadah*: "*Ashadu an la ilaha illa'llah wa ashadu anna Muhammadan abduhu wa rasuluh.*"

4. Islam – what all the Prophets taught

When we say "Islam," what we refer to is a comprehensive frame of reference for every aspect of human life, their thoughts, imaginations, daily activities, and spirituality. It is a system that stipulates an order and a set of standards by which it puts on scale how well these standards are reached. Its comprehensiveness lies in addressing both worldly and spiritual matters within its teachings, presenting this world and the hereafter in parallel, and thereby referencing and interrelating both. Despite their smallness, humans have managed to establish a connection with the Eternal Creator, the Possessor of Infinite Greatness, and have regulated their relationship with the entire creation accordingly, all thanks to Islamic teachings. Therefore, the further people immerse themselves in Islam, the further they will unfurl their true capacity towards infinity. All these meanings are inherent to Islam's nature – they are found in the very definition of Islam and they have found their true expression in the words and lives of the Prophets.

Prophet Adam articulated this definition for the first time. The Prophets who succeeded him continued to call people to Islam under the same definition and invited them to delve into its depths. After Prophet Adam, Prophet Nuh (Noah) declared,

وَاُمِرْتُ اَنْ اَكُونَ مِنَ الْمُسْلِمِينَ

I am commanded to be Muslim. (Yunus 10:72)

While Prophet Ibrahim and Prophet Ismail were building Baitullah (the House of God) in Mecca, the *qiblah*-landmark of the world and the angels' ground of worship from there to Sidrat al-Muntaha (the Lote Tree of the Furthest Limit),[6] they prayed as follows:

رَبَّنَا وَاجْعَلْنَا مُسْلِمَيْنِ لَكَ وَمِنْ ذُرِّيَّتِنَا أُمَّةً مُسْلِمَةً لَكَ

Our Lord! Make us Muslims, submissive to You, and of our offspring, a community Muslim, submissive to You. (al-Baqarah 2:128)

Likewise, Prophet Yusuf (Joseph) became a minister of Egypt, he saved his brothers from famine and miseries of hardship, and reunited with his parents. Yet, after attaining everything in a material and spiritual sense, he prayed as follows:

تَوَفَّنِي مُسْلِمًا وَأَلْحِقْنِي بِالصَّالِحِينَ

Take my soul to You as a Muslim, and join me with the righteous. (Yusuf 12:101)

In fact, there isn't another example of someone who was blessed in the same manner as Yusuf. While recounting the exalted status of Prophet Yusuf, the Messenger of God ﷺ stated, "The nobleman, son of the nobleman, son of the nobleman, son of the nobleman. That was Joseph, son of Ya'kub, son of Ishaq, son of Ibrahim, upon them be peace."[7] All of his forefathers were Prophets. Despite enjoying both material and spiritual blessings, Yusuf's last wish was, "Take my soul to You as a Muslim." This

---

6 *Sidrat al-Muntaha* denotes the limit, the final point, the furthest boundary of the realm of contingencies. Some have interpreted it as the final point which death-bound beings can reach (Gülen, *Emerald Hills of the Heart Vol. 4*, 'Sidratu'l-Muntaha', pp. 88–90).

7 Bukhari, Anbiya 18-19, Manaqib 13; Tirmidhi, Tafsir (12) 1.

should serve as the ideal aspiration for anyone who has devoted their heart to God and yearns for reunion with Him.

The statement "I have become Muslim" can be paraphrased as "I have submitted my will to God," and this is indeed repeating the same statement made by the Prophets Adam, Nuh, Ibrahim, Yusuf, and finally Muhammad, the Pride of the Universe ﷺ. This statement pronounced by the Prophets is an expression of taking a solemn pledge before God.

Submission to God in the true sense means a person's obedience to Allah in thought, imagination, and deeds. The following verse addressing the Prophet indicates this sentiment:

> Say: My Prayer, and all my (other) acts and forms of devotion and worship, and my living and my dying are for God alone, the Lord of the worlds. He has no partners; thus have I been commanded, and I am the first and foremost of the Muslims (who have submitted to Him exclusively). (al-An'am 6:162–163)

This address to Prophet Muhammad ﷺ can be expounded as, "O my Beloved! Everything is under the dominance of the Divine power. Therefore, submit to God, Who has absolute dominance of this world and the next, Who dispatches and administers everything from systems to atoms. There is nothing comparable to Him. He is the Sole One with regard to Divinity and Lordship (*uluhiyya* and *rububiyya*). So, say, 'it is God's command that tells me to say I am the first one among you who accepts and fulfills the things He reveals to us.'"

In his letter to the Byzantian emperor Heraclius, Prophet Muhammad ﷺ invites him to submit to God and embrace Islam.[8] This invitation can be interpreted as if he said to Heraclius the following: Concerning the ship that will take you to the coast of deliverance through these dreadful waves before you, leave the captaincy to God and His Messenger Muhammad. Otherwise, you will be subjected to the troubles to be caused by huge waves and will not be able to find peace and contentment.

Also, it was stated in the same letter to Emperor Heraclius that, "God will reward you twofold." This holds special significance for those in administrative positions. This statement applies to anyone in a posi-

---

8 Bukhari, Bad'al-wahy 6; Muslim, Jihad 74.

tion of authority, whether it's the head of a family, a district governor, or a state leader. If such a person embraces faith, those under their care will likely follow suit, resulting in a double reward—both for themselves and for those they lead. Conversely, if they reject the Divine Message and turn a deaf ear to it, they risk leading others astray into disbelief and misguidance. In such a case, they would not only bear the burden of their own sins but also the sins of those they influenced.

5. Obedience to the Prophetic message

Humans can acquire a certain level of understanding by studying the universe, leading them to acknowledge the existence of a Creator. However, this realization alone doesn't surpass the beliefs held by individuals like Waraqa ibn Nawfal or Zayd, the cousin of Umar ibn al-Khattab, who lived as a *hanif*[9] or a believer in monotheism prior to the coming of Prophet Muhammad ﷺ.

In a similar vein, consider the scenario of hearing a knock at the door while indoors. The immediate assumption is that someone is outside. From the rhythm and intensity of the knock, one might deduce that it's a conscious being. However, this deduction is limited to logical inference without visual confirmation. Any speculation about the identity behind the door remains just that—a conjecture.

Plato's allegory of the cave offers a distinct perspective on this truth. He suggests that the understanding of a person inside a cave regarding beings outside might be based on the shadows or reflections cast onto the cave wall from the outside world. However, true knowledge about those beings can be obtained only if someone from the outside enters the cave and gives clear information about those beings. If we compare the situation of such a person and the mission of the Prophets, we can say the following: It is only with the description and teachings of the Prophets that

---

9   *Hanif* (upright, true believer) is a term used for people who kept up a monotheistic belief without falling to idolatry or associating partners with God during the Era of Ignorance. Those who observed worship based on what remained from the religion of Prophet Ibrahim (pbuh) were also termed as *hanif*. Arabs in the pre-Islamic Period would call *hanif* those who followed the religion of Ibrahim (pbuh). See, Ibn Manzur, *Lisanu'l-Arab* 9/58.

people can thoroughly believe in the existence of a Creator and obtain definite information about Him. For example, points like God's Names and Attributes, what He requires from us in terms of worship, and how to perform these worships, can only be known by the teachings of a Prophet.

The universe is created like a book, presented for people to ruminate on. The beings and course of events therein, which are supposed to be thought-provoking for us, continuously flow in a certain harmony.

It is absolutely certain that beyond all of these things that happen, there is a certain Power which administers them. Yet, without paying heed to the words of Prophets, suppositions or imaginings about any force like a grand spirit or the Ten Intellects (*uqulu ashara*)[10] of the medieval cosmology, or some sort of force within every substance that allegedly governs everything, do not amount to anything meaningful but lead only to confusing people's minds. Yet Allah, who reveals His existence through countless phenomena in the universe, transcends all measures and forms. Islamic teaching affirms that God Almighty Himself is exalted far beyond whatever we think of or anything that may occur to our mind on this issue.[11] The Divine Essence or God Himself (*Dhat*) cannot be grasped by the human mind; He can only be known through His Divine Names and Attributes. True comprehension of all these can only occur when the mind, heart, and spirit fulfill their true functions under the guidance of the Prophets. The only solution against falling into mistakes on this matter is to pay heed to the word of the Prophets, who are the representatives of the Straight Path (*sirat al-mustaqim*). Remaining connected to the teachings of the Prophets, who depend solely on God and His revelation, ensures that we walk and remain steadfast on the Straight Path.

All problems find solutions when we turn to the teachings of the Prophets, and the unknown becomes clear under the light of their guid-

10   Based on Aristotelian metaphysics of causation, al-Farabi (d. 950) developed a theory of cosmology in which creation has come about through a process of emanation from God via "ten intellects." It suggests the universe to be eternal, and that God does not have a choice whether or not to create it. For reasons like these, this cosmology has been rejected by Islamic scholars.

11   Ali al-Qari, *ar-Raddu ala'l-qailin bi wahdati'l-wujud* 1/16.

ance. They were sent as examples and guides to humanity, illuminating the path forward. Indeed, God Almighty, recognizing humanity's need for guidance, ensured that every society received a Prophet. No matter which part of the world or what segment of history, you will hear the voice of a Prophet saying, "O my people, worship God! Do not associate any partners with Him." The Qur'an expresses this truth as follows:

> And assuredly, We have raised within every community a Messenger [to convey the essential message]: Worship God alone, and keep away from false deities and powers of evil [who institute patterns of faith and rule in defiance of God]. (an-Nahl 16:36)

With the *qunut* prayer[12] Muslims recite everyday they declare their loyalty to the pledge they made to God Almighty:

> O Allah, I seek help from You, ask forgiveness from You, and believe in You and praise You for all the good things and are grateful to You and we part and break off with all those who are disobedient to You. O Allah, You alone do we worship and pray exclusively to You and bow before You alone and we hasten eagerly towards You and fear Your severe punishment and hope for Your mercy, for Your severe punishment is surely to be meted out to the disbelievers.

God appointed a Prophet from among each people who spoke their language, facilitating understanding and connection.. This truth is expressed in the following verse:

> We have never sent a Messenger who did not use his own people's language to make things clear for them. (Ibrahim 14:4)

Another verse emphasizes the same meaning in a direct address to the Messenger of Islam:

> (O My Messenger) We make it (this Qur'an) in your tongue and easy (to recite and understand) so that you may thereby give glad tidings to the God-revering, pious ones, and warn, thereby, a people given to contention. (Maryam 19:97)

---

12   *Qunut* prayer is the name of a supplication offered during salah at a specific point while standing. This version of qunut is the narration preferred by the Hanafi school.

The blessed Messenger, who lived in the Arab society as an Arab, needed to speak Arabic. Whichever society he may have lived in, he would have spoken their language. This was the case with every Prophet, so that every matter would be told to everyone clearly.

6. The last Prophet

The harmonious line of the Prophets which started with Adam (pbuh) reached perfection with the Last Prophet, Muhammad ﷺ. While truths were yet like seeds with Adam (pbuh), they sprang new shoots out of the ground with Nuh (pbuh), they flourished and blossomed with Ibrahim (pbuh), and with the Last Prophet the truths started completely bearing fruit; the greenery turned into an orchard and the world became a bed of roses, because he has a universal mission, which is expressed by the verse, "We have not sent you (O Muhammad) but as an unequalled mercy for all the worlds" (al-Anbiya 21:107).

This vast mercy extends to everyone's benefit. In fact, when Archangel Gabriel, who delivered revelations to the Messenger of God throughout his mission, was asked if he had benefited from this overarching mercy, he affirmed that he had. Gabriel explained that he was not assured of his own ending until the Qur'an referred to him as "*amin*" (trustworthy, safe one).[13] The Qur'an refers to Gabriel as the "*Ruhu'l Amin*" (Trustworthy Spirit) in ash-Shuara 26:193.

The ampleness of this mercy from which even Gabriel benefited should be a sufficient example to give an idea of the extensiveness of Prophet Muhammad's ﷺ blessed magnetism. Thus, as believers, our hearts should never be heedless of the fact that we are followers of a faith whose sphere of mercy even encompasses the angels.

Islam reached its pinnacle with the Prophet: humanity made an incredible leap forward at his time; material and spiritual revolutions occurred in human mind and thought. The social structure was saved from primitiveness and turned to a direction of prosperity and civilization. Towards the end of his mission and his life, the Prophet made his final address to humanity. Among those final words, he also recited the verse by which God Almighty states, "This day I have perfected for you your

---

13 Qadi Iyad, *ash-Shifa* 1/17.

religion [with all its rules, commandments and universality], completed My favor upon you and have been pleased to assign for you Islam as religion," (al-Ma'idah 5:3) and declared that the religion was completed.

The revelation of this verse is such a blessing that once a Jewish man said the following to Caliph Umar: "O the leader of the believers! There is a verse in your Book that had it been revealed to us, we would have made the day of its revelation a day of celebration." When the Caliph asked which verse it was, the man mentioned the verse above. Upon hearing this, Caliph Umar smiled and said, "We know very well when and where this verse was revealed. It was Friday and the Prophet was standing at Arafat (on the eve of the Hajj)." By saying so, he pointed out that the day was a festivity for Muslims in two ways already.[14]

That was indeed a day of festive for Muslims, but that particular day also involved an aspect of sadness, for the same verse was giving the news of the (soon to be) passing of the Prophet. The Messenger of God ﷺ, who did not only bring a religion, a system, but also communicated it and practiced it perfectly, was being summoned to the presence of God, once again with Divine decree. In one hadith, the Prophet gives a beautiful example for his being the last ring of the chain of the Prophets:

> My example in comparison with the other prophets before me, is that of a man who has built a house nicely and beautifully, except for a place of one brick in a corner. The people go about it and wonder at its beauty, but say: "Would that this brick be put in its place!" So I am that brick, and I am the last of the Prophets.[15]

Prophet Muhammad ﷺ was the completion of a poem that started with Prophet Adam; if it were not for him, it would not have been possible to hear the name of Prophet Adam, to know Prophet Musa, and to know Prophet Isa (Jesus) correctly. Humanity only gained true knowledge about past nations and what happened to them thanks to him. Just as he is the Messenger to the entire world, his message similarly needs to be heard by the entire world, because he holds the keys to everything that needs to be affirmed; in other words, it has become possible only within

---

14   Bukhari, Iman 33, Maghazi 77, Tafsiru's Sura (5) 2, I'tisam 1; Muslim, Tafsir 3, 4, 5.

15   Bukhari, Manaqib 18; Muslim, Fadail 23.

the frame of the essentials he brought to understand and believe the true faith in God, the Prophets, Scriptures and the Afterlife.

7. Faith, actions, and worship

a. Faith and actions

Religion encompasses both belief and conceptual aspects, as well as a practical dimension that guides daily routines. *Iman* (faith) constitutes the conceptual aspect, whereas worship, acts, and deeds constitute the practical aspect of Islam. However, deeds come after acceptance of iman. In this regard, what is to be practiced is complementary to the required theoretical acceptances. Theoretical principles or aspects cannot stand alone or last long if they are not put into action or practice.

That's why it's essential for individuals to align their lives with their beliefs and reinforce them through practical actions. As Nursi maintains, belief cannot be sustained without acts of worship. Iman can only be upheld with practices like the daily prayers (salah), disciplining the *nafs* (carnal soul) through fasting and abstinence, purging the heart of selfishness and stinginess while fostering generosity and benevolence towards others, and actively promoting good deeds while discouraging wrongdoing. These practices are fundamental to Islam and necessitate not just belief, conviction, and intention, but also tangible actions and unwavering commitment.

In essence, each pillar of Islam acts as a support, reinforcing iman from various angles. In this respect, worship refers to the way people both affirm belief and submit themselves in humility to God. A believer demonstrates their distinction through their actions, distinguishing themselves from those without faith. It is only through practical worship and devotion that a believer truly demonstrates their faith in and relationship with God. To the degree they strengthen that relationship, they will spiritually flourish and activate the inherent angelic aspects in human nature; this is the true meaning of worship, which should be profoundly observed (*ubudiyya*). This bond needs to be protected for a lifetime. For this reason, the Messenger of God stated that "the best deeds are those done regularly even if they are few."[16]

Considering that the minimum level of worship is the five daily prayers, a person neglecting them will be devoid of that great merit and will fail to take the path to purify their heart from dust and rust and then to establish a relation with God. Addressing the Prophet, God Almighty commands "observe and (continue to) worship your Lord until what is certain (death) comes to you" (al-Hijr 15:99). And this means, "reveal your character by observing worship until death comes."

Acts of worship strengthen the connection between our hearts and spirits with the unseen realms (*lahut*). In other words, strengthening our relationship with God relies on harnessing the inner qualities we are given. Just as specific exercises improve our physical endurance, flexibility, strength, and balance, certain acts of worship refine and elevate our spiritual faculties and subtleties dispelling fearfulness and hesitation in devotions. In this state, bodily fatigue, the allure of food, or material pleasures are unlikely to hinder our worship of God.

In this respect, just as unbelief consists of a series of customs, acquisitions and routines, so does servitude to God. A person may not be able to observe worship in full consciousness all the time. The manners, patterns, and routines ingrained in our spiritual hearts and faculties empower individuals to effortlessly bridge any potential gaps in their relationship with God. For instance, particularly in colder regions, waking up before dawn and performing ablutions with cold water can be challenging for the carnal soul, which prefers the comfort of a warm bed. However, individuals overcome these difficulties through the acquired habits and manners they've developed, rising to pray despite the obstacles. Consequently, they prevent any gaps from forming in their relationship with God. This commitment enables the heart and spirit to better focus on worship, experiencing spiritual delight and contentment with the gentle breezes of Divine Grace and Mercy during worship.

Human nature inherently encompasses both animalistic and angelic aspects. Activating the angelic side of human nature requires prioritizing worship and restraining the animalistic tendencies. As individuals

---

16 Bukhari, Libas 43; Muslim, Salatu'l-Musafirin 218.

engage in acts of worship and delve into their inner meanings, the angelic side flourishes, leading to spiritual progress and growth.

On the contrary, when acts of worship are performed without mindfulness of God and consumed by worldly concerns, they become mere rituals devoid of spiritual depth. Instead of serving as a gateway to the spiritual realms, they merely follow established patterns. Consequently, the individual's relationship with God fails to evolve, and the spiritual dimension of human nature remains underdeveloped.

Whoever makes endeavors for spiritual progress, flourishing is always possible. Consider, for instance, a mystic in any tradition who explores different paths and teachings, abstains from food and drink for extended periods, maintains a state free from carnal desires for months, and immerses themselves in a lifetime of spiritual and transcendent experiences. However, every person has a different objective and intention in their search for such a progress. For some of them, having some sort of a spiritual experience in their soul as a result of their abstinence is enough for a progress. Yet in reality they are at the bottom of a well and keep jumping up and down. All the progress they attain, thus, is not more than the depth of that well. The real progress, however, is finding serenity, gaining peace in absence, being saved from the suffering of eternal nothingness—even though temporarily—and seeking a solution against the weight of being called to account beyond the grave.

Today, people who are devoid of the correct understanding of Divinity remain doomed to the narrow frame of their belief; they can barely make any progress pertaining to the spiritual realms. They observe some forms of abstinence only to have an inner spiritual experience. On the other hand, for those on the right path of belief, the acts of worship they observe is like a locomotive in its right tracks. The worshipers arrive at a different station at every stage of life, gain insight into things that exist or happen around us, seek out and feel delight in the Divine Names and Attributes, and become enraptured before the greatness of God Almighty Himself. This is a journeying that transcends reason or cognition, as the journeyer speaks with the speaking of God Almighty, sees with His seeing, hears with His hearing, and holds with His holding. During this journey, after traversing towards God (*sayr ila'llah*) and within God (*sayr fi'llah*), the journey back from God (*sayr min Allah*) commences, signifying a return from the Creator to humanity. In other words, the course Prophet Muhammad ﷺ followed involves returning to be among people, holding people by the hand and guiding them to maturity, and allowing them to experience the delights and reflections gained along the journey. This road that believers follow toward the otherworldly realms, with thousands of others following behind, extends to infinity, for the journeying to God has no end. The worshipper who advances in this spiritual journey and reaches the level of inner witnessing experiences delights and encounters Divine Grace and Mercy as the subtle capacities (*lataif al-rabbaniyya*)[17] unfold with them.

b. Reflections on worship

The human spirit flourishes and finds its true strength by means of worship to God. Establishing a relationship with God through worship is unique to humanity. There is no such relationship with Him concerning animals; God Almighty creates them and directs them to act in accordance with the natural disposition of their species. God demands humans to establish a relationship with Him so that they avoid spiritual deterioration and asks them to obey and observe servitude for their Creator, Sustainer and Nourisher. This subsistence encompasses their body, reason, and inner world. All these spiritual faculties (*lataif*) will die when connection with God is severed, as feelings like desire, resentment, hatred and the like are potent enough to extinguish them. Even when animalistic traits like grudges and hatred assert their influence, despite all adversity, a servant must stand in prayer, therefrom behold the Sublime Throne (*Arsh al-Azam*) and attain the delight of true servitude. This allows the angelic aspect to cleanse these impure inscriptions and reveal their true identities for proper functioning.

As long as humans observe worship, their relationship with God Almighty endures. Every obstacle that arises between a servant and the Creator aims to sever this relationship. In an address to the Prophet, God decrees in Surah al-Muzzammil (73:8), "and devote yourself to Him whole-heartedly."

---

17   Mostly rendered as "Godly faculties" or "the spiritual intellect," *lataif al-rabbaniya* are the inner, finer, special organs or faculties of perception in Sufi spiritual psychology; and subtle human capacities; singular form is *latifa*.

With this address, it is as if Allah is saying to the Prophet to purge his heart of everything other than Him, for doing this would be more fitting to a Prophet. This state is, in the terminology of mystics, "detaching oneself from anything but God," and according to erudite scholars it is to "regard anything that holds you back from God as worldly and leave them behind."

Here, it is necessary to expound a little on the word "*tabattal*" (تَبَتَّلْ) mentioned in the verse above and translated as "devote yourself." The verb is used in the imperative form and means "exert yourself in this respect even if you do not want to." By exerting oneself in this manner, the encounters with inner witnessing will become more frequent and profound. However, there must be this self-push at the beginning. In another place, the Qur'an in Surah al-Muddaththir (74:1-5) commands, "O you cloaked one [who has preferred solitude]! Arise and warn! And declare your Lord's [indescribable and incomparable] greatness! And keep your clothing clean! Keep away from all pollution [evils]!", and also in Surah al-Kahf (18:28) "and do not let your eyes pass from them, desiring the attraction of the life of this world, and pay no heed to him whose heart We have made unmindful of Our remembrance, who follows his lusts and fancies, and whose affair exceeds all bounds [of right and decency]"; this means "do what becomes you and do not set your sights on worldly riches or their owners."

God Almighty elevated His beloved servant with these verses in such a manner that the Messenger established his throne in the hearts of all humanity for 14 centuries. From all this, we can infer that it is allowed to remove, when necessary, any obstacles that might sever one's relationship with God. Through worship and devotion, Divine inspirations flow into a person's spirit and increase accordingly, directly proportional to the strength of one's relationship with God. Thus, the conscience attains a very pleasant and expansive state as well.

The verses, such as the following in Surah Ibrahim (14:24) ,"Do you not see how God strikes a parable of a good word: [a good word is] like a good tree–its roots holding firm [in the ground] and its branches in heaven…" and in Surah Fatir (35:10), "To Him ascends only the pure word, and the good, righteous action (God) raises it…" state that the words and deeds that come from the bottom of one's heart, pure and unadulterated, and only seeking God's good pleasure, rise to Him. Regarding every word and action, if there are ulterior motives behind them, they will lack the blessing and prosperity that come with sincerity.

The Messenger of God said that three types of people are the first to be called to give their account on the Day of Judgment. The hadith is as follows:

> …The first of those who will be called before Him will be a man who memorized the Qur'an, and a man who was killed in God's cause, and a wealthy man. Allah will say to the reciter: "Did I not teach you what I revealed to My Messenger?" He says: "Of course O Lord!" God says: "Then what did you do with what you learned?" He said: "I would stand (in prayer reciting) with it during all hours of the night and all hours of the day." Then God would say to him: "You have lied." And the Angels will say: "You have lied." God will say to him: "Rather, you wanted it to be said that so-and-so is a reciter. And that was said." The person with the wealth will be brought, and God will say to him: "Was I not so generous with you, such that I did not leave you having any need from anyone?" He will say: "Of course O Lord!" God says: "Then what did you do with what I gave to you?" He says: "I would nurture the ties of kinship and give charity." Then God will say to him: "You have lied." And the Angels will say to him: "You have lied." God will say: "Rather, you wanted it to be said that so-and-so is so generous, and that was said." Then the one who was killed in God's cause shall be brought, and God will say to him: "For what were you killed?" So he says: "I was commanded to fight in Your cause, so I fought until I was killed." God will say to him: "You have lied." And the Angels will say to him: "You have lied." God will say: "Rather, you wanted it be said that so-and-so is brave, and that was said." Then the Messenger of God ﷺ hit me on my knees and said: "O Abu Hurairah! These first three are the creatures of God with whom the fire will be enflamed on the Day of Judgment."[18]

---

18   Tirmidhi, Zuhd 48; Ibn Hibban, *es-Sahih* 2/136.

A servant needs to exercise self-supervision for the purity of intention while worshipping and trying to keep an unwavering intention. For all acts of worship have a value to the degree they are observed for God's pleasure.

True worship, sincere supplications, devout devotions, and adherence to Divine commandments are the indicators of one's relationship with God. False fervor and superficial enthusiasm hold no validity on the path to Him. Genuine expressions of devotion include heartfelt sighs in the stillness of the night, prayer rugs dampened with tears, and hearts ignited by Divine commands,[19] "O people, worship me alone!" Such deeds serve as a means for people to be purified from sources of impurity and to become eligible for Paradise. Just as gold or silver is processed, refined and extracted from impurities, God refines people through servitude so that they can be purified to enter Paradise and behold the Divine beauty. The consequence of such cleansing and purification of people by means of servitude is also stated in the following hadith: "The best of you are those who, when they are seen, Allah the Mighty, the Majestic, is remembered."[20]

> As servitude to God cleanses people and brings about total purity in all senses, God Almighty decrees: "O people, worship your Lord who created you and those before you…" (al-Baqarah 2:21).

Worship regulates life in every way, shaping our days, months, and even dividing our daily hours into specific segments. The five times of worship mark significant milestones or stages in one's lifetime, from birth to death. Their spaced repetition fosters a conscious positive self-conditioning, maintaining a constant awareness of God, which significantly reduces the inclination to commit bad deeds. Friday brings a distinct break to the colors and continuity of the weekdays. Fasting divides the year and organizes the months through the Blessed Months. Thus, hours, days, months, and our entire lifespan are imbued with the joy of servitude to God.

---

19 To cite a few, see the Qur'an 2:21, 3:64, 6:102, 7:59, 11:61, 20:11-15, 21:92, 51:56 and more…

20 Ibn Ma'jah, Zuhd 4.

Chapter 2

Salah

1. The importance of salah

Salah is the most comprehensive form of worship and has great importance in Islam. In the Qur'an, verses on the articles of faith are usually followed by references to salah. It was so critical in the life of the Companions of the Prophet that they doubted whether a Muslim who did not pray salah was a true believer or not. Observing salah in deep reverence and awe (*khushu*) is a precursor to the inspirational blessings to come. Salah is therefore acknowledged to be the most perfected act of worship for all souls.

Salah is a form of prayer that is in perfect compliance with the nature of humans, who are created with an aptitude to reach God, to interpret the creation, and to scrutinize the universe with different understandings of sciences. In order to achieve the perfection inherent in their nature, a person can only attain it through acts of worship such as salah. By fulfilling this duty, they embody the qualities of a true human being as expected by God.

It is a fact beyond doubt that the human has been created with perfection in both body and spirit. One cannot help but admire the proportion and harmony in the human body. Roman geniuses of art grasped this beauty very well, but they failed to attribute it to Almighty God. Rather, they tried to express these feelings in tangible ways such as paintings and sculptures and thus limited all these into a narrow frame. With such admiration for humanity one tends to think that if God were to allow prostration to anyone other than Him, it would be the human. In a way, the Divine command for the angels to prostrate before Adam is used to prop up this idea. Having said that, prostration in Islam is a matter of worship and it is absolutely forbidden to do so to any one but Allah. Muslims prostrate before God only.

Thorough observance of worship and humbling oneself before God, one receives inspirational and surplus blessings (*waridat*). In Surah al-Mu'minun (23:1-2), God Almighty decrees,

قَدْ أَفْلَحَ الْمُؤْمِنُونَ ۞ الَّذِينَ هُمْ فِي صَلَاتِهِمْ خَاشِعُونَ

> "Certainly, the faithful have attained salvation, those who are humble in their prayers..."

If we consider what this verse may imply conversely—which is not an appropriate method in all cases—we can infer that those who do not observe salah with awe may not be saved. Although we do not take such an interpretation as our foundation, we do view it favorably as a cautious approach, acknowledging the possibility and keeping it in consideration. In this regard, just as a hungry person relishes every bite of food while eating, or a thirsty individual savors every sip of water while drinking, or like someone on the verge of suffocation experiences the refreshing sensation of fresh air while inhaling, we should strive to feel the significance of the salah we engage in. It's not merely a task to be performed carelessly.

Salah, as an act of worship, merits dedicated time and complete concentration before its commencement. Actually, the salah and the preparations beforehand have the potential force to maintain this concentration. They function as integral components of the salah process, with each sequential step serving as an instrument to facilitate it.

Before observing the prescribed prayers, one is advised to eliminate waste from the body by visiting the washroom and relieving oneself. Then, by making *wudu* (ablution), the ritual purification by water, the process significantly balances the kinetic energy in our body, bringing further relief. Later, the sound of the blessed call to prayer guides us towards a different level of appeal and profundity. Then we walk to the place of worship in awe and respect, as if we were going to meet God; with the sweet chants and tunes by the *muadhin* (the clergy calling to the prayer), a different realm prevails. People observe the *Sunnah* prayers by themselves and finally the *muadhin* recites the *iqamah* (the second call to commence the *fard* salah), which signals that it is time for the prayer to start collectively, congregationally. Every one of these are like invitations to gain inner depth to observe the obligatory part (*fard*) in full concentration, to feel God. All of these preparations enable worshippers to maintain a constant and sincere focus on God.

Striving to deeply experience salah is an ideal goal, and the preparations made prior to salah can be regarded as strategies employed in order to achieve this depth of feeling. In other words, just as protocols or procedures are developed to achieve certain objectives, these preparations serve as a means to fully realize salah in the perfect sense. None of the elements, like the *adhan, wudu, iqamah, Sunnah* prayers and other deeds, in themselves are the actual purpose. Rather, they are but the means established to allow humans—the very beings blessed with the perfect pattern of creation—observe worship in a manner befitting them.

Salah is considered the epitome of true humanity, serving to foster closeness to God by aligning both inward and outward aspects of human existence. Therefore, it must definitely be observed with a serious inner profundity. Being conscientious about observing it properly, or feeling remorse when failing to do so, is an important level of spiritual progress for a person. Yet, very few people manage to accomplish observing it at that level. "Few" is in relative sense here, for everyone has their own experience of salah. For example, one individual in prostration may not even wish to rise back up... another may feel oneself in the heavenly gardens... another may feel themselves as being at the very outskirts of Paradise... and another can perceive themselves ahead of certain spiritual levels and beings. Individuals can attain these and other levels of observance according to their abilities. Here it should be noted that even if we cannot reach our target, as long as we maintain our intention to strive to perfection, it is always possible for us to find fulfillment in accordance with our intentions. Let us not forget that the intention of a believer is better than their action.[1]

Even if individuals meticulously fulfill all the requirements for observing salah, they may still not experience a fully profound connection

---

1   Tabarani, *al-Mu'jam al-Kabir* 6/185-186; Bayhaqi, *Al-Sunan al-Sughra* p.20.

with it for various reasons. Some conditions that arise during salah are always beyond our control. For example, no sooner than the salah begins, your children may come and climb on you. This even happened many times to the Messenger of God ﷺ. His blessed grandchildren jumped on his shoulders while he was praying, especially during prostration. Additionally, unexpected loud or intense noises can cause one's attention to sway from salah, preventing it from reaching its peak level of concentration.

In the pursuit of achieving full composure, some obstacles may stem from human nature itself. For example, daydreams or thoughts of other matters may intrude into the mind during salah, causing a mental barrier. In such cases, one will continuously feel as if they are obscured by fog and smoke, hindering their focus. Even a person like Umar ibn al-Khattab, who was such a devout person, once erred in prayer because his mind drifted to the ongoing problems of that time in Iraq.[2]

Another aspect of this matter pertains to the atmosphere where salah is being observed. Obviously, there will be great differences between the salah observed in a completely trouble-free atmosphere compared to the one observed in the face of many sufferings, hardships, and different concerns; the difficulties mentioned in the latter scenario may actually serve for a more deeply observed salah.

In this latter scenario one's focus and peace during prayer might be spoiled by various distractions and interruptions maybe a thousand times. However, if one can still observe the salah as intimately as one breathes despite such distractions, this depth of feeling transforms salah into something of a different hue, a value that may be beyond our full comprehension. This is what matters most.

For this reason, the salah observed during times of hardship, distress, disasters and danger is much more blessed in comparison to salah observed during normal times. When we consider the way *salat al-khawf* (prayer of fear) is observed, the place and significance of salah becomes much clearer. When a massive army of non-Muslims came to erase Muslims and Islam off of the earth, the Messenger and his Companions were forced to take their place on the battlefield to defend themselves. Despite

---

[2]   Ibn Sa'd, *Tabaqat al-Kubra*, 7:441

the perilous situation, when it was time for *fajr* salah, the Muslims did not falter or skip the mandatory prayer; instead, they performed it in accordance with the instructions laid out in the Qur'an:

> When you (O Messenger) are among the believers [who are on an expedition and in fear that the unbelievers might harm them] and stand (to lead) the Prayer for them, let a party of them stand in the Prayer with you and retain their arms with them (while the other party maintain their positions against the enemy). When the first party have done the prostrations [finished the *rak'ah*], let them go to the rear of your company (and there, hold positions against the enemy), and let the other party who have not prayed come forward and pray with you, being fully prepared against danger and retaining their arms. Those who disbelieve wish that you should be heedless of your weapons and your equipment, so that they might swoop upon you in a single (surprise) attack. (an-Nisa 4:102)

Certainly, observing salah in such a fashion may come as strange to some considering the impending attack. Yet it shows the place, weight, and importance of prayer in people's lives. Also, observing prayer in such times and instances is far more valuable and rewarding compared to the prayers observed in comfortable times and instances.

In short, when we feel the responsibility of prayer and, despite all the unfavorable circumstances, search for a suitable slot of time with the consciousness of "I must observe salah no matter what," there is an immense and profound quality in that salah. I don't think one can reach the profundity of such a salah even in spiritual retreats or even at the Ka'ba, if he or she does not have the same level of consciousness.

a. The first worship to be questioned about

Salah is the first deed a believer will be taken to account for before the Divine Presence. Other acts of worship, serious sins, or crimes will be addressed later. We should not draw the wrong conclusion from this that other acts of worship are unimportant; on the contrary, we should understand the importance of salah in light of this fact. If the person does not observe salah, then they are experiencing the greatest loss of their lifetime.

Observing worship like fasting, *zakat* and Hajj are comparatively easier than salah. Salah has a difficulty of its own. The Companions viewed those who did not observe salah as hypocrites, but not those who did not observe the fasting or Hajj. The scholars mention abandoning salah mostly as an example of "hypocrisy in actions" (*nifaq a'mali*).

Observing servitude to God five times a day, depending on one's depth of consciousness, exalts that person's spiritual degree beyond what anyone would imagine. One should not dismiss salah as unimportant. One who abandons the salah may do the same for one's faith one day. A specific meaning and essence of *mi'raj* (ascension) is inherent in salah. Having said that, everybody feels salah in their own capacity and as much as their spiritual abilities allow. Undoubtedly, the most perfect *mi'raj* was indeed that of Prophet Muhammad ﷺ.

As soon as the person passes away, the first situation they will face is being called to account for salah. A hadith states this as follows: "On the Day of Judgment, a person will be firstly brought to account for salah among their deeds. If this account is complete, then the person is saved. If it is not complete, then the person is in loss."[3] Therefore, what takes one to either the pitfalls of Hell or the mansions of Paradise will be the importance they gave to salah.

Accordingly, a believer should observe the five daily prayers without missing any and look forward to strengthening their connection with God at every opportunity. For, every prayer a person observed in this world will meet and help them on the day of the Judgment, when they need help the most. While describing the dread of that day, the Messenger of God stated that "Whoever will be called to account [about his deeds on the Day of Resurrection] will surely be punished." We read this as whoever is examined "thoroughly" at the Reckoning, a reckoning which is long and tough and thorough. Upon this, the Prophet's wife Aisha asked how that aligns with the verse, "Then, as for him who will be given his Record in his right hand, surely he will be reckoned with by an easy reckoning, and will return in joy to his household [prepared for him in Paradise]" (al-Inshiqaq 84:7-9) The Prophet explained, "That is the presentation of deeds but whoever is examined thoroughly at the

---

3   Abu Dawud, Salat 144-145; Tirmidhi, Mawaqit 193; Nasai, Salat 9; Ibn Majah, Iqamah 202.

reckoning is doomed – or will be punished." May God Almighty be our helper with His grace and munificence on the Day of Judgment. We will be in dire need of His help. May He make our small deeds big, forgive our wrongdoings, and spare us from punishment. The following is the Qur'anic depiction of those who are ruined due to abandoning salah:

> Dwelling in Paradise, they will ask questions to one another, about the disbelieving criminals, "What has brought you into this pit (of Hell)?" They reply as follows: "We were not of those who observed prayer; nor did we use to feed the destitute (and meet their needs). We used to plunge in words of falsehood together with those who plunged (in them). And we used to deny the Day of Judgment. [we were always thus] Until what is certain to come did come upon us." (al-Muddaththir 74:40–47)

What catches our attention first in the verse above is that not spending for the sake of God and abandoning prayer are mentioned together. The opposite of this is observing salah and supporting the poor. These two points are mentioned together in many verses of the Qur'an. One of them pertains to regulating the believer's personal life and to their individual *mi'raj* (ascension), while the other paves the way for establishing a sound and healthy society with integrity and unity of spirit, as well as progress in unison. Therefore, these are inseparable parts of two worships and indispensable to one another.

The first worship made obligatory on Muslims is salah; it will be the last thing for them to abandon. Some commands of Islam have been neglected and thus abandoned over time. For example, transactions in markets may no longer comply with Divine orders, societal disorder and instigations may spread everywhere, and countless people may succumb to temptations. However, one can assume that even in such an environment, the only thing that will continue in terms of worship to God will be salah. May God Almighty not let us witness an era when salah is abandoned! Quite the contrary, we presume that we are on the verge of a fresh spring and revival. The Almighty Creator allows us to perceive Him as stated in a hadith, "I am just as My servant thinks I am," which signifies that God will interact with His servants according to their perceptions of Him.[4] In this vein, we pray to Him to increase these revivals, to let all people run to stand before His presence in salah, and to have the honor of having a *mi'raj* with their salah even if it were in the last moments of their lives. May He thus let us all behold His Divine Beauty in the next world.

b. The identical sibling of iman

Iman and the prescribed prayers (salah) arise from the same source. They are like identical twins. Belief constitutes the theoretical aspect of religion and religious life. Consolidation of the theoretical aspect and internalizing it as a character trait in oneself is only possible through salah and other acts of worship. For this reason, it can be said that the salah is "practical *iman*" and "*iman* is a theoretical salah." Those who view religion merely as a matter of conscience and argue there is no need for worship and devotions unwittingly fall into contradiction. Indeed, the prescribed prayer is the pillar of religion.

The daily prayers are a river of repentance and forgiveness, flowing towards eternity. A fountain of purification in which a believer is cleansed at least five times each and every day. The prayers are such an important duty that they need to be observed at all times and circumstances, even at times of war as previously explained. They are a secure stronghold, a vital means to gaining nearness to God, and the shortest path to His presence. For these reasons, from the time of our Prophet until the present day, saintly individuals have always placed salah at the center of their lives. Not content with observing only the obligatory prayers, they have made it a habit to perform voluntary prayers (*nawafil*) every day.

c. The index of all acts of worship

As it bears the meaning and elements of all other acts of worship in its essence, salah is considered to be their index. Believers may engage in other acts of worship during specific segments of life, but salah is distinct. It establishes a direct link between the servant and their Lord. It constantly maintains their relationship with His Grace and Mercy. In this respect, it is almost impossible to compare it with other forms of worship.

---

4   Bukhari, Tawhid 15, 35; Muslim, Dhikr 2, 19, Tawba 1.

The daily prayers become a means of delight and happiness in this world and the next as long as they are performed with a heart filled with reverence and awe before God, the Owner of Infinite Mercy and Munificence. Therefore, as he was the one with the greatest responsibility among mankind, Prophet Muhammad ﷺ placed the utmost importance in salah. He did not settle for just the five daily prayers; he maintained his active relationship with God in the night as well. As His wife Aisha (r.a.) narrated, he never abandoned the *tahajjud* (night) prayer because he saw it as incumbent on him. He would persist in observing it even during times of sickness, even if he had to do so while sitting.[5] Thus, he never allowed any shadows to remain unilluminated by prayers in his life, which he entirely devoted to the worship of his Lord. In other words, He never succumbed to a state of heedlessness and not remembering God, not even for a moment.

Salah is a form of worship that encompasses certain aspects not found in other forms of worship. It represents a proactive response to the call of God, uniquely structured to align with that response. In this regard, salah possesses a distinctiveness. While other forms of worship are specific to certain times and therefore observed within particular time frames, salah, on the other hand, is continuous and unceasing. Take fasting Ramadan for example. During the blessed month of Ramadan, we embark on observing the fast and soon find that the month has come to an end. Fasting is a noble act of worship carried out internally. Only God knows whether a person truly abstains from food and resists desires or appetites. Therefore, only He will bestow the rightful reward for it. We must wait an entire year to welcome Ramadan once more.

Another pillar of Islam which is mandatory but performed once a year is "*zakat*." *Zakat* is not a form of worship everyone can observe since it requires certain conditions. One must meet the required criteria of wealth. When the time comes, you give the designated amount allocated from your wealth as *zakat*, fulfilling your obligation. In this regard, it can also be seen as a one-time act of worship. However, *zakat* also brings prosperity and blessings to the wealth for which *zakat* is given. While initially, it may feel challenging to part with a portion of your wealth,

---

5   Muslim, Salatu'l-Musafirin 141; Tirmidhi, Salat 348; Abu Dawud, Tatawwu 26; Nasai, Qibla 13, Qiyam al-Layl 2, 64.

you are giving for the sake of God, and as you act in accordance with the Divine command, your heart finds contentment, and you feel gladness and peace.

The same holds true for Hajj. Special to Hajj and umrah, the believer enters the state of ihram, a special condition. Attaching their heart to God alone, the believers enthusiastically say,

لَبَّيْكَ اللَّهُمَّ لَبَّيْكَ، لَبَّيْكَ لَا شَرِيكَ لَكَ لَبَّيْكَ، إِنَّ الْحَمْدَ وَالنِّعْمَةَ لَكَ وَالْمُلْكَ، لَا شَرِيكَ لَكَ

> "We are at Your service my God! There is no deity but You; You are one, You have no partners. All praises are due to You. Blessings are from You, the sovereignty belongs to You, You have no partners!"

With these words, they declare being at God's command. All of these acts are a means of standing in the Divine presence, communicating with Him, and being filled with the inspirational blessings flowing from His Grace. Every act during Hajj holds a special significance and occurs on specific days. At the conclusion of the numbered days, even if the believers are reluctant, they must depart from the holy sites, as it marks the end of Hajj. The believers leave with sadness and a yearning heart and return to their family homes.

During fasting, individuals turn to God by abstaining from eating and drinking. Similarly, during salah—albeit temporarily—there is a state of abstaining from worldly matters and completely turning to God.

Salah occurs five times a day and offers us inner peace, a tranquility that even a believer can hardly attain in Arafat during Hajj. It grants us the blessing of standing in the Divine presence and prostrations five times a day. Prophet Muhammad ﷺ said,

أَقْرَبُ مَا يَكُونُ الْعَبْدُ مِنْ رَبِّهِ، وَهُوَ سَاجِدٌ، فَأَكْثِرُوا الدُّعَاءَ

> "The closest that a person is to his Lord is when he is in prostration in prayer, so increase your supplication when you prostrate."[6]

We reach the peak of this nearness when we place our head on the ground in humility before His greatness. Then, in this state of rever-

---

6   Muslim, Salat 215; Abu Dawud, Salat 148; Nasai, Mawaqit 35, Tatbiq 78.

ence, we glorify God by reciting, "*Subhana Rabbiy al-A'la*" (Glory is to my Lord, the Most High).

Likewise, salah bears in its essence the quality of regularity, recurrence, and repetition. Staying regular with your five daily prayers each and every day, or in other words, its recurrence several times a day for a lifetime, almost goes side by side with *kalima tawhid* (*la ilaha illallah Muhammadun Rasulullah*). Just as we heed the Messenger's call to recite the kalima *tawhid* one hundred times each morning and evening, and thirty-three times after every salah, salah itself revisits us periodically. It even blissfully interrupts our sleep, inviting us to spend a part of the night in worship rather than solely indulging in worldly pleasures. The Qur'an puts this as, "Their sides shun their beds at night, calling out to their Lord in fear [of His punishment] and hope [for His forgiveness, grace, and good pleasure], and out of what We have provided for them they spend" (as-Sajdah 32:16).

The Messenger of God said that when the body of a person is placed in the grave and the footsteps of those leaving after the funeral have barely ceased, the angels come and question the person. Right at that moment, something of light comes and sits beside the head of the person; this is his prayer. Another thing of light comes and sits beside his feet; this is the rest of his good deeds. Another thing of light sits at his right; this is his fasts. Another thing of light sits at his left; and this is his *zakat*. They protect him against the troubles of the grave from the right and left.[7] Accordingly, for those who did not abandon salah in the worldly life, salah will not leave the person alone in the grave even though all friends and loved ones will leave. For salah became indispensable for that person every day while living.

Worship falls into two fundamental categories: those that are observed with financial means and those observed with physical action. Although salah is seen as a bodily form of worship, we cannot claim it does not have a financial aspect, as some *fiqh* scholars argue. The "value of time" was not something commonly known in the past. Globally, "time" came to be recognized as something with a financial value only with the emergence of capitalism and communism. However, in Islamic teach-

---

7   Ibn Hanbal, *Musnad* 6/352; 4/287, 295; Abdurrazzaq, *al-Musannaf* 3:582–583.

ings, it already had value, and its worth was known. When we consider that a person devotes time for both salah and ablutions, their clothes gradually wear out over time during salah, and they have to pause their business activities during salah, it becomes evident that salah indeed has a financial aspect as well.

Moreover, salah serves the purpose of purifying the heart and cleansing the *nafs* (carnal soul). During salah, a person turns to God from the heart, humbly bowing down the *nafs*, and breaking its arrogance through prostration. Therefore, salah holds significance in terms of the spiritual advancement of the human spirit.

Another unique aspect of salah is that it allows the person to stand in prayer alongside angels, side by side, in the same rank. Scholars of Islam acknowledge that angels indeed stand by the believer. They base their argument on that people who pray give greetings to the right and left upon finishing salah, thus greeting the angels, along with the congregation, who also accompany worshippers in salah. During salah, the person feels and experiences *sakina* (serenity, tranquility, peace of reassurance), which descends upon the place where angels are present. Thus, salah carries the hue of the presence and worship of the angels.

Some angels are constantly in a state of bowing, while others remain in prostration, all expressing their reverence to God. In a way, the human version of salah mirrors the worship of angels. However, while each class of angels perpetually performs only one type of worship, human beings engage in all of them during a single salah.

When we look at the creatures on earth, we see that some of them stand on two legs, some on four, and some lie on their belly; this is how they demonstrate their worship of Allah through the tongue of their disposition. As for human worship, it has the quality of representing the worship of all creatures and presenting it to God on their behalf. In addition, the postures during the prayer signify certain things in nature and guides human beings to understand the unique qualities and superior abilities they possess compared to what is given to other creatures. While standing, the believer says, "Praise be to You, my Lord, that you did not create me as a vertical and motionless object like a tree. Thanks to the joints You gave me, I can bend down and get up, and I can make all kinds of movements effortlessly." While bowing in (*ruku'*), "Praise be to

You, You have not created me as certain creatures (like cattle) which constantly remain in horizontal positions." And during prostration, "Praise be to You, for You have not made me a creature constantly creeping on the ground." Concerning all these positions and postures God Almighty states:

واللهُ خَلَقَ كُلَّ دَابَّةٍ مِنْ مَاءٍ فَمِنْهُمْ مَنْ يَمْشِي عَلَى بَطْنِهِ وَمِنْهُمْ مَنْ يَمْشِي عَلَى رِجْلَيْنِ وَمِنْهُمْ مَنْ يَمْشِي عَلَى أَرْبَعٍ يَخْلُقُ اللهُ مَا يَشَاءُ إِنَّ اللهَ عَلَى كُلِّ شَيْءٍ قَدِيرٌ

God has created every living creature from water. Among them are such that move on their bellies, and such that move on two legs, and such that move on four. God creates whatever He wills. Surely God has full power over everything. (an-Nur 24:45)

In summary, salah is essentially an index that reminds us of all acts of worship in the entire creation.

d. Preparation for salah

Because of the blessed and extraordinary nature of salah in God's sight, the works done in the way of salah are also counted as if they were a part of the salah. Anything done in pursuit of an important task is as precious as the task itself, for "the intention of a believer is better than their deeds."[8] We rely on God Almighty's infinite mercy on this issue and say, from the *istibra* (ceasing of impurity) we make in preparation for salah to the steps we take on the way to the location of prayer, all relevant acts will be evaluated like salah and earn us rewards due for salah. The Messenger of God states,

لاَ يَزَالُ أَحَدُكُمْ فِي صَلاَةٍ مَا انْتَظَرَ الصَّلاَةَ

"As long as any one of you is waiting for the prayer, that person is considered to be actually praying."[9]

Another Prophetic narration is as follows:

8　Tabarani, *Al-Mu'jam al-Kabir* 6/185-186; Bayhaqi, *Al-Sunan al-Sugra*, p.20.

9　Bukhari, Adhan, 30. For narrations with similar meaning, see: Bukhari, Masajid 36, Buyu 49, Bedu'l Khalq 7; Muslim, Masajid 275.

While sitting under a tree with his friends next to him, Salman of the Companions takes a piece of branch in his hand and begins to shed its leaves by shaking it, and then says to those next to him, "will you not ask why I am doing this?" When those near him ask why, he answers thus: "The Messenger of God also did so and asked whether we would not ask why he was doing that. And when we asked why, he answered as follows": "When a Muslim makes ablutions properly, and then goes to observe salah, like these leaves are being shed, his [or her] sins too will be shed."[10]

From the moment a believer sets out for any location of prayer or to a *masjid* (mosque) – although they have not begun observing salah yet – they are counted as being spiritually in salah. God's Messenger expressed this situation plainly in another hadith. Accordingly, one night, God asked the Prophet whether he knew what those in *Mala' al-A'la* (the Supreme Assembly[11]) are competing for. When the Prophet replied he did not, God let him know what is happening in the heavens and earth. Then He asked the same question to the Prophet again. This time the Prophet replied in the affirmative and said that they were competing for the deeds which increase a person's rank and deeds which become atonement for sins. Those that serve as atonement are: "walking for observing salah, making ablutions thoroughly during intense cold, and waiting for the next prayer after having observed one. Whoever continues these, lives upon goodness (*khayr*) and dies upon goodness. Concerning sins, the person attains a (purified) state as if newly born."[12]

Accordingly, waiting for the next salah after having observed one is an important point among those in the highest heavenly assemblies. For example, you have just observed *dhuhr*, thus there is no obligatory prayer you are supposed to observe. You say to yourself "I wish the time for the *asr* prayer comes as soon as possible, so that I can stand in the Divine presence and observe it too…" This eagerness and waiting of

---

10 Ibn Hanbal, *Musnad*, 5/437; Darimi, Tahara 45.

11 The Supreme Assembly indicates the angels and those spiritual beings, the Noble Friends, who are closest to Allah.

12 Al-Bazzar, *Musnad* 11/42.

yours become a matter of competition among the angels for recording this good deed. From the moment a servant intends to worship, it means the person has stepped into worship.

The steps taken on the way to and from the mosque hold a distinct merit because mosques are blessed places where worship, supplications, petitions, and sincere intentions rise to God. Observing salah at home instead of the mosque might deprive the worshipper of both observing salah in the proper sense and the twenty-seven-fold more rewards that would come when observed with other fellow worshippers instead of alone.

The tribe of Banu Salima was located on the outskirts of Medina. As it was difficult for them to come to the mosque in time for salah, they feared they would miss out from the Prophet's teachings. So, they decided to move near the mosque. When the Messenger heard about their decision, he told them to remain in their present neighborhood, and said, "Don't you take into consideration the reward due for the steps you take while coming to the mosque?" They remained where they lived.[13]

Muslims are expected to observe salah in the *masjid*. All oriented towards the Ka'ba (the mosque of God), mosques serve as signposts on earth, pointing to the direction that leads worshippers to God. Therefore, the prayers observed in congregation are counted among those observed near the Ka'ba. The Ka'ba, a mosque commanded by God, serves as the central point. The other mosques in the periphery align their pulpits and direction towards the Ka'ba, the House of God. Given that all of us are not able to observe our salah at the Ka'ba all the time, by attending *masjid*s in close proximity, which are Ka'ba's counterparts throughout the earth, we can hope to gain rewards as if we observed our salah there.

e. The reward of prayer

Salah, performed five times a day, fosters personal growth and guides individuals towards attaining the desired status of *insan al-kamil* (a perfected being, a true human). It is hoped that people purify with salah so much so that they become a bright mirror to reflect the Divine Names and Attributes and manifest the color of the state the Divine commands

---

13   Bukhari, Adhan 33, Fadailu'l-Medina 11; Muslim, Masajid 280-281.

bring on. For example, one asks, "what does my God ask of me? What does He expect from me? Is it to stand in His presence obediently? Then I do this by standing in prayer with salah before Him. Does He require me to control my pride and overcome my arrogance? Then I fulfill this with bowing down (*ruku'*) before Him. Does He require me to give reverence to Him? Then I acknowledge His Greatness and therefore show deep and complete reverence for Him with my prostration." This is how a believer "takes the color of God" [14] and shows the will and readiness to obey Divine commandments. Namely, it is the relief of their inner world with faith in God. Actual faith, devotion, and worship colors the life of a person. Their forehead's gain a blessed luster and become honored with reflecting the truth expressed in,

سِيمَاهُمْ فِي وُجُوهِهِمْ مِنْ أَثَرِ السُّجُودِ

"Their marks are on their faces, traced by prostration" (al-Fath 48:29). Note that this is not necessarily a reference to a physical mark. Washed by their ablution their body parts will shine to be spotted from a distance in the afterlife, as described by the Messenger of God ﷺ:

> "Suppose a man had horses with white blazes on their foreheads and legs, among horses which are all black. Tell me, would he not recognize his own horses?"

Thus those who pray display all otherworldly hues of the Divine Realms. Surely, there cannot be any better dye than that.

Salah is a very pleasant deed for those who savor its taste. However, it is a weight and burden for those who fail to make a proper assessment of it. In instances where individuals are unable to observe their salah, devout believers may blame themselves excessively, as though they've committed an unforgivable sin. Meanwhile, others might view it as a burdensome obligation imposed by God, something to be endured merely to fulfill a duty.

A sane person remembers that they are not eternal in this world, and that death will visit them one day, and that signs of old age are actually heralds of death; thus they try to reciprocate God's blessings with

---

14   "[O Muslims, say], we take the color of God. Who is better than God in coloring? And We are those who worship Him [as He is to be worshipped] exclusively" (al-Baqarah 2:138).

their due; so they use most of the twenty-four hours given to them in this world in order to make preparation for the Hereafter. Such persons will not suffice with merely sparing one hour for salah, because salah allows their spirits to breathe, allows them to stand in Divine presence with material and spiritual purification, become eligible for a favorable passing to the afterlife and behold the Beauty of God (*Jamalullah*). In other words, salah will let them sense what is normally beyond senses and see what is beyond sight. By performing additional *nawafil* prayers amongst the five daily prayers, they try to increase their gains.

إِنَّ أَثْقَلَ صَلَاةٍ عَلَى الْمُنَافِقِينَ صَلَاةُ الْعِشَاءِ وَصَلَاةُ الْفَجْرِ، وَلَوْ يَعْلَمُونَ مَا فِيهِمَا لَأَتَوْهُمَا وَلَوْ حَبْوًا

The Messenger of God ﷺ said: "No prayer is more burdensome to the hypocrites than dawn and evening prayer. If they knew the blessing in them, they would come even if they had to crawl."[15]

Hypocrisy comprises deceiving others and acting insincerely. The insincerity of a hypocrite does not allow them to take all the trouble to attend the *fajr* and *isha* prayers, because the times for these prayers are the most difficult to leave behind one's comfort and languor. Those who truly believe, however, say "there is mercy in hardship"; that is, "no pain, no gain," and they pray *fajr* and *isha* prayers behind the imam in complete devotion to God, and thus observe servitude to the Almighty Creator. It should be noted here that scholars of Islamic law dispute on the degree of obligation (*fard*, *wajib*) of observing these prayers in congregation.

Salah is the worthiest thing for a person in this world. Some people work so hard for worldly gains, even though they might not even get them in this short life. It is pitiful that the same people shun spending a total of one hour to observe salah every day, a practice that will reward them with Paradise and seeing the Beauty of God (*Jamalullah*).

Many people complain that their income is not enough, that their compensation does not correspond to the amount of work they do. Bosses, employers, and politicians always give promises to people, yet many of them can hardly keep them. However, if the one who promises is God Almighty, He definitely fulfills what He promised. If He promised that He will let believers pass the "Bridge of Sirat" to Paradise as quick as

---

15   Bukhari, Adhan 34, Mawaqit 20; Muslim, Masajid 252.

lightning, bless them with beholding His Beauty, reward the tears they shed during their prayers and supplications, and appraise them as "priceless" should they pray, He absolutely will. God Almighty, Who has absolute power over everything and Who lets believers affirm this several times a day by saying "هُوَ عَلَى كُلِّ شَيْءٍ قَدِيرٌ" (Indeed, God has power over all things) definitely fulfills His promises. He is equally capable to fulfil the punishments He decreed for engaging in the things He forbid.

In the same vein, we should consider the same thing about the warnings, cautions and threats He makes. God has the absolute power to count sins against us. God has the absolute power to carry out the punishments He decreed for what He forbids, but He also has the will and power to forgive. He therefore leaves the door of forgiveness and mercy open all the time.

God Almighty, who never breaks His word, promises Paradise to His servants in return for their salah. Believers ascend to the heavenly realms by means of a special "staircase" of salah. Observing salah five times a day is like adding a five-step-stringer to one's life to go higher up each day. Believers who have continued observing prayers will be overjoyed upon encountering the mercy God will bestow on them after their passing. The Qur'an depicts the situation of a believer in the next world as follows:

> Anyone who is given his Record in his right hand will say, "Here is my Record, read it. I knew I would meet my Reckoning," and so he will have a pleasant life in a lofty Garden, with clustered fruit within his reach. It will be said, "Eat and drink to your heart's content as a reward for what you have done in days gone by. (al-Haqqa 69:19–24)

May Almighty God include us among those righteous people.

We are sent to this world so that we undergo training and become qualified for the exalted ranks of the other world. Everything here consists of a process of learning and training, making up for our faults, getting rid of our undesired aspects, making spiritual progress as much as we can, and thus being eligible for Paradise and for beholding Allah. The worship to effectuate these purposes best is salah, for salah is too great to compare with other acts of worship. It is the main pillar of religion. It is like the mast of a sailing vessel.

As the staircase of ascension (*mi'raj*) salah serves as the greatest means for our spiritual progress, and we continue to observe salah until the end of our lives, until we meet His Mercy. When we make that ascension, salah will speak on our behalf like, "O Allah, these people did not let me down while in the world. So, do not let them down here, please!" However, if we failed to observe salah as perfect as we should, from ablutions to its physical moves and other acts of goodness, then it will say, "May Allah let you down, just like you let us down."

If there is no inclination for salah in a society particularly among their educated and intellectual circles, it means that the religious life there is withering away. Considering the wretched condition of Muslim peoples today, we can say that those who are too arrogant to prostrate before the Majesty of God present sycophancy to so many little ones like themselves, and we may then better understand the reason for that wretchedness.

People who do not believe that they will be called to account for everything they did replace their fear of God and feeling of responsibility by misappropriation, dissipation, and the like. However, real believers cannot be like that as they bear the concern for being called to account for even minor things. Therefore, they take their steps accordingly. A believer who sincerely comes to the prayer five times a day and renews their covenant with God essentially says, "O Allah, I have not forgotten that I am Your servant; here I have come to Your presence to confess this. When I leave after salah, I will arrange my life accordingly, and will not cease to be mindful of You for even a moment. I will take my steps heedfully with a consciousness of Your omnipresence and witnessing. Let alone violating the rights of other people, I will not even step on an ant." Believers must think this way, otherwise they will contradict their own previous statements and become liars. For a believer who stands and bows forty times and prostrates eighty times a day before God and thus proclaims and confesses His Lordship and Greatness, there can hardly be any deflections as such in their lives.

To the extent we reveal our humbleness before Him with worship, God will honor us and let us rise to the uppermost level of humanity. Otherwise, as long as we live as slaves to our own whims and interests, only run after worldly desires and pursuits, and thus neglect, miss, and fail to observe the prayer constantly and attentively, we might seem to be winning but, in fact, will be losing so much for the other world. May Allah let us succeed at remembering Him and the Afterlife in all circumstances. May He let us act in such a way that we always remember Him. May He let us be conscious of the Reckoning and the Day of Judgment, when the record of our deeds is opened, so that we adjust our acts accordingly. The ideal believer is such a person that on seeing them you remember the Afterlife and God and your heart gains its right course.

How fortunate are those who run to the prayer and *masjid* to pray five times a day, who dive into the rivers and waterfalls of salah and ablution, who are cleansed of material and spiritual impurities, who then stand in the presence of Allah in that purified state and ask Him for prosperity here and in the hereafter.

2. Salah as a form of worship

a. Ta'abbudi worship

In turning to God, engaging in worship, and offering supplications lies a hidden secret of servitude. Even if a person may not fully comprehend the meanings, reasons, or wisdom behind an act of worship, decrees, or prohibitions, they still observe it solely because God commanded it, thereby demonstrating their obedience and servitude. This is called *ta'abbudi*. Besides, through this act of servitude, one may experience benefits such as the spiritual nourishment and awakening of the heart, spirit, feelings, and the inner spiritual faculty known as the *sirr* (secret). One's subtle faculties may turn towards God as a result of worship. Other than these, upon reflection, one may discover additional reasons, wisdom, and benefits too.

For example, it can be understood by reason that *Zakat* (charity) is Islam's bridge between the rich and poor as it enables them to come together and care for one another, raising amicable feelings and harmony, thus preventing bloody clashes between the haves and have-nots. Considering the Hajj, one can infer that it is a journey of revitalization, and that it is like a congress or convention which brings the world's Muslims together. It can be deduced that thanks to *sawm* (fasting), the human carnal soul learns patience, self-control, obedience, and even finds physical health by following a kind of diet.

However, a believer never attaches their acts to those benefits and wisdoms. Because they know that what matters the most in acts of worship is their being *ta'abbudi*. Irrespective of their known wisdom or benefits, regardless of whether one fully comprehends them, adhering to Divine commands solely because they are decreed as such is paramount. It's acknowledging that there may be numerous wise purposes behind them, some of which our own understanding may not yet grasp. As is the case with *zakat*, fasting, and Hajj, it is possible to discuss the wisdom behind the differences of certain times of salah, differences between the number of *rak'ah*s (units) or particular acts like bowing down and prostration. However, a sincere believer does not attach his or her salah to these wisdoms. On the contrary, they take Divine Commands as basis of their belief and practice. In *Usul al-Fiqh* (Methodology of Islamic jurisprudence), this quality is termed as being "*ta'abbudi*."

An important aspect of *ta'abbudi* is that you do not seek a cause-and-effect relationship between what you do and what God grants you. For example, you observe your salah, and you may see many of your prayers that pertain to this world and the next are answered, and your heart, spirit, reason, and feelings feel satisfied. Your wishes are fulfilled in such a way that even you wonder how it happened. There is a subtle point here: *Ta'abbudi* acts reinforce more *ta'abbudi* acts. That is, it develops in you the feeling of observing worship just because it was commanded.

Consider the miracles of Muhammad, the Last Prophet of God ﷺ. Remember how the moon was split in two by a gesture of his finger; how he beckoned a tree, and it moved towards him. Remember how he passed his blessed hand over some little amount of food, and it became abundant to feed seven hundred people. In accordance with the cause-and-effect principle there is no rational explanation for these phenomena, but it is understood that only God Almighty granted such special blessings. In the same light, as individuals observe and compare their worship and the blessings it brings, they may notice an increase in their sense of *ta'abbudi*, especially as they are bestowed with more blessings in accordance with their limited attitudes, behaviors, and spiritual development.

In addition, being *ta'abbudi* bears much importance since it engenders a unique set of feelings or understanding, such as, not seeking anything in return for worship, fulfilling and interpreting deeds exclusively in accordance with Divine commands, and turning to God with utter sincerity. Furthermore, it supports and enhances the feeling of seeking out His good pleasure and approval.

There is also an aspect of *ta'abbudi* not only in obligatory acts of worship, but even in the essential commandments that regulate people's personal, familial, and social lives. The idea and intention of doing things solely for the sake of obeying God can also apply to the things a person does in their daily life like transactions, dealings, and interpersonal relations (*muamalat*). While common sense and practical wisdom typically guide daily interactions and transactions, individuals may still act in accordance with *ta'abbudi* principles even in these matters. Grounded in *ta'abbudi*, people may conduct their dealings based on divine command rather than solely relying on their own intellect, rationale, or personal interests.

When the person carries out their daily mundane dealings and worship as is commanded by God, it means that they are training and attuning themselves for sincere servitude to God. Said Nursi expands on this as follows: if a person observes certain daily acts for the sake of God with a sound intention—for example if the person has the intention of following the tradition (*sunnah*) of the Messenger of God and thus eats like him, acts like him, and tries to be like him at every act— then that person will have transformed even daily mundane acts into worship.[16]

The underlying essential of being *ta'abbudi* is to recognize God Almighty as the Absolute Ruler, the Ultimate Sovereign, and the True and Ultimate King. Human beings are His servants and therefore, they are His "property." The Owner has the absolute right of initiative and disposal of what He owns. Hence, God holds absolute sovereignty over determining what we should do and how we should behave in this world. On the other hand, God also bestowed upon humans the role of vicegerency (*khilafah*) among His creation. This entails granting them a relative form of ownership and the capacity for discretion over other beings. Humans must absolutely surrender to and follow the orders of the Absolute Sov-

---

16 Nursi, *The Gleams*, 11th Gleam.

ereign and Disposer of Affairs with a consideration of being *ta'abbudi*; as for ordinary tasks and disposal over things, they should make use of the relative right granted to them. While using this right, they should still know that the actual Owner of everything and the true Causer is God.

God Almighty created certain laws, which are His way of doing things, such as repulsion, attraction, friction, and gravity in the universe. For example, grass and trees grow and flourish as long as they find suitable ground and continuously receive sunlight and water. Plants' growing with water and yielding fruits and crops is also a law of God. Actually, God is the One Who creates the result to be obtained from watering, but He assigned watering as an apparent cause. Knowing this cause, we develop different methods of irrigation according to the conditions of our time, like science, technology and understanding, and we practice them. When sowing seeds, we adopt and implement whichever method is necessary to achieve the maximum expected result from those seeds.

However, even while sowing the seeds we know that our acts merely serve as an apparent cause. God is the One Who will give the crop. He makes them grow if He wills. If the crop will be twice as abundant, He is the One Who gives it if He wills. However, we say that He renders causes as a veil for His Dignity and Grandeur (*'izzah* and *'azamah*). "Divine Dignity and Grandeur require that causes serve as a veil before the operation of Divine Power. On the other hand, Divine Oneness and Majesty (*Tawhid* and *Jalal*) require causality to be dismissed from being perceived as the actual doer."[17] This is the understanding we follow. Even in such matters, we maintain a *ta'abbudi* mindset and observe worship to God accordingly. By adhering to causality because He granted us a relative right and ability for discretion over things, as well as commanded us to exercise this right, we truly embody the actual consciousness of servitude.

b. Worshipping without expecting anything in return

The comprehensive term "*ubudiyyah*" comes to mean obedience, submission, worship, devotion, and servitude to God. As for the believers, who have grasped the essence of *ubudiyyah*, they carry out all deeds

---

17   Nursi, *The Words*, (29th Word, First Purpose, Second Purpose, "Gleams of Truth").

solely for the sake of God's being pleased with them. They exclusively seek out the ways and gates leading to God's good pleasure. If God the Almighty Truth (al-Haqq) grants their soul to gain true strength, He elevates them to the level at which they have a fully functioning spiritual heart. At that level, they appreciate this also as another gift of the Most Merciful and Compassionate. No matter whether God grants them with such an ideal result or not, the believers remain devoted exclusively to the Exalted Creator. If they experience some extraordinary things and witness some wonders (*karamat*) happen, they evaluate them with a sincere attitude, like that of saintly servants of God, saying, "*A slave as I am, I am not worthy of this gift; why am I being granted this favor?* (Muhammed Lutfi) I sought the greatest treasure when I asked for You. If You are with me, it is fine if I do not have anything else; because only when I find You will I have found everything and will have been saved from poverty." By voicing this consideration, the person lives with a complete consciousness of servitude.

Those who harbor no other expectations find themselves fully committed to the path, free from the risk of wavering, unlike others who may easily be led astray. Their hearts, devoid of ulterior motives, pulsate with the following considerations:

> O God, You have granted me infinite blessings for free! I have already received everything in advance. You have given me the blessing of life, You honored me by creating me as human, You have brightened up my heart with the light of Islam and granted me the opportunity to walk on the path of Your knowledge (*ma'rifa*) and love (*muhabba*). You have bestowed me the means to serve for the good of my people and humanity. I have already received what I will and You have made me responsible for an enjoyable, comfortable and simple service. Now what falls to me is to gain Your approval by making good use of those bestowals of Yours... to observe worship and servitude to You as much as I can, and then seek refuge in Your mercy and munificence.

On account of such considerations, saintly persons mostly implore to God as follows in their prayers:

O my Lord! You bestowed upon us unmerited favors even without us feeling the need to exist, or anything else at all. And now we are in need of servitude to You with sincerity. We are in need of Your grace and generosity. We did not exist, nor could we even imagine about coming to existence; we never took and could not take becoming human into consideration. We never thought of them as our needs, but You bestowed them to us out of Your munificence. But from now on, we are in so much in need of You for everything, even to be able to stand... we need You so much to not stumble and fall... we need You so much to stay on the path to Paradise, to not be tripped by our weaknesses and to walk towards gaining Your good pleasure! O God, Who has blessed us with things without our knowledge of needing them! Here we are begging You for the things we need!

It is very important to know the Almighty Haqq to the degree we are supposed to know Him. It is very important for us to turn to Him as He turned to us. We seek this at His door again and say, "O God, please enable us to know You; let our hearts have their share from knowing You... let our spirits be sated with Your love. Please, do not let our hearts stray ever. Please give us the willpower to overcome Satan and the carnal soul!"

c. Shirk and riya in worship (associating partners with God and affectation)

Diseases such as affectation, where one seeks to display their religiosity for others to see or hear (*riya* and *sum'a*), originate from inherent character flaws and weaknesses in human nature, which manifest in various forms. At times, deeds are performed solely to gain attention or recognition, a clear manifestation of hypocrisy. Other times, actions may be embellished to appear profound, seeking admiration from those present. The following depiction of the Qur'an with reference to hypocrites and the manner they go to the mosque by dragging their feet can be given as an example to the first situation:

إِنَّ الْمُنَافِقِينَ يُخَادِعُونَ اللهَ وَهُوَ خَادِعُهُمْ وَإِذَا قَامُوا إِلَى الصَّلٰوةِ قَامُوا كُسَالٰى يُرَاءُونَ النَّاسَ وَلَا يَذْكُرُونَ اللهَ إِلَّا قَلِيلًا

The hypocrites try to trick God, whereas it is God who "tricks" them [by causing them to fall into their own traps]. When they rise to do the Prayer, they rise lazily, and to be seen by people [to show them that they are Muslims]; and they do not remember God [within or outside the Prayer] save a little. (an-Nisa 4:142)

During the time of the Prophet, the hypocrites made an effort to appear like Muslims, they observed salah with considerations of having a share of the perceived benefits and advantages that seemed important to them. They would come to the *masjid* unwillingly, pretend to carry out the prayer in their half-hearted way, and then seek to swiftly leave the mosque thereafter. In their attitude and behavior, the hypocrites showed no genuine concern for observing salah; their sole aim was to portray themselves as devout. This point about salah can apply to other forms of worship too. For example, if a person who has no concern for making *dhikr* (remembrance of God) but engages in useless chitchat for hours and then takes the prayer beads and starts *dhikr* to show off to others, his condition also falls within the frame described above.

At times, the intention behind an observed deed may not initially be to impress others, but the individual may succumb to the temptation of embellishing it to appear more profound. For example, imagine a man praying alone, if he does it haphazardly without compliance with the manners and he bows down very quickly to leave, doubtful of whether he was able to say *Subhana Rabbiy'al Azim* (glory be to my Lord Almighty) at least once; then after rising from bowing, he makes the prostration right away without straightening up properly, his demeanor in prostration not being different from the one while bowing. Then, the same man who quickly does the bowing and prostration in such a reckless fashion while alone adopts an attitude of observing salah with great care near others, then that person is committing a behavior that smells of *shirk* (associating partners with God), as stated in one hadith.[18]

Indeed, such behaviors are prone to be inflicted with *shirk*, because the person does not seek approval from God but only takes into consideration the approval of other people. However, any depth reflected outwardly can only gain value if it exists in the heart as well. Otherwise try-

---

18   Ibn Majah, Zuhd 21; Ibn Hanbal, *Musnad* 3/30.

ing to appear profound with the purpose of being liked by other people is a very dangerous condition, and—may God protect us from it—this will be recorded in that person's record of deeds as *shirk*.

Shirk, however, is what Islam primarily aims to rescue individuals from – for, Islam is but the name of the system of divine commandments that were revealed to eliminate *shirk*. Here, let me reiterate the fact that it is because He is God that He is the One that is worshipped, loved, and eternally besought; He is not God because He is worshipped. Hence, it is His right and our duty to align all our thoughts accordingly and devote them entirely to God Himself. We are meant to observe servitude to Him and steadfastly avoid associating partners with Him. Having other thoughts and intentions in our worship (other than worshipping Him only for His pleasure) ruins the essence of worship.

An ideal horizon all of us should seek to reach during worship and when we try to carry out certain services is to take solely God's approval and good pleasure into consideration. We should endeavor to fulfill our duty of servitude to Him even during unfavorable circumstances. We should be concerned if our thoughts spoil our sincerity and corrupt our worship. On the other hand, the attitude or mentality of seeking to look nice to others and to expect their appreciation and compliments instead of seeking to make God well pleased is doubtlessly an ugly and problematic mindset that does not befit a believer.

To put this in the Qur'anic way, everything to be done for God needs to be pure and wholesome. Not even a grain of the impure should be allowed into the pure, for that grain may cause it to be utterly corrupted. And this means nothing but making Satan pleased, whereas the purpose of a believer is rather making God well-pleased.

Minor shirk: Riya (affectation)

Sometimes one can be inclined to show off while praying. The Prophet said: "The thing that I fear most for my community is the minor *shirk* [associating partners with God]." When the Companions asked him what it was, the Messenger of God said that it is *riya* (affectation).[19] If "major *shirk*" is to accept things other than God as deities to be

---

19   Ibn Hanbal, *Musnad* 5/428, 429; Tabarani, *al-Mujamu'l Kabir* 4/253.

worshipped, then what does "minor *shirk*" refer to? Minor *shirk* is when a person does things – including worship – only to show off, and when he or she puts his or her personal desires at the center of all things they do. Beyond merely observing salah, it is crucial to consider how a person performs it and the emotions they experience during the act. First of all, salah must be observed for the sake of God and as a thanksgiving for the blessings He has already given. God grants people limitless bounties at every stage of their life.

God, in consideration of our spiritual needs and constitution, provides us with suitable environments and opportunities for prayer. He endows us with the ability for worship, opens our hearts to it, and grants us guidance. Moreover, to facilitate our fulfillment of servitude, He equips us with the capacity to meet its demands. Thus, if we genuinely desire, we are capable of observing the daily prayers, which is a major blessing.

Sometimes, a person intends to observe salah but may be unable to do so, for instance, due to paralysis. Similarly, someone might be unable to attend Jumu'ah or Eid prayers because they are in prison. Therefore, while we have the opportunity we should worship God at every step of this life, with our hearts filled with infinite gratitude.

When believers stand before God in salah, they first express their thankfulness, for they are completely indebted to Him. If God were to reclaim all that belongs to Him from us, nothing would remain. Accordingly, we can only stand before Him with the blessings He has bestowed upon us.

Obviously, the salah is purely a bestowal from God to us. We stand before Him to express our gratitude to Him with the things He bestowed upon us. While this is the case, it is impertinent to forget about Him and to observe worship not for Him but for showing off to others. This is the actual meaning of *riya* (affectation). For this reason, there are instances where a person's intentional avoidance of *riya* can paradoxically resemble *riya* itself, as it may come across as artificial behavior.

Are we supposed to be extremely worried about *riya*? If we grow aware that all things belong to God, then we need not worry about *riya* anymore. Are we aware that we stand on the two legs given by Him? Are we aware that we worship God with the strength He provided? Are we aware that only God makes our hearts beat? Some scholars considered it also *riya* to abandon what one normally does with a concern of avoiding *riya*. As for showing off to people, they see it as associating partners (*shirk*) with God. This is the point that separates ordinary people from special servants of God; this is a matter of comprehension.

Let us be reminded once again that affectation is to display a merit that you do not really have. Hadith scholar Al-Samarqandi tells of the situation of someone who shows off his deeds as follows: A man fills his purse with pebbles while going out to the market. Those who see him speak as "Look! His purse is so full!" However, the stones in the purse do him no good other than making people talk about it. If he wishes to buy anything with them, he cannot. The same holds true for someone who does deeds to let others see or hear. People say good things about it, but that person gains no reward at all in the Afterlife.[20]

A man committing *riya* is like someone who sells what he does not own. Or like someone who stands on his tiptoes to reach the window reserved for him, which is far higher than his actual standing. As Nursi puts it, "There is a window of 'social standing' for every man through which he appears to others. If the window is higher than his actual stature, he will try to look taller with vainglory. But if the window is lower than his actual stature, he will try to appear lower with modesty. For the mature and perfected ones, modesty is the criterion of greatness; in defective ones, assumed greatness is the criterion of lowliness."[21]

Whoever commits *riya*, God will show them in the next world to whom they actually worshipped. And whoever committed *sum'a* (showing off by letting others hear), God will disclose it in the high heavenly assemblies (*Mala' al-A'la*).

Nevertheless, a devout individual must possess the integrity to exhibit their attitude, behavior, or thoughts authentically, without any pretense. For example, a person who has a strong relationship with God and a deep attachment to the Prophet, having ingrained these qualities as inherent character traits, will and must "walk their talk" regarding the principles of belief they have accepted in their heart. They should behave accordingly at every moment of life, reflecting their faith through their

---

20   Abu al-Layth al-Samarqandi, *Tanbih Al-Ghafilin*, "Ikhlas."

21   Nursi, *The Words*, Gleams of Truth.

actions. Such people will perform salah and all acts of worship with due regard to its conditions, pillars, duties and preferred acts. Surely, they will do so not with a consideration to let any person see or hear them but exclusively to fulfill God's commands and attain His good pleasure.

Doing unusual actions in salah

If a person involuntarily makes sounds like sighing or wailing during salah, there is no harm in it. If these expressions genuinely arise from a state of *jazba* (religious ecstasy), then they are beyond criticism. In this state, the person is so absorbed that they are not conscious of their actions, hence the sounds they make are unintentional. Then when others say, "you acted in such and such a way," the person will be surprised and say, "I do not even remember such a thing at all." Other than that, the person should not make any sounds that are not a part of the salah. The same goes for crying. A person should stifle crying (with religious feelings) as much as possible. But if the person cannot restrain that despite everything and is crying involuntarily, then there may not be any harm in it.

Those who witnessed and spoke about how Bediüzzaman Said Nursi was while beginning and during salah would express that his eyes looked somewhat strange, and his voice sounded unusual; this is a matter of concentration level and devotion. It is entirely inappropriate for anyone who has not reached such a level to merely imitate these behaviors and present them artificially.

There is the risk of *shirk* and *riya* during worship observed with other people. If a man who carries out salah carelessly while alone observes it in an elaborate fashion near others, this is—may God forbid—secret *shirk*. On the other hand, if a person who observes salah at length while alone observes it briefly near others, there is also a risk of *riya* for it, because this behavior too involves taking others' presence into consideration, attaching a significance to it and acting accordingly. they should do so similarly when near others. It should be neither lengthy nor brief, without any distinction. Consider a shepherd who observes salah near his flock. Does he ever concern himself with whether the sheep see him praying?

d. The consciousness of servitude in worship

Transcending physicality and the constraints of the body, ascending to the spiritual realm of the heart and spirit is achievable for everyone according to their spiritual level or status.

A person's fulfilling his or her duties of worship and, on top of that, striving for the exaltation of God's good name everywhere in order to glorify His word, serve as a purifying agent, akin to bleach on physical impurities. Through this process, one can ascend to higher levels of spiritual life and progress, ultimately earning God's approval and good pleasure.

Servitude must definitely be fulfilled conscientiously. Just as people show great care in serving their guests with the best food, utensils, etc. so must we show ultimate care and scrupulousness in our worship and devotions. This is a vital way to transcend animality and overcome the carnal soul, thereby accessing the spiritual realm of the heart and spirit. If one does not or cannot perform every act of worship, from salah to fasting, with the same care as they would in doing the sweetest things, they have not truly freed themselves from animality or subdued the carnal soul. One may perform worship by doing its necessary rituals and can be saved from responsibility. However, when not done mindfully, the life of heart and spirit[22] will not thrive with such worship.

To attain higher spiritual levels in the domain of heart and spirit, believers must adhere to certain principles. Firstly, they should consume only lawful sustenance. Secondly, they should avert their gaze from prohibited sights. Thirdly, they should heed the guidance of the hadith which states, "Anyone who safeguards for My sake what is between his jaws and what is between his legs, I will safeguard paradise for him."[23] Consequently, one should refrain from engaging in unnecessary conversation and harboring feelings that lead to sinful behaviors.

---

22 The "life of heart and spirit" refers to a spiritual state or level of consciousness where one's heart is fully alive and awakened to the divine presence. In Sufi terminology, it signifies a deep spiritual connection and awareness, where the heart becomes the locus of divine illumination and guidance. It's a state where one experiences profound spiritual insights, inner peace, and closeness to God.

23 Bukhari, Riqaq 23; Abu Ya'la, *Musnad* 13/549.

In short, one must show ultimate care for worship and maintain an iron will and magnanimous mood, in a sense to see even death more likable than committing sins, since sins paralyze a person's spiritual life. Together with that, hearts must be made responsive, if they are not, they should be empowered to be so; note that as a result of this insistence and endeavor, even the most callous hearts can become responsive in time. Depending on the person's condition, such attainment may take weeks, months, or even years; however, for the sake of gaining God's good pleasure, whatever sacrifice made in this respect is worth it.

3. Observing salah mindfully

وَتَقَلُّبَكَ فِي السَّاجِدِينَ

The verse "... (Allah sees, knows) your strenuous efforts in prostration among those who prostrate" (ash-Shu'ara 26:219) not only describes how the Messenger of God ﷺ observed salah outwardly, but it also teaches us how we should do it inwardly. Given that we are supposed to observe salah in the same way he does[24]—as stated in one hadith—then it is absolutely not right to reduce this responsibility to the outward form. Matters like grasping the meaning and essence of salah and offering it in such concentration always need to be considered within this frame.

Surely, it is not possible for our salah to equate with that of a Prophet in terms of both form and meaning; we cannot feel what he did. However, this does not mean that we should not walk in his footsteps. Everyone can and should strive to perfect their worship according to their relationship with God and the significance they place on Him in their heart.

A believer goes to pray willingly and with the enthusiasm of doing the most blissful act. We witness the most apparent examples of this at Jumu'ah prayer, Eid, and near the Ka'ba where Hajj is observed. The believers go to salah fast and eagerly as if they are going to attend a big feast and they stride quickly with a concern for not missing their worship. Their purpose is to get to the mosque as soon as possible and arrive in the presence of God and fulfill their servitude. Such a deep meaning can be felt in the way people rush to the Prophet's tomb as well. On seeing

---

24 Bukhari, *Adhan* 18, *Adab* 27, *Tamanni* 9; Darimi, *Salat* 42.

people carrying prayer rugs on their shoulders, still holding their shoes after the ablution, without pausing to brush their hair and beards, and running toward Him so enthusiastically, oblivious to those around them, one cannot help but be touched by the scene.

Salah bears the excitement of such a rush. This meaning can be sensed in salah which can be felt by believers. As for hypocrites, since they cannot feel that meaning, they come to salah in a manner of ridding themselves of a burden; since they cannot have this zest via belief, they carry it out like a chore. As for salah carried out like being rid of a burden, it will only be observed drowsily and by yawning; God describes this state of the hypocrites as follows:

وَإِذَا قَامُوا إِلَى الصَّلَاةِ قَامُوا كُسَالَى يُرَاءُونَ النَّاسَ وَلَا يَذْكُرُونَ اللهَ إِلَّا قَلِيلًا

> When they rise to do the prayer, they rise lazily, and to be seen by people; and they do not remember God save a little. (an-Nisa 4:142)

A hypocrite is in a constant state of laziness when it comes to practicing religion. They come to the Divine presence dragging their feet. They yearn to quickly conclude their prayers and exit, driven by their dual existence, their hearts devoid of the zest for salah. May God not allow such a feeling to nest in our hearts, which is considered a big stain on the heart profile of a believer.

فَوَيْلٌ لِلْمُصَلِّينَ ۞ الَّذِينَ هُمْ عَنْ صَلَاتِهِمْ سَاهُونَ

> And woe to those worshippers (denying the Judgment), those who are unmindful in their prayers. (al-Maun 107:4–5)

Sahw (mistake, lapse) means being distracted from Him while standing in the Divine presence. A weak narration explains this as follows: "A time comes when (thousands of) people fill mosques. They observe salah but there is no believer among them."[25] May God protect us from falling headfirst like that. We hope He forgives each and every one of us for the sake of the good people with whom we keep company and whose prayers are acceptable. When God grants His mercy on an entire group that has gathered to remember and glorify Him and angels wonder, "There was so-and-so amongst them; he was not one of them,

---

25   Ibn Abi Shayba, *al-Musannaf* 6/163, 7/505.

but he was just there for some need." Allah would say, "These are those people whose companions will not be reduced to misery." God Almighty forgives even such individuals, as they are part of a group with whom He is pleased. Anyone who joins them will not be deprived of His favor.[26]

Believers are anticipated to engage in salah fervently, experiencing the tranquility of complete devotion to God; this is the manner and attitude expected from believers. Heedlessness should not be anywhere near them. While coming to the Divine presence with enthusiasm and saying the exaltation "*Allahu Akbar*," they remember all truths about servitude to God, acknowledge His being the Absolute One to be worshipped and thus confess their own impotence and poverty before Him. When they say, إِيَّاكَ نَعْبُدُ (to You we worship) they bear considerations such as, 'Our Lord! We have come to Your presence by purifying our hearts. You alone do we worship, and to You alone do we ask for help. We have abandoned everything we ran after in the world, and we have removed all but You from our sight. Now we are petitioning for Your mercy. Maybe we have undertaken a very heavy task and thus will have difficulty at carrying this load; actually keeping our hearts with You all the time and letting them always tremble with Your awe is such a hard duty! However, our hearts are smiling now as they turn to the otherworldly horizon, Divine realm of Yours.' Afterwards they add, "O God! From You alone do we seek help with events that could cause hardship for us. Please support us and uphold our good causes. Let salah, this quintessence of prayer, pervade all phases of our life. We therefore say earnestly, وَإِيَّاكَ نَسْتَعِينُ (from You alone do we seek help and assistance).

And the next petition is, اِهْدِنَا الصِّرَاطَ الْمُسْتَقِيمَ meaning: "Guide us to the Straight Path, to the path of the Prophets, truthful ones and martyrs, which you accept as the main road!" After seeking refuge in God with these words, the worshipper bows down before God, before His greatness.

In the same way, as they bow for *ruku'*, believers say سُبْحَانَ رَبِّيَ الْعَظِيمِ, which can be paraphrased as "O my Almighty God! I proclaim that You are the Benevolent One to His servants, Who favors them with blessings" and thus renews their pledge of faith.

---

26   Bukhari, Daawat 66; Muslim, Dhikr 25.

While rising back from *ruku'*, the believer praises Allah, Who enabled us to rise anew after we bowed down under the weight of the reckoning, then continues with سَمِعَ اللهُ لِمَنْ حَمِدَهُ (God hears who thankfully praises Him). And after standing upright, the person affirms the previous phrase by saying رَبَّنَا لَكَ الْحَمْدُ, "Indeed, all praise and gratitude is due to You O God!" And sometimes, the person finds saying this not enough and adds (Al-lah اللهُ أَكْبَرُ كَبِيرًا وَالْحَمْدُ لِلَّهِ كَثِيرًا وَسُبْحَانَ اللهِ بُكْرَةً وَأَصِيلًا is the greatest of all, we praise Him much and our glorification is to Him day and night). When a Companion said this on rising from *ruku'*, the Prophet asked who said those words and the Companion answered that it was him; then the Prophet stated: "I like those words. The gates of Heaven were opened for them."[27]

In short, salah is an utter confession of one's worship and servitude to God. It is a worship in which all meanings and stages of life are sprinkled. Therefore, a believer, a servant of God, feels and experiences it with enthusiasm from the call to prayer (*adhan*) to the end of salah, finishing with wishing peace to all.

a. The true meaning of salah

There are *zahiri* (outward, external) and *batini* (inward, internal) conditions or pillars of salah. Fulfilling outward conditions completes the duty; when someone observes them in full, we deduce that he or she has done it well. Having a firm intention, being sincere and mindful are about the inward aspects of salah. While some scholars considered being mindful to be among the *arkan* (pillars) of salah, others accepted it as necessary (*wajib*) in *fiqh* categories.

Outward conditions are like the mold into which the salah is poured—without the outward conditions observed, inward aspects of salah cannot be attained. Washing your face three times during ablution is one of the pillars of salah; yet fulfilling this requirement properly does not cover the inward dimension of salah. That entirely depends on a servant's relationship with God.

Salah is an act that manifests the true nature or essence of being human. In the following hadith on this subject, the Prophet said:

---

27   Muslim, Masajid 150; Tirmidhi, Daawat 127; Nasai, Iftitah 8.

"When you get up in the morning, charity is due from every one of your joints. There is charity in every ascription of glory to Allah (*SubhanAllah*); there is charity in every utterance of praise of Him (*Alhamdulillah*); there is charity in every declaration that He is the only true Allah (*La ilaha illa'llah*); there is charity in every declaration of His Greatness (*Allahu Akbar*); there is charity in enjoining good; there is charity in forbidding evil. Two units of *Duha* (Forenoon Prayer) is equal to all this (in reward)."[28]

When the person is vigorous and busy with work in the morning, by running to stand obediently in the presence of God, the person profoundly appreciates and expresses the worth of the joints God bestowed upon them. As such, the *duha* salah can serve as a gratitude for all the joints. Moreover, the five daily prayers may also serve as expressions of gratitude.

Salah reflects and manifests the true essence of being a human. For this reason, after death, in the Intermediate Realm of the grave, salah will appear as a person with a beautiful face and serve as a guide for the deceased. A believer who wishes the salah they observe to appear to them not as a frightening being but as a beautiful person in the grave should observe it in compliance with its requirements and inner depths when alive.

For example, *at-tahiyyat*[29] is a form of glorifying and praising God, Who has given us countless blessings, through our tongue of servitude to respond appropriately to His exaltedness, majesty, and beauty. With the consideration that I am zero and He is infinite, and that in return for the blessings He gave I am not supposed to have the attitude of a creditor but of a debtor, and I should respond with worship and thanksgiving to Him and say *at-tahiyyat*, which is absolutely His right. If a person does not properly feel these considerations while praying alone, they can even repeat these phrases some, say, ten times. This mindset will assist the in-

---

28 Muslim, Salatu'l Musafirin, 84.

29 The *tashahhud*, also known as *at-tahiyyat*, is the portion of salah where the person kneels, sits on the ground facing the qibla, glorifies God, and sends greetings of peace to the Messenger and the righteous people of God.

dividual in observing salah by truly understanding its significance, with the understanding that "This is my duty and this is God's right." Failure to maintain such dedication would amount to a gross violation of the right and neglect of duty. Not only for *at-tahiyyat*, but this is true for all other elements of the salah. It is reported that Bediüzzaman repeated some words until he felt its meaning within while praying on his own. However, this is not for a person leading other people at prayer as the imam, because such behavior might confuse people in the congregation.

God Almighty states قَدْ أَفْلَحَ الْمُؤْمِنُونَ (*Prosperous indeed are the believers* – al-Mu'minun 23:1-2). In the continuation of the verse, as the first merit of such prosperous people, God mentions their being humble and fully submissive during prayer, overwhelmed by the awe and majesty of God, and having consciousness of *ihsan* (awareness of being seen by Him all the time). Everybody should then check their own conscience to see whether they are able to observe salah within this frame. To reach this level, individuals must firmly believe that their deeds will be scrutinized and judged in the Afterlife. The following verse shows us the way in this regard:

قُلِ اعْمَلُوا فَسَيَرَى اللهُ عَمَلَكُمْ وَرَسُولُهُ وَالْمُؤْمِنُونَ

Say: "Work, and God will see your work, and so will His Messenger and the believers." (at-Tawbah 9:105)

Specifically, ensure that your deeds are presentable to God, His Messenger, and believers in the truest sense of the word. As the verse suggests, individuals should endeavor to have righteous deeds that benefit both this world and the hereafter to the best of their ability. The practice of Prophet Muhammad ﷺ also confirms that. Our mother Aisha, the blessed wife of the Messenger, noted, "When the Messenger of God did something, he would do it soundly in a way to leave no flaws."[30] Muslim believers are obliged to adhere to the Prophet, so they should observe their deeds as the Prophet did. They should perform their worship beyond reproach. Given that salah is the most beautiful deed and that there isn't any greater act of worship, then every prayer observed in a flawed fashion will diminish our worship and servitude.

---

30   Muslim, Salatu'l-Musafirin 141; Tirmidhi, Salat 348; Abu Dawud, Tatawwu 26; Nasai, Qibla 13, Qiyam a'l-Layl 2, 64.

Against such shortcomings, we have to observe salah with scrupulous attention. Maybe you will need to force yourself artificially at the beginning. However, it will become a part of your nature in time. The Prophet would prolong his salah when he prayed alone. He did his best to observe salah so perfectly that it was difficult for other people to do likewise, as Ibn Mas'ud narrated.[31] However, he always preferred the easier way for his followers. When he led others as imam at prayer, he would always keep it much lighter.

A person who wishes to observe salah in the true sense of the word may have some difficulty at the beginning. Sometimes the person's moves might be artificial or forced. However, after some time the person will be able to "observe" it in accordance with the true meaning and value of salah. For such attentive observance, the Qur'an uses the word "*iqamah*" (to establish or setting the pillars up properly).

b. Feeling salah profoundly

Unlike angels and other spiritual beings, human beings have a physical form. Although sometimes their spiritual side takes prevalence or dominance on some individuals, human beings live mostly under corporeal pressures. For this reason, they cannot always profoundly feel the acts of worship they observe, salah being the first.

When directed to the One Who is infinite, our feelings, sensations, and perceptions might also occur without any limits. There is scarcely any limit to the actions done for the sake of God, to reach Him, to sense His presence, and to deepen oneself in such lofty aspirations. This is because God Almighty Himself is Infinite, and infinity applies to matters related to Him. A person can feel different things or levels during each salah. It is impossible to speak of reaching a final state of satisfaction, familiarity, or routine in salah.

Salah is observed in order to reach God. The failure to do so stems from us, from our *nafs* (the carnal soul). Any likely dullness on our side does not stem from salah itself but from the weaknesses and flaws of our own attitudes and perspectives. As human beings, we have many imperfections in sight, emotions, and senses. God expresses Himself to

---

31 See Bukhari, Tahajjud 9; Muslim, Salatu'l Musafirin 204.

us through different self-disclosures (*tajalli*) at every moment. However, since we do not think and reflect (*tafakkur*) about these enough, even the most lively, attractive, and colorful things suddenly lose their luster in our sight. Therefore, we cannot feel what we are supposed to feel from them; then everything remains limited only to form. Outwardly we observe salah, we physically move up and down, but that is not salah in the real sense. What really matters is observing salah by feeling each of its pillars with its due profundity.

While performing ablution, it is essential for a person to engage in deep reflection. As the water flows and trickles from their body parts, they contemplate being cleansed of their sins. This contemplation is so profound that the water used, which flows down or drips from the body during ablution, is considered ritually impure as it symbolically washes away sins. With such mindfulness, one takes utmost care to avoid even the drops of used water. While washing the face, the individual should reflect, "My face is being purified from deeds that may cause me shame in the Hereafter. Oh God, please purify my face on that Day when some faces will shine with purity and others will be darkened with sin!"

Feeling all of these profoundly is very important especially in terms of concentration in salah. If you observe salah with such profound feelings, a different door can be opened before you everyday. In a way, you perceive the matter in a different depth than what meets the eye. Sometimes, a door can be opened for you while standing in prayer, sometimes while bowing down, sometimes while sitting or prostrating. However, one must actively seek these moments to unlock heavenly doors. You need to keep your hand on the doorknob, metaphorically speaking, and your heart constantly connected to the divine, otherwise these doors will not open.

Some may then wonder, "what about the salah we observe without feeling these? Do they mean nothing?" With such salah, you will have fulfilled your debt towards God and *insha'Allah*, at least, you will not be held responsible for abandoning salah in the next world. However, you will have failed to reach the truth of salah, the desired meaning, essence, and effect of salah. Actually, salah is a gift for the earthly ones from the Heavens, decreed by God in order to be observed by feeling it, as if savoring a blissful treat.

Also, the essence and meaning of salah may not be disclosed right away. When someone experiences the essence of salah, they yearn to pray even while occupied with life's sweetest pursuits, finding joy in doing so. Although this may not happen every time, they often wish that life never ends, and that they always stand in prayer before God in reverence! However, it may take some months or years—sometimes ten, twenty or more years—for a person to unfold such acquisitions. As long as you keep on sincerely and obediently standing at His door, even if it takes forty years, salah can then unfold its mystery to you. How relevant is the Qur'anic command here: وَتَبَتَّلْ إِلَيْهِ تَبْتِيلًا "...and devote yourself to Him whole-heartedly!" (al-Muzzammil 73:8).

The verb in the verse above is inflected in the tafaul form in Arabic. It denotes forcing oneself (exerting one's all continually). Such an address was made to the Prophet in his early days of Islam; however, he had come to such a state over time that he stated it as, "I have a desire for salah, like you have a desire for eating, drinking, and intercourse."[32] Likewise, it takes one to earnestly persist in this regard, show patience and wait for salah to uncover the veils from the face of its meaning. Once he or she attains that meaning, they would not seek any other joy, even if it was a feast in the heavens. When invited to such feasts, they would say, "I must first observe my salah and cannot sacrifice it for anything." Even if the angel of death Azrail were to come to take their soul, they would ask the angel to hold it until they are finished with their salah. That is, an individual can develop such a state of mind and spirit over time that they will not want to miss salah even when it coincides with the time of death.

Every pillar of salah is lovable and graceful to the utmost degree. If the meaning of salah were to be cast as a statue, its grace would surpass any statue's competition. You would gaze upon it for a lifetime without turning away. As mentioned above, salah will accompany a person in the Intermediate Realm of the grave (*alam al-barzakh*) and will appear in one's dreams (*alam al-mithal*) and if it were observed flawlessly in this physical world, it will have a very pleasant, beautiful appearance in those realms.[33]

---

32 Tabarani, *Al Mu'jam al-Kabir*, 12/84.

33 Tabarani, *Al Mu'jam al-Kabir*, 3/263.

As is conveyed by another hadith, a new Muslim from the countryside, a Bedouin, came to the Prophet's mosque and observed salah. The Messenger of God ﷺ told the man that he had not observed salah. The man stood up and repeated the salah again in the same way. The Messenger told the man again that he had not observed salah. When the man said, "O Messenger of God! I do not know it any other way," the Messenger then taught him the manners of observing salah by explaining how he needed to act while standing, bowing, and in prostration.[34] This suggests that if you fail to uphold salah properly, you would have squandered it, and there is no assurance that salah wouldn't reproach you in the Hereafter, saying, "May God allow you to be wasted just as you wasted me!"

The imam who leads the prayer should take into consideration that there can be weak, ailing, pregnant, nursing mothers, infants, and the elderly among the congregation praying behind him. He should therefore keep recitation at a minimal length. However, this "minimal length" does not refer to, nor does it require in any way, reciting the words in a hurried manner, without proper articulation. The minimum number of repetitions of phrases in bowing, prostration, and other pillars of salah should be observed meticulously with proper recitation and articulation.

For example, during *ruku'* (bowing), it is a requirement to say "*Subhana Rabbiya'l 'Azim*" (Glory is to my Lord, the Most Great) at least once by articulating each word properly. Some scholars stipulate that it needs to be said at least three times. Therefore, we should say the due phrases in bowing and prostration, at least 3 times, by articulating each word unhurriedly and accurately.

Moreover, many recite Surah al-Fatiha very quickly. Such recitations are not of the Qur'an, because the Qur'an was not revealed in such a hurried fashion. Therefore, the salah observed with a hasty recitation of al-Fatiha is not acceptable. The obligation of reciting the Qur'an during salah is not fulfilled when done hastily, aiming to finish it in a single breath, and taking quick gasps when running out of breath. While words convey meanings, their form must align with the intended meaning.

---

34   Bukhari, Adhan 95, 122, Isti'zan 18, Ayman 15; Muslim, Salat 45.

Proper recitation during salah means pronouncing the words as they should be and trying to be conscious of their meaning. If this is not achieved, the person can repeat the same words for some 3-5-7-9-11 times until feeling their meaning. Companion Hudhayfa speaks of the salah of the Prophet as follows: "He bowed down for *ruku'*; his *ruku'* was no less than his standing (he had recited the surahs al-Baqarah, an-Nisa, and Al 'Imran while standing). He rose back to straighten his body (*qawmah*), which was no less than his *ruku'*. He prostrated himself; his prostration was no less than the preceding straightening (*qawmah*)."[35] A person must endeavor to observe salah like this while praying alone.

Given that salah is a very important act of worship, and that it is the *mi'raj* of a believer, which, in the words of poet Alvarlı Efe, makes the "ship of religion" move, then salah needs to be observed in the best way possible. Note that observing salah in the best way also means exerting one's willpower the best he or she can.

c. Performing salah with awe (hashyat) and reverence

One's salah gains its pure and clear nature in the sight of God to the degree of the quality of its content and purity. If it is observed in full humility, obedience, reverence, and awe, each of its pillars such as the standing, bowing, and prostration becomes like steps taken while making a *mi'raj* to God.

Regarding its outward aspects, such as standing, bowing, sitting and getting up, salah looks like a combination of regular physical movements. However, those seemingly simple acts gain great worth with the addition of inner components, particularly reverence and awe. They then rise to unparalleled value in God's sight, becoming the most precious deeds. If there were anything more valuable than salah, then God would have mandated that as a duty for humans five times a day instead.

The true value of salah in the eyes of God could also be understood by the way angels pray. God Almighty created angels as His honored creatures and assigned different angels to observe only one pillar of salah. For instance, some angels are solely tasked with prayer in the standing position. Even this act alone is enough for them to attain an

---

35   Muslim, Salatu'l-Musafirin 203; Abu Dawud, Salat 155.

exalted position in the sight of God. Similarly, there are angels whose sole duty is to pray in the bowing position, which allows them to achieve a worthiness to stand before the Sublime Throne (*Arsh al-Azam*). Likewise, there are angels designated solely for observing prostration.

In short, each group of angels achieves perfection and earns God's pleasure by diligently upholding just one aspect or pillar of salah. Therefore, God Almighty has blessed the followers of the last Prophet ﷺ with salah and its pillars that He gave the angels as a way to express their servitude to Him. Then each person should observe every pillar of salah as if it is a staircase allowing them to climb and complete their perfection and ascension with each step. Salah elevates angels to the peak of their potential for perfection. It undoubtedly yields the same benefit for people as well.

Given that salah can elevate each human being to such a status, then the person should not see it merely as a series of formalities to get rid of. On the contrary, when it is time, when they hear the call to prayer (*adhan*), they must come to the Divine Presence with the manner of fulfilling a very serious duty. They should never give in to heedlessness while in His Presence, and thus complete salah in deep submission, humility, reflection, and inner excitement.

Salah is a matter of awe, inner reverence, and mannerliness. As long as it is observed with such meaning, it always brings purity to our inner world and lets our thoughts gain rectitude. The salah which is not observed in such consciousness and conviction is a burden and cause of weariness for the person; let alone becoming a means of closeness to God, it can even cause the person to become distanced from Him. The Prophet ﷺ stated that if one's salah is not preventing him from evil and shameful deeds, it means that his salah makes no contribution to him and distances him from God:[36]

مَنْ لَمْ تَنْهَهُ صَلَاتُهُ عَنِ الْفَحْشَاءِ وَالْمُنْكَرِ، لَمْ يَزْدَدْ مِنَ اللهِ إِلَّا بُعْدًا

Essentially, salah does not distance a person from God; however, as a consequence of not shaking off heedlessness, not being saved from forgetfulness, not overcoming one's weaknesses, not going beyond the limitations the carnal self imposes on the person, and thus being unable

---

36 Tabarani, *Al Mu'jam al-Kabir*, 11/54.

to attach one's heart to God as it ought to be, the person causes themselves to drift away and become distanced from God.

While observing salah, one is supposed to fulfill all its inner and outer requirements as if they were holding a blessed rope of light to the Heavens; in case of experiencing a momentary lapse, they will turn their inner gaze to the most Sublime Realm immediately and thus fulfill the duty of worship and servitude in reverence.

Halaf ibn Ayyub was one of the great scholars of Hadith and *Fiqh*. It is told about him that he would never spoil his salah even when he was hurt. Once, he was stung by a bee while observing salah, but he did not budge. Another time a fly landed on his face, but he did not move a muscle. His friends noticed this strange situation with wonder. Halaf explained: "I met some criminals in the past. They were proudly telling one another how they remained steadfast without yelping even once while being whipped and punished by the sultan. By contrast, then, how can I, as a humble servant of God, not endure flies and bees while observing salah that is a *mi'raj* to God?"

Ali ibn Talib, may Allah be pleased with him (r.a.), never feared when he confronted even the most formidable adversaries; but his legs shook while in salah aware of the heaviness of that encounter with the Divine. Remember, even though he was just a boy during the Battle of the Trench, when the renowned warrior Amr ibn Abd al-Wud called for a challenger, Ali volunteered persistently, insisting to the Messenger of God ﷺ. When he confronted Amr, Ali was not overtaken by the opponent's provocations like "Boy, I smell milk from your mouth!" Afterwards, despite a break in his shield and a wound in his forehead by Amr's attacks, Ali defeated the opponent with his sword Dhulfiqar given to him by the Messenger. This was the valiance of Ali ibn Abu Talib. However, he would turn pale and turn weak in the knees before observing salah. When at the time of prayer he was asked why his face was so pale, Ali said, "I am going to fulfill the commitment of the trust."

نَّا عَرَضْنَا الْأَمَانَةَ عَلَى السَّمَاوَاتِ وَالْأَرْضِ وَالْجِبَالِ فَأَبَيْنَ أَنْ يَحْمِلْنَهَا وَأَشْفَقْنَ مِنْهَا وَحَمَلَهَا الْإِنْسَانُ

> Indeed, We offered the Trust to the heavens and the earth and the mountains, and they declined to bear it and feared it; but man [undertook to] bear it. (al-Ahzab 33:72)

The "trust" assumed by humankind as mentioned in the verse, and which Ali ibn Abu Talib (r.a.) was aiming to fulfill with salah, is to assume human self, consciousness, and cognition, by way of which one is expected to observe the phenomena, reflect on the signs therein that pertain to God, and bring about a "honeycomb" of knowledge (*marifa*) from them. So, when we are called to pray salah five times a day, we are coming to God's presence to fulfill this duty. This very thought caused Ali's legs to shake.

While heading to the mosque to pray salah, the Prophet's companion Abdullah ibn Umar (r.a.) would walk very slowly because he felt the weight of that responsibility. Those who saw him would say, "An ant walking along would definitely go faster." In truth, we all experience a sense of serious preoccupation, stress, and shakiness in the face of an important task. We become so absorbed that we barely notice our surroundings, oblivious to ordinary things and people around us. The *adhan* has a similar impact in our spiritual world; we rise from our places with an invitation to the Divine Presence; we ritually purify ourselves through washing completely; we try to shake off heedlessness as we are about to stand in the presence of our Lord; we stand in a consciousness of being called to account for our life. It is surely not appropriate to be heedless there. Standing in the Divine presence, turning towards the Ka'ba – a landmark of turning to God – we imagine it is towering before us. In other words, we submit ourselves to God in humility and obedience; we turn to Him with our heart and imagination in reverence; then we try to obtain God's mercy and His good pleasure.

There have been many prominent, leading figures and champions of spirituality in every era; for us too, it is always possible to attain the same level as our past generations did. Living in an era and environment abundant with fellow believers makes it easy and possible for us to shield ourselves against evils. However, regrettably, we have not achieved even one-hundredth of the level attained by previous generations.

For a state leader, it is not unlikely but very difficult to be a good believer, turning one's gaze from the ugly things of this world to the beauties of the next, and not becoming entangled by the benefits, pomp, and positions of this world. Similarly, it is very difficult for a king to lead an army and at the same time to run the state and make people pleased and prosperous. According to reports about him, the Ottoman Sultan Murad 1 was an exemplary figure in all these aspects. He was so devoted to prayer that he would not start his salah until he saw the vision of the Ka'ba before him; he would repeat the *takbir* of salah more than once, or even a third time, until he saw the Ka'ba. One day, he asked his spiritual mentor if it was because of some sin he had committed that he was unable to see the Ka'ba after the first *takbir*. Interestingly, he was assuming that everybody including his mentor would have a vision of the Ka'ba before them as soon as they said "*Allahu Akbar*" for the first time. He was regarding himself to be the only one who failed to do so after the first *takbir*!

This is the state of a righteous person during salah. To maintain a connection with the Divine Mercy, they imagine the landmark of the Ka'ba right before them, and the Bridge of Sirat[37] just under their feet; the Sirat spans over the raging fires of Hell with mountain-high sparks and provides passage to Paradise; even the Prophets sought refuge in God before its ghastly sight. One prays salah as if they were crossing over the Sirat Bridge, imagining Paradise to be to their right with the entirety of its splendor, Hell to their left with the entirety of its dread, and death to be behind them as it is uncertain where it will strike its decisive claw; thus they observe salah, their worship to God, with serious fear alongside immense hope. As long as a believer maintains this atmosphere during salah and continues to uphold it, he or she will steer clear of everything evil and shameful. Otherwise, they might receive a slap in the face by the decree, "there are those who pray and get nothing from their prayer but a sleepless night."[38]

In summary, salah is a deepening of consciousness, an inner illumination, and a means of gaining the good pleasure of the Lord. What constitutes salah's inward *khushu* (deep reverence, awe, and humility before God) is a mood and manner of worship where feelings of fear and hope, ease and dread, and awe and grandeur fill the person and where spiritual contentment, chills and thrills follow. It's as though a glimpse of

[37] Sirat is the bridge which every human must pass on the Day of Resurrection to enter Paradise.

[38] Ibn Majah, Siyam 21; Ibn Hanbal, *Musnad* 2/373.

your heart rises to your lips, brimming with hope and contentment—a moment where you perceive your prior state as impertinent before God's Majesty. Gathering yourself, you adopt a humble demeanor and affirm, "I must not worship with reluctance, arrogance, or caprice," continuing your observance of salah in that reverent mood.

As for the outward aspect of *khushu*, it refers to fulfilling what you are prescribed to say, recite, and perform in an accurate, precise, and serious manner. For example, it comprises knowing what is being said and meant in the recitations, and bowing, prostrating and sitting in the ideal way, as is described in the reference books of *fiqh* and catechism.

Only the salah observed by a believer with such feelings and precision will be salah in the true sense. Thus, it becomes possible for it to navigate the ship of one's body and being to the shores of deliverance and bliss.

d. Some crucial points to consider about salah

The pillars of salah like standing, recitation, bowing down, prostration etc., make up only the outward form of salah. In fact, what really matters with its pillars is the content and spirit. Just as eating and drinking are essential for our physical bodies, salah is nourishment for our spirit and heart. Salah should become an indispensable part of our character. The spirit can only find nourishment through salah observed in such a manner.

One point to consider is to focus on our hearts when we perform salah. While exercising, people tend to keep their mind relaxed and free from intense thoughts, so they are not exhausted. Similarly, for the development of the spirit, it is essential to set aside worldly concerns and become wholly oriented towards the heart and spirit during salah. It is a fact that there is a close relationship between the careful observance of the outward form and the content of salah.

Another point believers should pay attention to is that they should not adopt different attitudes, manners, or practices of other people during salah, nor should they attempt to imitate them. For instance, some individuals involuntarily move part of their bodies or exhibit different physical manners during salah, but this does not mean others can do the same. It's best for everyone to observe their own salah as prescribed by the religion.

Additionally, one should not be concerned about or doubt whether others' salah is valid or whether they have fulfilled (with salah) their duty towards God; the door to negative assumptions (*sui-zan*) about others should never be opened. Such assumptions or negative thoughts about others only lead to sin for the one harboring them. Remember, we are not meant to judge others' behaviors.

Another point is that the worshipper's mood and whatever is happening around them will definitely influence the salah being observed. However, one can overcome all these influences and interferences with consciousness, willpower, and concentration. Such influence may occur, but it should not distract from the focus on one's prayer. Using willpower, the worshipper can concentrate on and direct the heart to the status of perfection. Even during the moments when one is very open to inspirational blessings and abundant grace (*fayd* and *barakah*), the person should still try to take only God into consideration. If, during salah, a feeling of spiritual attraction (*jazba*) arises, potentially leading the worshipper to the Sublime Throne (Arsh), it is advisable for the worshipper to say, "O God, I do not seek this additional experience. Being a humble worshipper whom You are pleased with is sufficient for me."

The last point is that everyone has their unique experience of salah according to their own spiritual caliber and level. The experience a regular person has might look strange compared to Imam Rabbani's salah. Even the most devoted and exemplary Muslim figures never considered their salah adequate, and therefore criticized themselves, and continually asked forgiveness for it. What is important here is to pave the way for people with only basic assumptions about salah to acquire a true and firm conviction about this worship, so that as a single drop they can immerse themselves in a vast ocean and then transform into an entire ocean... Beyond that, we may expect from His Mercy to attain a status of grace, the nature of which we are yet to comprehend.

e. Concentration in salah

Believers start and continue to gain heavenly rewards and blessings through a sequence of daily rites and rituals. They believe that the water of ablution washes away their sins and with that they gain a state of spiritual vigilance. Then comes the *adhan*, the call to salah; with that the love felt for God and spiritual attraction to Him continue or even increase while listening to the *adhan* in reverence.

No sooner than the *adhan* finishes, believers start to observe the initial *Sunnah* prayer; with that they reach a further level of profundity, for *Sunnah* and voluntary prayers make up for the flaws of obligatory prayers and provide an extra degree of closeness to God Almighty. A *hadith qudsi* states this as follows:

> My servant cannot approach me with a deed more lovable than the prayers I have made obligatory for him (*fard*). [After observing the obligatory ones] Then My servant continues to get closer to Me by observing the voluntary (*nawafil*) ones, to such that I love him in the end. And after that, I become the ears with which he hears, the eyes with which he sees, and the hand with which he holds, and the leg with which he walks.[39]

Keeping these considerations in mind, believers practically express their desire for a closer connection to God by completing the *Sunnah* prayer. In doing so, they take another significant step towards better concentration and covering the remaining distance needed to become fully immersed in salah. They then become prepared to observe the obligatory prayer.

Devout and attentive servants of God do not make salah wait, but rather wait for it at all times. Having performed ablutions even before the *adhan*, such servants say with complete readiness, "I am fully prepared, my God! When You grant me an audience, You will see that my face and attention are completely turned towards You, awaiting admission to Your Divine presence."

In fact, if a person has not been able to attain this spiritual vigilance with the preparations that begin before the ablutions and continue with the *adhan* and *Sunnah* prayers, there must be something missing. However, even if such distractions occur, the *muadhin* who calls the *iqamah* before the obligatory salah helps eliminate any thoughts that might lead believers away from the thought of worship and that draw them towards things other than God. Then, believers who have achieved concentration

---

[39] Bukhari, Riqaq 38; Ibn Hanbal, *Musnad* 6/256.

utter the exaltation "*Allahu Akbar*" with profound reverence and begin their salah.

Another aspect of the matter is that, in the Prophet's Age of Bliss,[40] the commandments of Islam came anew, like a heavenly feast. Everyday, the Companions of the Prophet encountered different kinds of worship. For instance, one day they learned salah, and the next day they heard the *adhan*. When the *adhan* resonated through their ears, filling them with a distinct thrill and excitement, they observed salah imbued with those emotions. The Muslims of that time would find everything they heard or learned as original, highly appealing, and attractive; they would be almost mesmerized by those brilliant wonders. At every moment, they were receiving news from beyond the heavens, encountering new surprises everyday, and in a sense, they were living in a zone of constant surprises. They would continuously hear and listen to new surahs and ayahs with which they would virtually be showered, thus becoming equipped with sublime feelings and appearing in the Divine presence accordingly. Therefore, they did not feel a need for excessive exertion and effort to maintain the spiritual vigilance and concentration to prepare for worship. As they constantly breathed an air of togetherness with God, they were spontaneously overflowing with thoughts of the realms beyond and with spiritual feelings. When the time came to stand in the Divine presence, they could concentrate all of their feelings and spiritual faculties (*lataif*) on worship.

Since we are distant from the Age of Bliss, when revelation came abundantly like showers of blessings, we are not able to attain that level of concentration and spiritual state so spontaneously. We therefore must overcome the distance between that age and ours through our exertion, endeavor, vigilance of willpower, and determination. We must endeavor to sense the originality in the essence of religion by invigorating and stimulating our reflections deliberately. If we aspire to pray with the most sublime feelings and profound considerations like the blessed Companions did, we must also give due attention to our willpower in this regard.

We should always try to bear pure feelings and thoughts; while walking to salah, and even before beginning ablution, we should pro-

---

40   The term "the Age of Bliss," or in some renderings "the Age of Happiness," refers to the time when the Prophet Muhammad ﷺ lived and led his community.

ceed in line with these wholesome considerations. For instance, our final words before commencing salah should undoubtedly revolve around the Beloved, Almighty God; it's preferable to discuss a topic related to Him to ignite God-consciousness in our hearts. We should reflect on what saintly servants of God have said about salah and deliberately focus our senses and thoughts on it.

From this perspective, it indeed appears challenging for us to detach ourselves from all distractions and solely concentrate on preparing well and focusing on salah. Yet, we must not forget that the greater the hardship of a deed and the greater the difficulty in obtaining it, the greater the reward will be. Hence, in order to be imbued with beautiful feelings and experience worship fully, we must endure any hardships that may arise in the process, starting with the ablutions.

f. As if your last prayer

One should pray in a manner that sets an example for others, so that each salah becomes exemplary, where prostration brings insatiable joy, supplications to God become nourishment one never tires of, bowing becomes a unique expression of devotion, and articulate recitations turn into a harmony of living words. Muhammad, the Truthful Messenger ﷺ, tells us to observe salah as if it were a farewell prayer.[41]

So, if you were told that you will only survive long enough to pray one last time, then you would observe it with utmost care; but this is how you should observe salah each time. Salah observed with full consideration that, "this may be my last one," is a farewell prayer.

Salah is the most beautiful thing a person will do in life, and it must be so. The sweetest memories in life should be related to salah, because *mi'raj*—a believer's spiritual ascension to God—is realized through salah. It is through salah that one can reach Allah and join the company of the Prophets.

---

41 A man came to the Prophet and said: "O Messenger of Allah, teach me but make it concise." The Prophet said: "When you stand to pray, pray like a man bidding farewell. Do not say anything for which you will have to apologize. And give up hope for what other people have" (Ibn Majah, zuhd 15; Ahmad Ibn Hanbal, al-Musnad 5/412).

g. The three levels of salah

We can evaluate salah in three different levels:

1. Salah observed as fulfillment of an obligation: This level relates to the prayers observed in an air of familiarity, which remain limited to carrying out God's command. Compared to not doing the prayer at all, this is surely a better level. People observing their prayers in this way may rid themselves of the accountability of abandoning the obligation. However, they will be deprived of the spiritual blessings they could get from salah.

2. Salah that protects from evil: Salah protects people from shameful deeds and all things religion counts as evil.[42] God Almighty gave such a special quality to salah. However, being able to benefit from salah that much depends on capturing its gist or true spirit. Each consciously observed salah envelops the worshipper like a protective aura and prevents indecent things finding a way to reach him. The Prophet describes salah with the simile of the situation of a man who bathes five times a day in the river that passes in front of his door.[43] In fact, it is this quality of salah that it protects and cleans us from floods of sins that come upon us. Otherwise, it would not be possible for our soul to resist against so much ugliness.

3. A mi'raj-like salah: If a salah is observed in a way that each minute earns the reward of years, then it is a *mi'raj*-like prayer. It is quite difficult to realize such a prayer, and this is special to distinguished souls, but it is still possible. Given that it is possible, everyone should endeavor for such salah and try to realize it in at least some periods of their life.

It can be useful to make the following reminder here: Salah is first and foremost a religious obligation; therefore, even if it cannot be achieved at the desired level and quality, it must absolutely be observed. Abandoning salah on account of not observing it in the desired level is

---

42   "Recite what is revealed to you of the Scripture, and perform the prayer. The prayer prevents indecencies and evils. And the remembrance of God is greater. And God knows what you do" (al-'Ankabut 29:45).

43   See Bukhari, Mawaqitu's Salah 6; Muslim, Masajid 283–284.

not a sign of God-consciousness. It is on the contrary a sure sign of being a toy in the hands of Satan; it is an expression of being a plaything for Satan. Believers should not fall for this trick.

Besides, salah has certain pillars and certain times. No person has the right or authority to make arbitrary changes in them. Those who see such a right in themselves are definitely those whom Satan approached from the right and made them believe that is the right(eous) way. The things such people say merely signify nothing but their defeat by Satan. What they say does not reflect any scholarly knowledge either.

h. Salah lovers

Acts of worship such as habitual recitations (*awrad* and *adhkar*), supplications (*dua*), and supererogatory (*nawafil*) prayers should be performed consistently and steadfastly, so that they become ingrained character traits within us over time.

For instance, if you regularly observe four units of voluntary prayers, becoming accustomed to it and internalizing it as a habit, then one day you cease doing so or reduce it to two units, you might lament, "Oh no, I have erred today!" This understanding stems from the utilization and cultivation of certain inherent abilities in human nature and their impact on the human spirit.

God's Messenger is the guide for devoted worshipers. His attention, care for salah awakens in the hearts of those who follow his footsteps a profound eagerness for this essential worship. The Prophet stated that salah is the delight of his eye.[44] His every manner indicated that he felt a desire for salah much beyond what others feel a desire for other things. He would observe salah until his blessed feet were swollen and on occasion, he would bow down for *ruku'* only after he recited multiple sections (*juz*) of the Qur'an. His heart was full of awe before God; during his salah, his sobs would be heard as if a pot within him was boiling and he would humbly curl up in prostration with utter reverence. His meticulous care for salah also served as a means for Companions to become devotees and enthusiasts of salah.

---

44 Nasai, *Ishratu'n-Nisa* 1; *Sunan al-Nasai* 3939; Ibn Hanbal, *Musnad* 3/128, 199, 285.

So much so that, to put it in the words of Fudayl Ibn Iyaz, most Companions of the Prophet would reach the morning with pale faces, because they would spend most of the night in salah. They would sometimes keep standing (*qiyam*) for hours, and sometimes remain prostrated for a long time. While opening their hearts to God, the Companions would shake like trees on a windy day, and shed tears in awe and reverence, so much so that their tears would make the ground and their clothes wet. The delight they received from salah would make them forget the tiredness of their bodies and they would wish those minutes of audience and communion with God would never come to an end. In the morning, they would apply oil (cream) to their faces, kohl to their eyes, in order to conceal that they kept long vigils through the night and come out in public as if they spent the whole night asleep and were well-rested.

The Caliph Umar fainted due to blood loss after having been stabbed with a dagger. However, as soon as he was told it was time for salah, he exerted himself to stand up, but he fell back weakly after each attempt because of the blood he lost. He was truly a lover of salah. The fatal blow struck him just before he was about to prostrate and implore his Lord in salah.

The Caliph Ali was no different. How Ali felt before observing salah is mentioned above. Just like Caliph Umar, he was also stabbed. He was on the way to observe salah in the mosque and died on the pathway of worship.

The following is a noteworthy indication of the Companions' awareness of the meaning of standing in the Divine presence and their eagerness for salah. During the military expedition of Dhat al-Riqa, the Messenger assigned two companions, Ammar ibn Yasir and Abbad ibn Bishr, night watch duty at a stopover. When Ammar was taking a rest, Abbad started observing salah. A hostile polytheist, who kept an eye on them from afar, wanted to take advantage of the moment and fired arrows at them. A few of the arrows landed on Abbad's body; despite this, he continued his salah and woke his friend up only after completing his bowing and prostration. When Ammar leapt to his feet, he saw the polytheist escape and later asked his friend in surprise why he did not wake him despite being shot with arrows and losing blood. Abbad's answer was indeed one that could only come from a true lover of salah:

I was reciting a Surah (Kahf), and its verses were so sweet that I did not wish to spoil the salah without finishing it. But when the arrows came one after the other, I completed the salah and woke you up. I swear to God that had it not been for the concern for failing to defend this spot and not fulfilling the Prophet's order, I would prefer death than leaving the Surah halfway and stopping the salah.[45]

When believers start observing salah (in the true sense), they become completely oblivious of their surroundings. As the poet Gedai (pen name of Imam of Alvar) expressed, such persons get so enraptured that they even become unable to recognize themselves. It is not possible to think of other things anyway when one comes to God's presence to observe this duty; if one still is preoccupied with other things, then it means that the person is not able to give the honor of being in the Divine presence its due. A person should utterly turn away from all other things and devote oneself to Him wholeheartedly. Otherwise, one cannot benefit from the fruits of that deed if their heart and body wander in different valleys during salah.

Observing salah finds its true meaning within this conundrum: remaining in private with God; rooting out the world and its contents from the heart; even forgetting one's own soul and becoming self-oblivious; and then endeavoring to observe salah in this manner, even if it happens just once in a lifetime.

i. One hundred rak'ahs of salah everyday

The Companions of the Prophet would never get enough of worship, particularly salah. Moreover, they instructed their righteous disciples to also excel in salah. For example, Ata ibn Rabah would recite a hundred verses from Surah al-Baqarah even in his old age although he had grown frail and powerless. His concentration during salah would never let him feel the tiredness of his body.

Muslim ibn Ibrahim uses the following expressions about Shu'ba bin al-Hajjaj, one of the great imams of the third generation of Muslims (Taba al-Tabiun): "Whenever I went near Shu'ba—other than the *makruh*

---

[45] Abu Dawud, Tahara 79; Hakim, *Al-Mustadrak* 1/258.

(disliked) times[46] —I would see him while observing salah."[47] Abu Katan makes the following addition: "Had you witnessed the time Shuba waited in *ruku'*, you would say he probably forgot about the prostration. Had you seen him sitting between the two prostrations, you would think that this time he probably forgot the second prostration."[48]

In the era when these lovers of salah lived, observing a hundred units (*rak'ah*) of voluntary, optional (*nawafil*) salah was almost something ordinary. They would observe salah so much that most of them gave their last breath on the prayer rug. For example, when Abu Ubayda al-Basri, from the generation of the Tabiun, passed away, he was standing in salah. It was not at all rare to find people who, for decades, prayed through the night and observed the *fajr* prayer with the same ablution from *isha*, including Wahb Ibn Munabbih, Tawus Ibn Kaysan, Said ibn al-Musayyib and Imam Abu Hanifa.

Another exemplary person from that period is Junayd al-Baghdadi. Junayd never missed salah in congregation at all or even the first *takbir*, for some thirty years. If he felt that a bit of worldly thoughts made their way into his heart and he could not feel the truth of salah, he would re-observe that salah. He had taken it as a habit to observe four hundred units of voluntary salah everyday. For some thirty years, he dedicated himself entirely to worship, abstaining from sleep entirely after the *isha* prayer.

Another exemplary person is Abu Uthman al-Nahdi. He was one of those who were not able to see the Prophet despite living during the Age of Bliss. Abu Uthman was a person who observed one hundred units of salah between *maghrib* and *isha*. Likewise, Bishr ibn al-Mufaddal and Bishr ibn Mansur had taken it as a habit to observe four hundred units of salah everyday. One of the distinguished caliphs of the Abbasid state, Harun Rashid observed a hundred units of salah everyday—including

---

46 There are a few time slots in a day during which offering "optional" salah is considered reprehensible. For example, when the sun is at its zenith at noon is one of those times. Offering the "obligatory" prayers during these times is not forbidden if one did not perform until then.

47 Baghdadi, *Tarikhu Baghdad* 9/261.

48 Dhahabi, *Siyar A'lam Al-Nubala'I* 7/207.

during his term as the caliph—until he passed away, which is important and good example in terms of indicating the enthusiasm for worship which permeated souls in those times.

Actually, if we delve into the historical resources of Islam, we will find numerous examples related to this subject matter. We will see that people who observed hundreds of units of salah were not rare at all among the Righteous Predecessors.

Just a useful reminder here: There is no difficulty in religion; Islam is based upon ease. Although the Prophet himself observed salah until his feet were swollen, he only guided his ummah to what they are capable of and counseled against their undertaking anything beyond their capacity, including worship. In this respect, both issues of feeling salah thoroughly and observing many salahs remain as a matter of one's own devotion, spirituality and spiritual level. All believers are consistently encouraged to strive for higher levels of worship, both in terms of quality and quantity, but compulsion or coercion is out of the question in this respect.

Said Nursi said, "one hour in total will suffice for making ablutions and observing the five daily prayers (in a basic sense),"[49] he pointed to the ease in the essence of religion and drew attention to the objective rules. That is, when a ruling concerns all people, it is necessary to consider even those under the most difficult circumstances. With this essential in mind, Nursi pointed out that Muslims must observe their prayers even under adverse conditions, even if they have to squeeze them into an hour, including the ablutions. He also noted that there will be a share of worship and its reward on the record of deeds of a person who solely performs the prayer as a necessary act without feeling its true meaning in the heart. In other words, even if someone performs prayers merely as a ritual obligation without truly understanding or feeling its significance in their heart, they still earn some merit and reward for their act of worship. Nursi expounded that while there are various degrees from, say, a mere seed to a fully grown tree, salah similarly has its own degrees too, and that salah of any level definitely receives its share from the blessed light of worship.[50]

---

49   Nursi, *The Words*, Fourth Word.

50   Nursi, *The Words*, Twenty-First Word, First Station.

Nursi's remarks may serve to remind ordinary people to have hope. They are not meant to crush people's hopes entirely, but to prevent them from falling into utter despair and to emphasize their objective responsibilities. God Almighty rewards everyone's salah as He sees fit; however, the central point of the argument we're making is about attaining "the truth, spirit, and essence of salah."

In this regard, a believer should, at a bare minimum, definitely observe at least the obligatory (*fard*) salahs with a quality of "establishing" (*iqamah*). In his *Isharat al-I'jaz*, Nursi explains that *iqamah* of salah refers to observing the *arkan* (i.e. standing, bowing, prostration, etc.) properly, solemnly, and unhurriedly, performing it in continuity and regularity, and maintaining it as perfect as one can along the way. Muslims should genuinely try to maintain all of these aspects with utmost enthusiasm and never allow this feeling, considerations, and conviction to fade away. With this enthusiasm, one should run to that spring of fresh water at least five times a day, to purify themselves from aberrations, offenses, and sins. Then turning to God Almighty with a pure frame of body, mind and spirit, one should embark on another *mi'raj* (rising to the Heavenly realms and the presence of God) at each prayer time.

4. The seeds of salah

Special phrases and particular compilations of sentences are like the seeds of salah. The special phrases like *Allahu Akbar*, *SubhanAllah*, and *Alhamdulillah* are repeated all throughout salah. In this way, their meanings are embedded in all of the actions and recitations of salah. Nursi notes that from the start with the opening *takbir* to the end with the peace greetings, at every moment with every word, state, and attitude of ours during salah, we praise and glorify God with *SubhanAllah*,[51] we voice our feelings of gratitude and praise with *Alhamdulillah*, and we express our reverence with *Allahu Akbar*.

The first *takbir* (saying *Allahu Akbar*) in salah is termed as the *takbir* of prohibition (*tahrim* or *ihram*) because it marks the beginning of the term for prohibited acts during salah. Actually, this *takbir*, which marks the beginning (*iftitah*) of the prayer, is a pledge in the form of forbidding

---

51   There is no one exact or precise definition in English, but it is generally understood that with *SubhanAllah* we mean "Allah is perfect," "all praise be to God," "all glory be to God," "how free of any imperfection is Allah," and "may He be Exalted."

to oneself anything other than God during salah and stepping in the special Divine Realm, leaving anything worldly behind. This means weaving the spirit of *tasbih* (glorification), *tahmid* (thankful praise), and *takbir* (exaltation) into all minutes and seconds of salah from that moment on, effectively making a pledge to become totally imbued with salah.

If angels were to illustrate how the reflection of such a worshipper would show in *Alam al-Mithal*,[52] their illustration would most likely look like the form of salah, for he or she has become an embodiment of salah.

If you wish to establish salah by properly giving it its due, you should detach yourself from all things other than God, open your heart exclusively to Him, and put the seal of your consciousness on every word that streams from your lips. For example, while saying *Alhamdulillah*, you should know well what this phrase means and expresses; and taking it into profound consideration, you should say, "all praises and gratitude exclusively belong to God Almighty, regardless of who says them and to whom; and proclaiming this truth is a duty of mine and a right of the Creator of the universe. Thus, let this phrase ascend to God, carrying with it the deep meanings you infuse into it."

You should be filled with the same profound feelings when proclaiming that God is Rahman and Rahim. While voicing the truth "Master of the Day of Judgment," you should impress upon it the weight of its meanings like a stamp and submit it to God Almighty accordingly. Salah should be a *mi'raj* for you as well and you should also try to feel the truths that the Prophet ﷺ felt there as much as your discernment allows.

After internalizing all the meanings of salah, you would gradually ascend through all levels, just as in the case of Messenger Muhammad ﷺ; you would meet with Prophet Adam at the First Level of Heaven, Prophets Yahya (John the Baptist) and Isa (Jesus) at the Second, and Prophet Yusuf (Joseph) at the Third, and at other levels with Prophets Idris (Enoch), Musa (Moses), and Ibrahim (Abraham), may God's peace and blessing be upon them all. By learning from the lives of each Prophet, and imbued with the color of their blessed presence, you would be permitted to take one more step, feeling as if you were admitted to the Divine chamber of audience.

---

52   *Alam al-Mithal*: The world of representations or ideal forms.

At the end of your salah, after you give the greetings of peace, you should raise your hands in supplication out of concern that you might not have fully complied with the manners of being in the Divine presence. With this, you turn once more to the gates of Divine Mercy with phrases of *tasbih*, *tahmid* and *takbir* (*SubhanAllah* for glorification, *Alhamdulillah* for praise, and *Allahu Akbar* for exaltation), and repeat each of those blessed phrases that will consolidate the meaning of worship.

While reciting such phrases, you might have thoughts like: "O Lord! Here I offer once more a concise summary of the blessed phrases I recited in detail during salah. Although I have already said them in salah, I still cannot get enough of them. Allow me to remember You God again, once more with these expressions after salah..."

Given that it is necessary to establish salah with such immense feelings and thoughts, we cannot do it haphazardly; we need to fulfill the necessary preparations prior to it and observe it in a way that suits its meaning.

Tafakkur in salah

Tafakkur literally means to deeply think on a subject, systematically, and in great detail. The words meditation, reflection and contemplation in English all correspond to *tafakkur*.

The phrases of *tasbih*, *tahmid*, and *takbir*, which can be seen as the essence of salah, are at the same time essentials of servitude and are crucial components for a believer's world of *tafakkur*. In other words, these very important phrases serve as the self-expression of a believer, imbued with reflection. Moreover, each of these phrases expresses the admiration of a believer for the truths in the universe. Let us next delve deeper into these assessments we briefly outlined.

"Salah is the ascension of a believer."[53] Indeed, the Prophet ﷺ ascended to the heavens with his body and spirit, reached peaks beyond all stations, with God's grace he saw things he needed to see, and then came back. With good concentration, a believer can always attain these horizons in imagination, soul, and mind, and thus can experience a relative "ascension" in the shadow of the Messenger of God.

---

53   Razi, *Mafatih al-Ghayb* 1/214; Suyuti, *Sharh Sunan ibn Majah* p. 313.

While realizing this ascension in mind and soul, a person witnesses God's signs related to his or her own inner world and also the outer world; they establish connections and find correlations between these worlds and the verses of the Qur'an. Although their feet are on the ground, they feel their heads above the heavens and that they have reached realms beyond this one. If a person pays attention and listens to their own spirit a little, they can always feel this atmosphere.

What appears before you after that are colorful views with some help from the verses of the Qur'an; while those views may have sourced from your soul, they can also be pictures born from the universe... and you meet such colorful things in each of those pictures! In fact, there is such a profound harmony between the entire universe, all existing things, the human body, and the relationship between humanity and the universe that it couldn't be more perfect.

Before such a view, you cannot help but say, "there cannot be any other hand involved in this; It is only God behind this splendid orderliness and harmony." By feeling it wholeheartedly, you proclaim this Holiness as "*SubhanAllah.*" As soon as you make the *takbir*, you say, "*Subhanaka Allahumma wa bi hamdik...*" You combine praise and glorification adding, 'Praise be to God for letting us feel this. O God, we glorify Your Holiness and proclaim that You do exist; You have no partners; You are the Exalted and Glorified One!' While all these reverberate all around as the voice of a sincere heart, you feel a complete state of ecstasy and immersion (*wajd* and *istighraq*).

Right after these profound considerations, the person may sometimes see and feel those stunning phenomena, magnificent order in the universe, and the marvelous arrangement of the systems and galaxies, as well as the miraculous run and operation of the entire creation. Then they cannot help but say, "this is the work of such an astonishing and great power!" In order to take a deep breath with *tafakkur* once more, they say, "*Allahu Akbar*" and bow down. Depending on the verses they have recited or on what they have reflected on, and the blessings God bestows graciously, they overflow with feelings of thankful praises to God. They tend to see the things bestowed as a reference for further blessings and feel a sense of joy and elation. Thus, their thoughts and feelings well up and always resonate in a mood of journeying to God. They establish a relationship between the words recited and what they feel and sense. They then voice these emotions and sentiments in each phase of salah with pure and holy words, sacred phrases, and sentences (*kalima tayyiba*) and continue the journey, deepening further and further.

The pure and sacred words of glorification, praise and exaltation of Allah, like *SubhanAllah*, *Alhamdulillah*, and *Allahu Akbar*, which are repeated many times in salah, are in a way the sounds of servitude and markers of the different phases of the truth of journeying and ascending to God (*mi'raj*).

While observing our servitude before God Almighty, we articulate all of our witnessing, feeling, and sensing by means of *tasbih*, *tahmid*, and *takbir*s: for all the material and spiritual blessings God gave us we say "*Alhamdulillah*"; for glorification to declare the truth of there never being any partners to Him "*SubhanAllah*"; for acknowledging our insignificance and proclaiming His greatness "*Allahu Akbar*"; we say all these and more, assuming ourselves as spokespersons for the entire creation and their worship. Thus, we strive to fulfill and offer a universal servitude in response to His Lordship over all things.

Surah al-Fatiha is the summary and quintessence of the Qur'an, a precise table of contents of the Qur'anic message. It is possible to see all truths of the Qur'an concisely within that *surah* (chapter). Beholding God Almighty's greatness in it, we feel utterly awed and say, "*Allahu Akbar*," to acknowledge His Grandeur. Sometimes we feel to be floating among the blessings of Paradise; we perceive ourselves surrounded by the means provided to guide us toward that Paradise; and as we witness Divine Grace allowing us to ascend a spiritual staircase—similarly experienced in acts of worship such as fasting, *zakat*, Hajj, and the like—we express our gratitude by saying "*Alhamdulillah*." And sometimes we gratefully recall and acknowledge all these by affirming that God is the One Who maintains the relationship between this world and the next. Indeed, all of these meanings and much depth are succinctly encapsulated in Surah al-Fatiha.

As for (the reciting of) *at-tahiyyat*, it reminds us of the *mi'raj* even more clearly. The Ascension is an expression of the fact that the Prophet surpassed the basic servitude required of him and ascended to the peak of spiritual perfection. God Almighty opened a door of servitude to the Prophet and required him to pass through it in accordance with due manners. And the Prophet passed through it with a profundity, perfection, and closeness to God never to be accomplished by anyone else, until he was as close to God as "two bows' length," or even closer (an-Najm 53:9)—a level of proximity in Divine realms that we may never fully grasp or comprehend, but only believe and acknowledge.

The *mi'raj* took place more as a result of the Prophet's servitude than in relation to his being a Prophet. It was the most difficult time for him; people had completely turned their backs to him and to his message, and apparently there was no worldly cause left to resort to. Yet, he never made any concessions from his servitude. At a time when all the circumstances were to his disadvantage, the *mi'raj* occurred as a manifestation of the light of Divine oneness' particularity (*ahadiyyah*) within the mystery of its universality (*wahidiyyah*).

To better understand this, we need to revisit the early period of Islam. During an inauspicious period, the ruling tribe of the Quraysh began to persecute the early Muslims, their larger families, and supporters, and started to impose a brutal embargo. The Muslims and their supporting relatives were banished to a valley on the eastern outskirts of Mecca and were thus confined within a narrow pass. The Quraysh declared "that no one should marry Muslim women nor give women for them to marry; that no one would trade with them; and that all people should cut off all relations and business with the Muslims and their supporters." The banishment lasted for three years and caused extreme privation. During such unfavorable conditions, the Prophet did not alter his opinion, attitude, conviction, or mission in the slightest. Furthermore, during that period, two major misfortunes along with all those adversities took place: The Prophet's uncle, Abu Talib, and the Prophet's beloved wife, Khadijah, passed away. That year was named "The Year of Sorrow." In order to heal him from these sufferings and losses, God Almighty honored His Messenger with the Ascension (*Mi'raj*), for an audience in His Divine Realms and Presence in order to console his heart and make up for others' disgraceful attitudes. God crowned His beloved servant, conveying that "In spite of everybody and everything, I am here, and this is worth all the worlds."

The *mi'raj* was possible as a result of the Prophet's prayers, worship, fasting, and suffering, and his teaching people about their meaning. These became like a staircase that served as a means for ascension to the *Mi'raj*. No other Prophet was blessed with such a great honor except Muhammad, the Messenger of God ﷺ. Each Prophet may have had an experience of ascending to the Divine presence within his own soul and may have been honored accordingly. However, the blessing of beholding the heavens and paradises with qualities unknown to us was a blessing exclusively granted to Prophet Muhammad ﷺ. So, with the honor of following such a treasured and magnanimous Prophet, we also endeavor to experience that *Mi'raj* thanks to salah.

5. *Dhikr* and *tawbah*

Dhikr means remembrance of God. It is a form of worship. It lets a person gain closeness to God in the fastest way. It is an influential airstream that disperses dark clouds of heedlessness (*ghaflah*). It is a person's living by feeling the meaning of life or by receiving and deducing a Divine message from almost everything while walking through the corridors of existence. In this sense, there is a strong connection between *dhikr* and salah.

Salah potentially has a reminding power in itself. God Almighty speaks to us this truth in the verse, "…so worship Me and keep up salah for My remembrance" (Ta-ha 20:14). The verse also points to the strong connection between *dhikr* and salah. On account of this paramount importance, God frequently emphasizes the five daily prayers in the Qur'an.

We can even say that *dhikr* in other forms of worship remains at a secondary level in comparison to the *dhikr* in salah. Had there been any other form of worship that would replace salah for remembrance of God to that degree, and if there were any other form of worship that would disperse heedlessness from one's horizon of sight, thought, comprehension and judgment, then God would have commanded and encouraged that worship to be observed five times a day instead of salah.

For example, fasting is also a form of worship, but it is a hidden form of worship, others cannot know whether a person is fasting or not. In fact, fasting has a special place in God's sight on account of its being hidden. This is stated in a *hadith qudsi*,[54] "Fasting belongs to Me and

---

54 *Hadith qudsi* are the sayings of Prophet Muhammad ﷺ as revealed to him by God. The meaning is from God, but the wording is by the Prophet. For the hadith above, see Bukhari, Tawhid 35; Muslim, Siyam 160.

Only I give its reward." Had there been any continuity with fasting as in salah, God Almighty would have held us responsible for it every other day, as Prophet Dawud practiced. In this regard, it can be inferred that this very powerful reminder effect of salah is definitely not found in any other worship. It is possible to discuss a similar capacity for powerful reminders in overall worships like the Friday Prayer and the Hajj, and their reminding quality can be regarded as a form of *dhikr* at a significant level. However, since they do not occur every day, let alone five times a day, it is not feasible for them to replace salah at all.

Salah is like a bath that cleanses people of sins and washes away the moral filth, dirt, spiritual dust, and rust on human beings. Those who are spiritually bathed five times each and every day through salah become cleansed of their sins and purified. The verse below voices this truth:

> Establish the Prayer (O Messenger) at the beginning and the end of the day, and in the watches of the night near to the day. Surely good deeds wipe out evil deeds. This is advice and a reminder for the mindful who reflect. (Hud 11:114)

It is understood from this verse that each salah observed is added to the totality of good deeds, which eventually wipe out the person's bad deeds. In addition, the end of the verse, "This is advice and a reminder for the mindful who reflect," brings the reminder of the power of salah to our attention once more.

Now that we have discussed the relationship between *dhikr* and salah, let us now look at the relationship between *tawbah* and salah. *Tawbah* is a person's turning to God in repentance and his or her opening up to Him. It is a process of reconstructing the pure and delicate innermost feelings inherent in our nature, which become distorted by sins.

Every person who commits a sin is counted to have taken a step toward unbelief. As Nursi puts it, "Each sin has a path that leads to unbelief."[55] Accordingly, one who commits a sin has taken one step away from God and one step nearer to Satan. If the person turns to God again with repentance, they are considered to have changed their bad deeds into good ones. So, from Nursi's perspective once more, repentance means

---

55 Nursi, *The Gleams*, Second Gleam, First Point.

redirecting human tendencies and abilities, prone to evil, towards goodness, thus reinstating the potential to do good within oneself.[56]

This situation holds true for salah, as it instills a consciousness of *tawbah* in a person in the true sense. Although the person may not literally pronounce the words of *tawbah* five times a day, the salahs they observe function as a practical form of *tawbah*. In salah, there are so many prayers and verses that bear the meaning of repentance and seeking forgiveness, anyway.

For example, believers begin salah by saying, "*Allahu Akbar.*" Here the *takbir* is almost like a hammer of reason and consciousness which batters useless things in the mind in order for the believer to be detached from other pursuits and turns to God with ease. In salah, there is the point of being detached from all things other than God, accepting the Divine call and then turning to Him in full submission. However, each person can only realize such devotion in accordance with their own inner stature or caliber.

Then the worshipper servant says, سُبْحَانَكَ اللَّهُمَّ وَبِحَمْدِكَ. "*Subhanaka*" (سُبْحَانَكَ) here can be explained as follows: "There is nothing in creation that can be associated as Your partner. You are the exclusively Unique One in Your Being, attributes and operations. Neither my actions nor the events occurring in the universe can be attributed to anyone except You. Here, I reject any notion of associating any partner with You. I glorify and exalt only Your Name."

As for "*bi hamdika*," (حَمْدِكَ) it means "I thankfully praise You." "*Subhanaka*" is an expression of glorification to the exclusion of all kinds of shortcomings. It exhibits a complete servitude to Him in the face of the universal self-disclosure of His oneness (*wahidi tajalli*). After such an expression of *tanzih* (God's absolute exclusion from faults), a person reciting, "*bi hamdika*" virtually says, "I may not be able to comprehend this meaning thoroughly, but You are the One Who makes me feel this meaning. Otherwise, I cannot feel and sense anything on my own. Therefore, while I am glorifying You on the one hand, here I also present my indebtedness and gratitude solely to You."

---

56   See, Nursi, *The Words*, 26th Word, Second Topic, Seventh Way: (Prayer and trusting God greatly strengthen our inclination to do good, and repentance and seeking God's forgiveness defeat our inclination to evil and break its transgressions.)

The following expression *"wa tabarakasmuk"* (وَتَبَارَكَ اسْمُكَ) means "Your name is a source of abundance (*barakah*). Please favor us—Your servants with some of your blessings from Your immense treasure! For You give so many blessings even to those who deny You or associate partners with You. And despite all my sins and wrongdoings, here I am turning to You and taking refuge in Your holy name, which is a source of blessings. Here I wail in Your presence." Muhammed Lutfi Efendi expressed this poetically:

Kerem kıl, kesme Sultanım keremin bînevâlerden /
Kerem kesmek yakışır mı Keremkâne gedâlerden

Beneficence, o my Sultan, do not deprive the poor ones of Your beneficence /

Does it ever befit the All-Beneficent to deprive His slaves of His beneficence?

With the phrase *"wa taala jadduk"* (وَتَعَالَى جَدُّكَ) we say, "Your Supremacy is transcendent. Hence, a sultan is supposed to act in a royal manner that befits him, just as asking befits a beggar. I may have erred countless times, yet here I am at Your gate, humbly bowed, for I have no other refuge but Yours. Sins do not become me, but forgiveness is a testament to Your glory and eminence."

And the last phrase of this prayer *"wa la ilaha ghayruk"* (وَلَا إِلَهَ غَيْرُكَ) means, "how can I turn to anyone else; there is none other than You, the Truthfully Worshipped One and Eternally Besought of All."

Indeed, from the exaltation (*takbir*) *"Allahu Akbar,"* to giving the greetings of peace to both sides, salah is an act of turning to God permeated with *tawbah*; so, this very turning to Him can gradually take the servant to the horizon of *ihsan*.

6. Salah and refinement of the heart

Tenderness of the heart is a sign of faith. Its outward expression is mostly a person's tears. Tears are a means of relief for the ardent lovers of God who burns with total devotion, affection, and fervor of heart. Prophet Muhammad, peace be upon him, stated, "If a single tear drop comes out of a believer's eyes with fear of God and flows down his cheeks, God does not let Hellfire touch those cheeks."[57] Tears are the only elixir to extinguish the flames of Hell in the next world and the fires of longing and grief in this world.

The Qur'an expresses appreciation for tenderness of the heart in some verses and states that genuine believers will prostrate themselves upon hearing the verses of God (al-Isra 17:107). In another verse, it warns believers so that they laugh little and cry much (at-Tawbah 9:82). The following supplication of the Prophet also shows the significance of having a tender heart: اللَّهُمَّ إِنِّي أَعُوذُ بِكَ مِنْ قَلْبٍ لَا يَخْشَعُ "I seek refuge in You O God against a heart that does not shiver with awe."[58]

A person with a refined and shivering heart will be open to self-criticism and self-supervision, and such people will frequently interrogate themselves. They don't attribute personal ownership to their successes and achievements, and they never feel they have done enough. As a result, they consistently question what more they could do or how they could improve thus they become exemplary people and heroes of good work.

For a person with a refined heart, there is no such thing as having enough worship or finding it sufficient. After having fulfilled the *fard* (obligatory) salahs, how many additional optional salahs a person chooses to observe is a matter of personal discretion. One might reflect on their previous salahs and realize they weren't performed with the desired peace of heart. "Then let me observe some optional, supererogatory salahs (*nawafil*) to make up for them," they would say. A believer may choose to pray in single a day salahs as many as would normally be prayed in multiple days, considering that the life is short and no one knows when he or she will breathe their last.

Optional prayers are like fillers for the cracks and flaws in one's worship (جَبْرًا لِلنُّقْصَانِ). They make up for the shortcomings in our *fard* (obligatory) prayers. How many optional prayers a believer should do is a decision they can take depending on his or her conscience. To cite an

---

57   Bayhaqi, *Shuabu'l Iman* 1/491.

58   Muslim, Dhikr 73; Abu Dawud, Witr 32; Muslim, Dhikr 73; Abu Dawud, Witr 32; Tirmidhi, Daawat 68.

example: a person may have observed salah for some time without properly turning their heart to God Almighty, which can be considered a deficiency in "intention" (*niyyah*). Later on, they come to realize that the true essence of intention lies in what the heart truly wills and turns towards. When they comprehend turning to God (*tawajjuh*) as completely eradicating everything except God from the heart, and as abstaining from and disregarding all else in that moment except God, and when they acknowledge that they have never prayed salah with such an intention before, then it could be said that they had never truly prayed salah until that realization. However, each individual should act according to their own level of understanding, conviction, and devotion in this matter.

Some sources of the Hanafi school of jurisprudence (*fiqh*) notes that "saying the intention by mouth is better." Although it is not known what evidence this is based on, some people traditionally do so. For this reason, when a person is beginning salah they make their intention loud enough to hear themselves and enunciate, "here I make an intention to pray salah for the sake of God..." If they are really able to maintain their heart's total turning to God with such an utterance, then good for them! However, if people remain at the level of mere words and start praying by only speaking certain words without even being conscious of their acts, and if the heart is not able to focus on where it should, then it indicates that the desired outcome is not being attained.

Once someone grasps the true essence of intention in awareness of connection with the Divine, they may reflect, "I have observed all of my salah without missing anything so far; however, I am not sure whether I was able to give them their due. Therefore, I feel the need to re-examine them or offer *nafila* salah to compensate for any deficiencies." If God grants the person some more time to live further in this world, they can make up for the missed salahs by observing a full-day's salah everyday.

In addition, while the *fard*s of the five daily prayers are observed with much care, the *Sunnah* prayers of those five times must also be observed with care. Twelve *rak'ah*s (units) among the *Sunnah* prayers are *mu'akkadah*, i.e., strongly ordered by the Messenger of God ﷺ. The *Sunnah* of the *Asr* prayer is not commanded as strongly as the others, but it is also among deeds regarded as meritorious. Similarly, the first four-unit *sunnah* of the *isha* isn't mentioned in the Six Books of major hadith references. However, scholar Ali al-Qari, in his significant work, *Fath-u Bab al-Inayah* points out, based on a hadith found in Said ibn Mansur's *Sunan*, that the Messenger of God ﷺ observed a four-unit salah before the *fard* of *isha* (night prayer) as well.[59]

The *tahajjud* prayer is also very important. It is performed at night after the *isha* prayer. It is hoped that people who light up their nights with *tahajjud* will have a similarly brilliant life beyond the grave. The *tahajjud* is like a lantern to be used against the darkness of the grave, and a safe haven that protects the person against the torments therein.

Each salah serves to illuminate a section of a person's life in the next world. As for *tahajjud*, it is like the travel provisions beyond the grave and provides illumination in *Barzakh*.[60] The Qur'an mentions *tahajjud* in a few places:

> O you enwrapped one! Rise to keep vigil at night, except a little; Half of it, or lessen it a little, Or add to it (a little); and pray and recite the Qur'an calmly and distinctly [with your mind and heart concentrated on it]. We will surely charge you with a weighty Word [and with applying it in your daily life, and conveying it to others]. Rising and praying at night impresses (mind and heart) most strongly and (makes) recitation more certain and neat. For by day you have extended preoccupations. And keep in remembrance the Name of your Lord [and mention It in your Prayer], and devote yourself to Him whole-heartedly! (al-Muzzammil 73:1-8)

> And in some part of the night, rise from sleep and observe vigil therein (through the Prayer and recitation of the Qur'an) as addi-

---

[59] Ali al-Qari, *Fath-u Bab al-Inayah* 1/467.

[60] Al-Barzakh refers to the intermediary stage between death and the Day of Judgment. It's a realm or state where the soul resides after death, awaiting the final resurrection and judgment. During this period, individuals experience a state of consciousness appropriate to their deeds in the worldly life, and their deeds continue to have an effect on their spiritual state. It's considered a transitional phase before the Day of Judgment when souls will be resurrected for their final fate.

tional worship for you; your Lord may well raise you to a glorious, praised station [of nearness to Him and give you leave to intercede with Him, as He wills, on behalf of His servants, in the Hereafter]. (Isra, 17:79)

Their sides forsake their beds at night, calling out to their Lord in fear [of His punishment] and hope [for His forgiveness, grace, and good pleasure], and out of what We have provided for them [of wealth, knowledge, power, etc.], they spend [to provide sustenance for the needy and in God's cause, purely for the good pleasure of God and without placing others under obligation]. (as-Sajdah 32:16)

And remember and mention the Name of your Lord (in worship) in the early morning and in the afternoon; And during part of the night prostrate to Him, and glorify Him a long part of the night. (al-Insan 76:25-26)

The significance of night prayers is underlined in a Prophetic tradition narrated by Bukhari and Muslim: Abdullah ibn Umar had a dream and asked its interpretation from the Messenger of God ﷺ. In his dream Abdullah sees that two formidable persons hold him by the arms and bring him near a deep pit of flames. When he fears that they will throw him in the pit, they say, "do not fear; there is no need for you to fear." The dream was related to the Messenger of God. The Messenger responded as follows: "Ibn Umar is such a good person; if only he observed the *tahajjud* prayer too!"[61] God showed a sight from Hell to Ibn Umar in his dream and prompted him to take action against it.

In addition, other *nafila* salahs like *duha* (forenoon) and *awwabin* (after the *sunnah* of *maghrib*) will also compensate for our shortcomings in *fard* practices and be complementary to them. God Almighty will fill the gaps in our *fard* salah with *nafila* ones.

As told in a hadith that supports this meaning, salah is the prime matter for which we will be questioned. God Almighty will ask, "Are the salahs of my servant complete?" If the reply is affirmative, He will allow that person to pass on. If the salah is missing, God asks whether the

---

61 Bukhari, Tahajjud 2, 21, Fada'il Ashab al-Nabi 19, Tabir 35, 36; Muslim, Fada'il al-Sahaba 139, 140.

person has *nafila* ones. If the reply is affirmative, He orders the missing parts to be completed with the *nafila* ones. As a manifestation of Divine Mercy, *nafila* ones will "count as" acceptable substitutes in order to make up for the missing *fard* prayers.[62] This "counting" can be interpreted as a making-up or compensation that happens directly by Divine Will, that is, God Almighty wills and makes up for our shortcomings in the Afterlife with our salahs.

In summary, our diligent attention to both obligatory (*fard*) and voluntary (*nafila*) prayers, coupled with due care of the heart, will not only bring us fervor and joy in this world but will also serve as a steadfast companion and advocate on the demanding journey to Paradise in the next world. Salah is a means that allows us to become closer to the Exalted Creator. It is an unbreakable rope we can hold on to save ourselves eternally; a very safe anchorage in the rough waters of life; an unshakable support to hold onto during turbulence; a source that wells up with a clean life; a rampart that protects us against shameful deeds and assaults of evil, as is stated in the following verse:

> Recite and convey to them what is revealed to you of the Book, and establish the Prayer in conformity with its conditions. Surely, the Prayer restrains from all that is indecent and shameful, and all that is evil. Surely remembrance of God with salah is the greatest merit. God knows all that you do. (al-Ankabut 29:45)

7. The salah of the Messenger of God

God Almighty discloses to us in the Qur'an how the Prophet set about and observed salah:

وَتَقَلُّبَكَ فِي السَّاجِدِينَ

> He [God] Who sees you when you rise [in the Prayer, and in readiness to carry out Our commands], as well as your strenuous efforts in prostration... (ash-Shu'ara 26:219)

With the verse above, God relates how His Messenger stood in

---

62 Tirmidhi, Salah, 188; Abu Dawud, Salah 144; Ibn Majah, Iqamahtu's-Salat 202.

prayer, took pains in prostration, and bore the responsibility of his mission while observing salah and its pillars. Thus, God tells us what a heavy duty of servitude Muhammad ﷺ was responsible for and how he exerted himself for fulfilling this responsibility. Such a state of the Messenger in prostration is an expression of the due reverence needed to be shown to God Almighty; and this statement of God Almighty is also an appreciation for him. Actually, salah is counted and registered by God so as far as the worshiper is conscious of being in the presence of God. However, as long as the person's inner world and spiritual faculties (in particular *sirr*[63]), are detached from the Divine presence, that act of worshipping stops being actual salah and proves itself fruitless. For God Almighty does not look at the body, but to the heart and the love and enthusiasm in it and gives His judgment accordingly.

Our blessed mother Aisha, may Allah be pleased with her (r.a.), reports that while observing salah, the bosom of the Prophet gave off a sound similar to that of a mill stone or of a boiling pot.[64] While standing in salah before God, he would become like a vaporizer releasing the scent of awe owing to God's Grandeur. This state was surely due to his endeavor and sincerity in realizing his servitude to God at the highest level.

Salah was an act of worship that the Prophet had a strong desire for. No other thing gave him the pleasure he received from salah. This is why he called salah "the light of his eye" (جُعِلَتْ قُرَّةُ عَيْنِي فِي الصَّلاَةِ).[65] In another hadith, the Prophet's statement supports this notion: "God gave every Prophet a strong desire towards something. My desire is towards worshipping at night."[66]

63 "*Sirr*" refers to the innermost secret or mystery, the deeper spiritual truth or reality that lies beneath the surface of outward appearances. It's often associated with the hidden aspects of divine knowledge, the inner dimensions of reality, and the personal connection between the individual and the Divine. In the spiritual journey of Sufism, uncovering the *sirr* involves delving into the depths of one's being to attain deeper insight, wisdom, and closeness to God.

64 Abu Dawud, Salat 161; Nasai, Sahw 18.

65 Nasai, *Ishratu'n Nisa* 1; Ibn Hanbal, *Musnad* 3/128, 199, 285.

66 Tabarani, *al-Mu'jamu'l Kabir* 12/84.

The Prophet had such a profound servitude to and connection with God, as well as such a profound attestation and proclamation of God's Oneness, that we can hardly understand its depth yet. The hadith related above is the clearest example that illustrates his intense passion for worshipping God. Moreover, what his wife Aisha (r.a.) narrated also exemplifies this:

> One night I awoke to find that Allah's Messenger was not beside me. I thought that he might have gone to another of his wives. I groped around and my hand touched his foot. Then I understood that the Messenger of God was observing salah. He was prostrating. I listened and heard him weeping and pleading as follows:

> "My God! I seek refuge against Your wrath, to Your good pleasure. I seek refuge in Your forgiveness from your punishment. My God! I seek refuge in You from You [from Your majesty to Your grace, from Your wrath to Your mercy, from Your grandeur and majesty to Your clemency and beneficence]. Here I confess that I cannot praise You as You praise Yourself."[67]

Afterwards he said:

> "Closeness to You is a means of dignity; one who is close to You is dignified. Your glory and eminence are so great. You army is invincible. You never break Your promise. There is no other deity than You, and no one to be worshipped but You."[68]

Another example of his profundity in servitude is narrated by the Companion Abu Dharr: "One night, the Messenger of God recited the verse [al-Maidah 5:118], 'If You punish them, they are Your servants; and if You forgive them, You are the All-Glorious with irresistible might, the All-Wise,' and he observed salah in tears until dawn."[69]

Another example is narrated by Companion Ibn Masud: "One night I offered the *tahajjud* prayer with the Prophet ﷺ and he kept on

---

[67] Muslim, Salat 221–222; Abu Dawud, Salat 148.

[68] Tirmidhi, Daawat 90; Abu Dawud, Adab 97; Haythami, *Majmu' al-Zawa'id* 10/124.

[69] Muslim, Iman 346; Nasai, *Sunan al-Kubra* 6/373.

standing till an ill-thought came to me." We said [other companions listening to Ibn Masud], "What was the ill-thought?" He [Ibn Masud] said, "It was to sit down and leave the Prophet (standing)."[70]

One more example is from his beloved wife, our mother, Aisha (r.a.):

> One night when the Messenger of God stayed near me, we went to bed together. A little while later he said, "O Aisha, [if you] permit me; let me observe worship for my Lord." I said, "by God, I want you to be near me so much, but I wish you to observe servitude to God more than that." Upon this, he got up, made ablution with the water from the waterskin hanging on the wall and started to observe salah. He wept to the degree of making his beard wet with tears. Then he went into prostration and wept. The ground was wet with his tears. Then he leaned on his side and continued to weep. Bilal [ibn Habashi] came near him and told him that it was time for *Fajr* Prayer. On seeing him cry, Bilal said, "O Messenger of God! Why are you crying? Has not God forgiven your sins for the past and future?" The Messenger of God replied: "O Bilal, Why should I not cry, tonight I received the revelation of the verses (meaning): "Surely in the creation of the heavens and the earth and the alternation of night and day [with their periods shortening and lengthening], there are signs [manifesting the truth] for the people of discernment. They remember and mention God [with their tongues and hearts], standing and sitting and lying down on their sides [whether during the Prayer or not], and reflect on the creation of the heavens and the earth. [Having grasped the purpose of their creation and the meaning they contain, they conclude and say]: "Our Lord, You have not created this [the universe] without meaning and purpose. All-Glorified are You [in that You are absolutely above doing anything meaningless and purposeless], so save us from [having wrong conceptions of Your acts and acting against Your purpose for creation, and so deserving] the

---

[70] Bukhari, Tahajjud 9; Muslim, Salat al-Musafir 204.

punishment of the Fire!"[71] ... What a pity for those who read these verses but do not reflect upon them!"[72]

When describing his prayer, the Prophet's wife Aisha says: "He would stand in prayer in such a way that one could not describe its beauty or length. He would bow down in *ruku'* in such a way that one could not describe it. He would make prostration in such a way that one could not describe it."[73] Thus she tried to describe with these words the beauty of how the Messenger of God observed salah.

It is not possible to find a single act of worship that the Prophet began to practice but later abandoned entirely. He indeed abandoned certain *nafila* acts for the sake of ease for his followers. For he reckoned that if he continued to observe everything as intensely as he did, it would be too difficult for everybody to follow his example. He exceedingly made up for those gaps by observing much more of salah at night, and he gave his duty as a Prophet its due. He spent his life with full spirit and consciousness, and tried to make further progress on the journey to God. Certainly, his life and the manner in which he lived until his death demonstrate that he did not think or behave otherwise. His blessed home already opened directly to the mosque, as he always preferred to have one foot in the mosque. When he retreated to *i'tikaf*,[74] he would do it within the mosque. At times, he would look into his home through the curtain, while making sure the other half of his body remained in the mosque. If he were to go somewhere, he would always pass through the mosque and pray there first. When he came from elsewhere, he would first come into the mosque, pray, and then go to his own quarter. Salah had become a path for him. The mosque was a place he frequented, essentially like a ramp to reach the realm between "contingency and necessity" (*imkan* and *wujub*).

71   Al Imran, 3:190–191.

72   Ibn Kathir, Tafsiru'l-Qur'an 1/442.

73   Bukhari, Tarawikh 1; Muslim, Salat al-Musafir 125.

74   *Itiqaf* is an Islamic practice consisting of a period of staying in a mosque for a certain number of days, especially during Ramadan, devoting oneself to worship during these days and staying away from worldly affairs.

8. Diseases that disrupt salah

a. *The waswasa (evil suggestions) of Satan*

Satan defied God's command to prostrate himself before Adam. He was therefore guilty of self-inflicted degradation, which banished him from Divine Presence. In order to prove that man did not deserve a position superior to his, Satan asked for respite and made the pledge to avert believers from every kind of goodness:

> Now that You have allowed me to rebel and go astray, I will surely lie in wait for them on Your Straight Path [to lure them from it]. (al-A'raf 7:16)

Satan lives in loyalty to this pledge and always tries to lead Muslims astray by approaching them from all directions. With reference to the words in his pledge, the Prophet ﷺ expresses Satan's slyness as, إِنَّ الشَّيْطَانَ يَجْرِي مِنَ ابْنِ آدَمَ مَجْرَى الدَّم "Satan travels through the veins of the son of Adam."[75]

Satan approaches a believer more during salah, because salah encompasses the meaning of all other worships, and no other worship can reach the effect and level it entails. Since salah has such a profound quality, Satan tempts a person particularly during salah; he gives evil suggestions to the believer's heart and throws arrows of doubt and suspicion into their mind; Satan busies the person with worldly matters and thus tries to spoil the salah.

The Prophet taught us that "when the *adhan* (call to prayer) is made somewhere, the devil goes away from there begrudgingly and runs as far as he can until he can no longer hear the *adhan*. He comes back again when the *adhan* is over. When the *iqamah* begins, he goes away again, and returns when it is over to come between the person and their hearts. Then he starts making evil suggestions like 'remember this,' 'think about that!' etc., with things that were not in the person's mind at all. So much so that the person comes to the point of not knowing how many units

---

[75] Bukhari, Itikaf 11, 12, Bad'i al-Khalq 11, Adab 121, Ahkam 21; Muslim, Salam 23, 24.

of salah (*rak'ahs*) they observed."⁷⁶ With this hadith, we learn that Satan rather pesters people who realize a *mi'raj* by means of salah; he does not visit hearts in ruins which are already empty and detached in terms of religiosity. Satan leaves them alone because he believes they have already succumbed to his influence, having abandoned any space in their lives for acts of worship, and some of them have either lost faith in God or never had it to begin with. With this state of theirs, they become devils of their own and are busy with leading one another astray. Therefore, Satan always targets hearts full of faith, infiltrating their thoughts and memories to sow doubt and confusion.

A person devoted to worship is so fortunate that despite being tempted by the worst evils, they are able to lead a life more decent than others and maintain good morals. Their primary focus is on serving and worshipping God, striving to maintain a vigilant heart in His presence day and night. That's why after saying that he will lead people astray, Satan adds, with reference to such people, إِلَّا عِبَادَكَ مِنْهُمُ الْمُخْلَصِينَ "Except Your servants from among them, endowed with sincerity in faith and Your worship" (al-Hijr 15:40; Saad 38:83).

Satan himself admits that he will have no power over some people and that he will not be able to entice and deviate them from God's way. These individuals comprise, primarily, the Prophets, and then those who overcome their carnal souls and its urges; who are not lured and corrupted by the worldly life; who are able to take this world and what it contains under their feet; who manage to stand up again after they have erred or had a lapse, but continue their progression in asking forgiveness; and through their five daily prayers, they maintain inner peace and purity, prioritizing the struggle against their own carnal souls over involvement in the affairs of others.

Satan will naturally pester flourished hearts. He will approach people who humbly prostrate themselves in love and awe before God's majesty and confess their defects, weakness, poverty, and humility. He will try to corrupt their prayers by means of his evil suggestions. However, one hadith gives us the following glad tidings in this matter: "When the

---

76   Bukhari, Adhan 4, al-Amal fi's-Salat 18, Sahw 6, Bad'i al-Khalq 11; Muslim, Salat 19, Masajid 83.

son of Adam recites a verse of prostration and he prostrates, Satan withdraws, and he weeps, and he says: 'Woe to me! The son of Adam was commanded to prostrate, and he prostrated, so he will go to Paradise. I was commanded to prostrate and I refused, so I will go to Hellfire.'"[77]

When we are in prostration, totally nullifying ourselves, Satan will bring to our attention all sorts of mundane and profane things, such as, our worldly position, business, the season's yield, the office, the family, possessions, etc. He will try to divert our attention to every worldly thought, matter, issue, or predicament. We, however, will regain our consciousness, realizing that this is in fact our *mi'raj* (ascension) and that we are a few steps away from arriving to the top level of the staircase that leads us to Divine Mercy.

So, we will refute Satan, "O you the accursed one! Our Lord, the Almighty Creator promises Paradise and Divine Beauty for us, then what is your offer?" Thus, by delving deeper into prostration, we strive to save ourselves from all mundane and evil suggestions.

b. Satan's stealing from salah

When Satan is unable to make you abandon or delay your prayer, one of his tricks is stealing from your prayer.[78] Looking around during salah is referred to as Satan's stealing from it. That is, Satan is unable to take away the salah in its entirety but steals a certain portion of it. He cannot steal its pillars (*arkan*) but instead he strives to make you look here and there. When he manages to distract your heart or mind, your gaze starts to wander. Satan steals your looks away from where they ought to be.

Salah is a trust (*amanah*) so you should not let Satan steal anything from it. The amanah includes everything that Allah has entrusted to you and instructed you to take care of and guard. It comprises the sense of responsibility and accountability for one's actions before God, too. So, if you wish to be entirely trustworthy you should observe your salah in ac-

---

[77] Sahih Muslim 81.

[78] Bukhari, Adhan 751. When Aisha (r.a.) asked the Messenger of God ﷺ about looking around while praying, the Messenger said: "That is something that the Satan steals from a person's prayer."

cordance with the truth of salah represented in the *Alam al-Mithal*.⁷⁹ In order not to experience any disturbance there, you should not let down salah in this world, and you should prevent the hand of "the thief" from reaching out to it.

As you turn to God Almighty with the entirety of your heart, feelings, and spiritual faculties, you should not allow anything to be stolen from it. It is rather difficult for beginners to achieve this with complete perception and awareness. However, God can open that door one day. Be steadfast, give your most important and suitable time to salah, and exert yourself. *Insha'Allah*, that day will come and it will be possible to observe it properly and beautifully.

c. Laziness for salah

Given that *iman* (faith) is the prime factor and essential of every matter, the issue of laziness towards salah primarily needs to be approached within this frame. Remember that the pillars of faith form a believer's view of the world and their actions. Let us now briefly reflect on salah in the light of the pillars of faith one by one.

Belief in God is the sole essential and assurance of having peace of mind and heart. Hearts devoid of faith in God can never make up for this gap with anything else. The Qur'an says:

أَلَا بِذِكْرِ اللهِ تَطْمَئِنُّ الْقُلُوبُ

> Be aware that it is in the remembrance of God that hearts find contentment. (ar-Ra'd 13:28)

Belief in the Prophets is an important factor that saves a person from seeing the past in darkness and the future as fraught with sources of anxiety. Thanks to our belief in the Prophets, particularly in the Prophethood of Muhammad, the Sultan of the Prophets ﷺ, we believe we will pass over the most dangerous bridges of this world and the next within the twinkling of an eye, like lightning. We also believe that we will attain blessings we cannot even imagine by means of the *Shafa'at-i Uzma* (the great intercession) of the Prophet ﷺ.

---

79   The Imaginal Realm or the Realm of Representations or Realm of Ideal Forms. It defines the realm where all ideas, thoughts and actions are manifested.

Belief in the Scriptures entails belief in the narrations in Divine Scriptures, particularly the descriptions of the Afterlife, and the portrayals of Paradise and Hell. They all instill in believers a perpetual metaphysical vigilance, zeal, and vitality. A person who internalizes the apprehension of the Day of Reckoning from books will endeavor to make every moment of life meaningful.

Belief in the Angels assures us that even in moments of solitude, when we perceive ourselves as isolated, we are never truly alone. We are accompanied by the Angels, who observe and record our every action. This awareness encourages us to exercise self-restraint, regulate our behavior, and adhere to moral principles, thereby imbuing our lives with profound significance.

Belief in Divine Destiny entails embracing, without doubt, the conviction that everything that occurs in our lives—whether it seems favorable or not, whether perceived as success or failure, deficiency or advantage, and regardless of whether the outcome is beneficial or detrimental—is ordained by God Almighty.

Belief in the Afterlife instills a sense of accountability in our actions, resulting in numerous worldly and spiritual benefits too numerous to tally. We believe that we are on this earth for a relatively short time and during this time we must prepare ourselves for the eternal life after death. So, this temporal and transient life is a test. Belief in the Resurrection, Judgment Day, the Reckoning, Paradise and Hell, and rewards and punishments, accordingly, are all part of this belief. The entirety of the Prophets, saintly servants of the past, the righteous, are in the Afterlife now. Meeting the Messenger of God ﷺ in person is a cherished aspiration of every believer in Islam and will be realized only in the Hereafter. Therefore, the faith in meeting them and the belief in the gains that faith yields are really something special.

Belief in the entirety of these essentials is paramount, as it positions a person correctly within their religion and leads to true and lasting contentment and peace. Any disturbance to this peace can then be consciously and willingly eliminated, followed by the observance of acts of worship to sustain it. In essence, the root of laziness towards salah can be traced back to weaknesses in the aforementioned essentials of faith. Conversely, those with perfect faith will never encounter such obstacles.

Salah is an act of worship that serves as a reminder for each of the essentials of faith we touched on above. Salah always holds the potential for a profound reminder and deep delight, underscoring our weakness, helplessness, and poverty before the Almighty God. It guides us towards solutions for problems that may seem insurmountable. The fundamental basis and essence of all these is faith in God, the All-Powerful Creator. We can elucidate this final point further by considering the verses of chapter Fatiha:

اَلْحَمْدُ لِلّٰهِ رَبِّ الْعَالَمِينَ — *Hamd* (all praise) is due for God, Who creates, maintains, grows and develops everything from a single particle to celestial systems. After having belief in such a Sustainer Who holds and helps people against many adversities and saves them from perishing, why should we be hopeless at all?

اَلرَّحْمٰنِ الرَّحِيمِ — He is compassionate and merciful to everybody with or without belief, in this world and the next. Verily, His mercy prevails over His wrath.[80] So why should we give in to hopelessness?

مَالِكِ يَوْمِ الدِّينِ — He is the sole Master of the Day of Judgment. On that day God will present even the pettiest deeds of every servant done in the world and call them to account there. However, Lord Almighty, Whose mercy (*rahma*) prevails over His wrath, will lend a helping hand to us there too.

إِيَّاكَ نَعْبُدُ وَإِيَّاكَ نَسْتَعِينُ — You alone do we worship, and from You alone do we seek help. We declare and confess our being Your servants before Your Divinity. But what an honorable servitude it is! Our King is You O God, the King of kings. We are so dignified and honored to bow before no creature but You. We denounce everything You have denounced. It is only from You we want.

اِهْدِنَا الصِّرَاطَ الْمُسْتَقِيمَ ۞ صِرَاطَ الَّذِينَ أَنْعَمْتَ عَلَيْهِمْ غَيْرِ الْمَغْضُوبِ عَلَيْهِمْ وَلاَ الضَّالِّينَ — Guide us to the Straight Path. The path of those whom You have favored, not of those who have incurred (Your) wrath (punishment and condemnation), nor of those who are astray!

Since a person cannot know what the best form of help to them could be, out of the Grace and Mercy of His Lordship, God teaches us first what to ask from Him, and commands us to say, "guide us to the straight path."

---

80 "Verily, My mercy prevails over My wrath." Bukhari 3194, Muslim 2751.

Now, presenting to God such servitude infused with *tawhid* (God's unique oneness) and performed with consciousness, and then begging for His help, are actually a confession of one's inability to properly express thanksgiving and worship in response to God's blessings and favors. For a person who is aware of their *ajz* (impotence, helplessness) and *fakr* (poverty), it is a declaration of seeking refuge in the Bounteous Lord of Absolute Power and Majesty. How can such a person ever be hopeless?

A person who manages to observe salah with such depth of feeling and contemplation is unlikely to neglect or miss it due to worldly and mundane distractions. Therefore, it's absolutely necessary to educate people about the true essence of salah and faith, helping them to deeply feel and experience it as much as possible.

Salah serves as a means for individuals to fully develop, much like sunflowers turning their faces and hearts towards the sun. By turning to God five times a day, one can revive their faded feelings and consciousness anew. They can regain vitality and hence renew their pledge to Him. From this aspect, salah is one of the greatest blessings of God to us. Its absence is like the absence of the sun. From a perspective of common causality, as there will be no sunflowers without the sun, there will be no true human in the absence of worship. Then, it is indeed us who are actually in need of worship.

Moreover, when a person diligently observes salah and becomes spiritually attuned to the presence of God, they naturally steer clear of many objectionable practices in their professional life as well. Particularly the *dhuhr* and *asr* salahs (the midday and afternoon prayers) in the daytime enhance and boost the person's feelings of self-supervision and self-accounting. As they reset and reactivate such a mechanism of inner control, they keep away and save the person from falling into wrong. As for the *maghrib*, *isha*, *tahajjud*, and *fajr* salahs, they are the locus of the manifestation of Divine blessings, secrets, and mysteries, as is implied in the following lines by scholar Ibrahim Haqqi:

> *When you remain truly helpless,*
> *He suddenly pushes the veil aside,*
> *And becomes a cure to every trouble...*

Salah is a *jabri* (compulsory) factor that regulates a Muslim's daily life and brings orderliness to it. A person who appears in the presence of God five times a day will naturally put their life in a certain order. They start working after *fajr*, and after working intensively for some 6-7 hours and feeling tired, they gain fresh vigor with the *dhuhr* prayer. They keep working until *asr*. With the *asr* prayer, a new session of mental and emotional rest begins. People who do not recognize and experience these essentials during salah will be caught in a whirlpool of unease, drifting from one depression to another. In summary, those who claim they lack time for salah due to their busy schedules are essentially shutting their eyes to Divine truths. This predicament often stems from a weakness in faith, a lack of understanding or belief in the fundamentals of faith, and a failure to comprehend the significance of salah, as touched upon earlier. To overcome these obstacles, one must cultivate a high degree of certainty in faith (*yaqin*), and actively apply it in their daily lives.

d. Weariness of worship

One great trouble among Muslims today is that we have lost our luster for our acts of worship. It is such a pity that mosques and the people who attend them, resemble withered leaves struck by the fall; some yawn, some lie down, others engage in worldly chatter even near the *mihrab* (central niche in the direction of prayer), and some eagerly await the end of salah to leave as quickly as possible. I do not want to make negative assumptions, but the outward reality, even though there can be exceptions, often reflects the situation of people who lack a proper relationship with God, who do not know the Prophet well, who attend the mosque or observe salah only by imitating their forefathers (out of tradition), and who merely go through the motions. Therefore, the condition of the mosque and the people within it may not hold much significance for others, and worship fails to serve as a practical demonstration of the beauty of Islam. If we can effectuate a practical state of thorough belief, many can embrace Islam. Regrettably, we fail to demonstrate the captivating essence of Islam.

Being Muslim must be a voice in itself, the voice of meaningful difference. Our religious practice should carry weight, resonating with others. When they witness our genuine sincerity, devotion, submission, humility, love, and awe in our acts of worship—our standing, bowing, prostration, recitation, supplications, and tears born purely out of love, respect, and connection to God—then they can truly admire our worship. They become deeply moved, inspired to join in, and feel compelled to worship alongside us. When Islam and its acts of worship are not represented at this level, they do not resonate with the people around us, for people do not see the spirit of salah and its heavenly attraction in mere formalistic movements up and down.

As Muslims, we find ourselves grappling with a spiritual weariness in our worship, almost as if we've grown tired of servitude. Our perception of Islam has become overly simplistic, lacking depth in our hearts. With familiarity comes contempt, and Islamic values have lost their vibrancy in our eyes, appearing faded and lacking luster. They fail to evoke excitement within us; we cannot observe worship as if relishing the sweetest delicacy. If a few individuals were to exude love and enthusiasm during salah, it would undoubtedly have a profound impact on other souls.

Salah that yields nothing but tiredness

The Messenger of God ﷺ remarked on the salah observed without a proper frame of mind, focus, consciousness and reverence as follows:

رُبَّ صَائِمٍ لَيْسَ لَهُ مِنْ صِيَامِهِ إِلَّا الْجُوعُ، وَرُبَّ قَائِمٍ لَيْسَ لَهُ مِنْ قِيَامِهِ إِلَّا السَّهَرُ

> There are people who fast and get nothing from their fast except hunger, and there are those who pray and get nothing from their prayer but a sleepless night.[81]

The inward meaning of one's salah is closely related to one's own inner profundity. Wherever salah is mentioned in the Qur'an, this inner profundity is also emphasized. For example, where the Qur'an talks about the people who attained salvation, the relation between salah and *khushu* (awe) before God is brought to our attention:

قَدْ أَفْلَحَ الْمُؤْمِنُونَ ۞ الَّذِينَ هُمْ فِي صَلَاتِهِمْ خَاشِعُونَ

"Prosperous indeed are the believers. They are in their Prayer humble and fully submissive [being overwhelmed by the awe and majesty of

---

81   Ibn Majah, Siyam 21; Ibn Hanbal, *Musnad* 2/373.

God]."⁸² Awe before God finds its real meaning only in salah. Therefore, a person in salah should not see, feel, or think of anything else but salah.

A person who observes salah makes a supplication to God both in words and action for the things they need. However, human beings are unable to provide and obtain everything they need on their own. By standing in obedient reverence before the greatness of God they ask everything from God. When it comes to one's immaterial and spiritual needs, salah is the nourishment of the heart and the heavenly ascension of the soul. In the face of all troubles, it lets the soul be relieved and the heart take wing and soar.

When the Prophet was weary of the worldly affairs he had to deal with, he would ask Companion Bilal al-Habashi to make the call for salah by saying,

يَا بِلَالُ أَقِمِ الصَّلَاةَ أَرِحْنَا بِهَا

"O Bilal, call *iqamah* for prayer: give us comfort by it."⁸³ Salah is not a task that a lazy and lethargic person would take on. It is a duty that a person with a vigilant heart and deep feelings will observe before God.

For a person whose mind is preoccupied with managing worldly affairs during salah, their physical tiredness will be their only gain. We ask from God's infinite Mercy that He not let anybody have tiredness as their only gain from salah. May He render our heart and feelings always responsive to Him and be totally in awe of Him.

It is not desirable for believers to lack mindfulness while reciting the Qur'an or glorifying God. It is essential that you put yourself in the proper frame of mind, eliminate all distractions, and maintain a proper focus on offering your supplications. Even if one falls short in this regard, their recitations or supplications still resonate with some aspect of their inner being, offering potential benefits, nonetheless. It is our hope that even such a small effort will have an impact, much like how tiny droplets of rain can awaken seeds in the soil. What falls to humanity is then to benefit from salah more profoundly. In order to advance towards deeper considerations, one must push themselves a bit. It is necessary to let each word reach into the depths of the heart with perception and awareness.

82   Al-Muminun 23: 1–2.

83   Abu Dawud, Adab 85.

Doing something consciously will allow our actions to flourish a thousand-fold.

On the other hand, abandoning salah by saying "I cannot recite with proper awareness, and I do not get delight in my worships as I should" is also mistaken, for such a thought is but a deception of the carnal soul. What really matters is fulfilling our duties without missing anything, even in the face of all adversities. Sometimes a long silence is far more eloquent than a long sermon and can convey much more meaning. In the same vein, trying to maintain our enthusiasm for salah under all difficult conditions is more valuable and auspicious than observing a wholly felt salah under favorable conditions. For example, we cannot know which one is better: the salah we observe in a mosque with an excited heart or the salah we observe alone, prostrated in full comprehension of our nothingness before God Almighty. Therefore, even those with constant inner contentment might be mistaken in their own evaluation, for it is not possible for us to be sure about what God will definitely be pleased with.

A memory and the importance of being careful in salah

One of the people I will never forget is Celal Efendi, father of respectable teacher Mehmed Kırkıncı. Celal Efendi was an esteemed person living in Medina; he passed away and was laid to rest there. When I went to visit him, he was very old. Despite his old age and ailments, he did not make any concessions from his salah and he observed the *nafila* (voluntary) ones by standing. Since he was having trouble getting up and down, he needed to lean on his bed so that he could stand up. After a salah he had completed in this manner, he asked me, "My respected teacher, I observe salah this way by leaning on my bed for support; is my salah valid?" I will never forget that scene. What a beautiful consciousness! Trying to observe servitude against all odds, but still not being satisfied with what he has been doing and seeking something better.

Salah is a capital that will save us in the Afterlife. Therefore, it is necessary to be very careful and sensitive about it. May God Almighty let its worth resonate in our souls and may He accept our salah by forgiving our flaws and shortcomings.

9. Salah and communicating the message of God

Every act of worship has a place and weight of its own. From the secondary to the primary, from the most essential matters to the finest details, all responsibilities of a believer are in serious harmony and there is no non-conformity between them at all.

The same holds true for faith and practice. Just as there cannot be true submission (*islam*) to God without faith, faith cannot be perfect without true submission to God. One should have sound faith in what needs to be believed Islamically in order to be a sound Muslim. If a person observes the commands of Islam without having sound faith they may start showing laziness about religious practices and rulings. So, a Muslim must have both sound faith and full practice. Faith not supported by deeds will weaken and disintegrate in the long run; unfortunately, today's generations are a living example of this.

The Prophet's Companions would both communicate the message of God and observe salah because salah means a person's renewal of the covenant with God five times a day. In fact, the act of renewing one's faith throughout the day, not merely five times but perhaps even five hundred times, holds profound significance. And only with this consistent and constant commitment can we cultivate the love, enthusiasm, and sincerity necessary to fulfill our work in God's cause.

The Qur'an speaks about the *salat al-khawf* in some detail.[84] *Salat al-khawf* is a method of performing salah in the event of an imminent attack or other form of immediate danger. With this salah, we learn that salah and congregational prayers should not be neglected even during the most intense times of danger and threat. In order to attain Divine blessings and abundance, people must carry out salah on account of His commandment. For example, the Companions observed salah during warfare and did not neglect it. While early Muslims were praying even during times of danger, some people today do not give up their comfort for the night prayer. They only give lip service to the matter.

However, what we rather need today is to have spiritual health, welfare of the heart, and the attainment of inner purity. The Qur'an (al-Maidah 5:105) counsels us on this with, عَلَيْكُمْ أَنْفُسَكُمْ "Your responsibil-

---

84   See Surah Nisa 4:101–103.

ity is your selves [so consider how you are faring along your own way]." God loves those who observe worship for His sake and who revere him. Some people unfortunately say, "I am a servant of God and I am doing exactly what I am commanded," however, they still commit thousands of acts of transgressions.

As for genuine believers, they accept fulfilling their salah as an essential for being able to communicate the message to others. Note that God Almighty reminded Jesus, peace be upon him—even him—that,

يَا عِيسَى عِظْ نَفْسَكَ فَإِنِ اتَّعَظَتْ فَعِظِ النَّاسَ وَإِلَّا فَاسْتَحْيِ مِنِّي

"O Isa, firstly give counsel to your own soul. If your soul does accept, then you can give counsel to people; otherwise, feel ashamed of Me."[85] It is important to observe our own responsibilities first; only then, we can ask others to do the same. Only then, our words will be sincere to have an impact on others – even if we give examples from other people, our audience will perceive the fact that we are actually "walking the talk." Otherwise, a person, let's say, who does not observe *tahajjud* should tremble before recommending it to others without practicing it themselves in the first place. Preaching without practice will have no effect at all. God states in the Qur'an (as-Saff 61:2),

يَاأَيُّهَا الَّذِينَ آمَنُوا لِمَ تَقُولُونَ مَا لَا تَفْعَلُونَ

"O who you Believe! Why do you say what you do not do [as well as what you will not do]?" It is as if He were saying, "are you not ashamed of it!"

Salah cannot be seen as separate from struggling for the sake of God. While the latter is an important obligation, salah is a person's most important struggle against one's own carnal soul. While returning from a military campaign, the Messenger of God told his Companions that they were passing from the lesser struggle to the greater one. When they asked what the greater struggle was, the Prophet replied that it is their struggle against the carnal soul.[86] A person who does not observe salah is a loser against their carnal soul.

If you believe you've committed yourself to glorifying God's name by communicating His message to others, then you must carefully consider the significance of such a duty and wholeheartedly embrace it. Glo-

---

85   Ibn Hanbal, Zuhd 1/54; Abu Nu'aym, *Hilyat al-Awliya'* 2/382.

86   Bayhaqi, Zuhd 1/165; Baghdadi, *Tarikhu Baghdad* 13, 523.

rifying the name of God is a call to have faith; it is an invitation to accept the Prophet, the other articles of faith, and Islamic teachings. Glorifying God's name entails earnestly striving for His exalted names to resonate everywhere, ensuring that the beauty of the message He revealed to His Messenger is cherished even in the farthest and darkest corners of the world. Glorifying God's name involves working harmoniously to ensure that the meaning and beneficence of the proclamation of faith are accurately comprehended and upheld everywhere.

Accordingly, if you are calling people to know God, to give an ear to His message, to read the Divine messages in the face of the creation, and to observe servitude to *Ma'bud-u Mutlaq* (the absolute One to be worshipped), should you not then personally take heed of His message, read His Divine manifestations in the creation, and thus become a genuine and sincere servant?

Salah is the basis and quintessence of worship. If you are calling others to servitude to God but you yourself are not properly observing a worship like salah, will others not call you a liar? If you observe salah every time in a manner of getting rid of it as soon as possible and merely going through the motions in a formalistic fashion, will it not be contradictory to what you say? Is it not meaningless to invite others to a task you deem so worthless that you get rid of it like a chore? If you invite people to the truth, should it not be a very serious matter in your sight? If you are not earnest about a given matter, how can you ever convince others about its being worthy?

Salah's influence and a person's relationship with God

Success of the efforts made for the sake of God only depends on God's acceptance and His giving value to them. God Almighty will never let those who do not have a sound relationship with Him be spiritually influential. As for those who do not maintain a profound relationship with God, they cannot reach anybody's heart; they cannot guide anyone to the truth; they can't prevent someone from remaining ordinary, nor can they assist in elevating a person to the spiritual realm of the heart and soul. Only those who tread the path of God are heard and their words and actions hold significance in His sight.

In this regard, those who devoted themselves to serving the Qur'an should assess their own true worth by looking at (the level of) their relationship with God. They should also know that things that remain as mere formality has no worth in His sight. As emphasized in a hadith, God Almighty does not regard your outward appearances or wealth, but rather, He evaluates the fervor of your heart, your inner depths, and the sincerity of your actions that stem from the depths of your soul.[87] If your behaviors are not a sincere reflection of your heart, then all of your efforts are in vain. Then those who devote themselves to serving faith should avoid being the object of Divine admonition, "Why do you say what you do not do [as well as what you will not do]?" (as-Saff 61:2)

They should strive to avoid being questioned, "Why did you deceive others by not practicing the truths you preached? Why did you tarnish the noble image of Islam by not aligning your actions with your words?" In this regard, along with observing the obligatory salahs properly, they must also pay close attention to the following three points in order to become paragons of salah

The three conditions for being a paragon of salah

1. When the Messenger of God ﷺ sets forth an objective for us, he firstly states that there are a hundred degrees in Paradise, with Firdaws being the highest. He then tells us to ask for Firdaws when we ask for Paradise from God.[88] Thus the Prophet points out that we had better seek high ideals. Additionally, he taught us the manners of making wishes beyond asking for Firdaws and he taught us supplications that indicate what we can ask from God. It is thanks to the prayers we learned from him that day and night we are able to supplicate to God saying, "O Lord, fill us with a desire to behold Your beauty (*Jamal*), let our hearts be excited with a zeal for reuniting with You, and bless us with beholding Your beauty in the next world." Thus, we declare that we seek to witness His beauty and to gain His good pleasure. The prayers we learn from the Prophet always counsel us to aim for high horizons.

---

87   See Muslim, Birr 34; Ibn Majah, Zuhd 9.

88   Bukhari, Jihad 4; Tirmidhi, Jannah, 4; Ibn Majah, Zuhd 39.

Likewise, we should have high ideals in attaining the truth of salah. We should therefore ask from God the fervor and enthusiasm of the Righteous Predecessors[89] in worship; we should search for the self-possession and stability of servitude they had; and we need to ask for Divine help in order to establish salah in a conscious fashion. Maybe each of us should say, "O God, in however profundity the Prophet observed salah, I am asking you to bless me in the same way. Let my soul, too, feel the meaning of salah. I also wish to observe salah like the Prophet did and feel it in all the atoms of my being. I wish to be closed to all other considerations other than You during salah, and to become completely immersed in salah. Please, O God, grant this blessing to me as well!"

Asking to worship like a Prophet does not mean asking to become a Prophet. Since we are supposed to follow Prophet Muhammad ﷺ, the Pride of humanity, in every matter, this is actually a demand for taking him as an example and a demand for deepening our salah. Such a petition of yours will never go wasted. If you keep praying like that in an eager and insistent manner, God will not leave you deprived of what you ask for. God willing, you attain togetherness with God through this path. When you demonstrate such eagerness, the Eternal Lord will respond in a manner befitting His Exaltedness, Supremacy, and the vastness of His Mercy. In this regard, the willingness for sublime things and the pursuit of lofty goals are expressions of aiming for the highest. Similarly, when it comes to establishing salah, one should always aspire for the highest standards.

2. A wish for realizing the truth of salah is a prayer by tongue and heart. Its practical dimension necessitates reading the works written on this subject. If a believer who wishes to observe salah in a conscious fashion has not read a few books about it, has not made any effort to learn about the considerations of spiritual masters on this subject, and has also neglected the theoretical aspect of salah, then that person cannot be sincere at this wish.

---

89   The honorific expression of "*al-salaf al-salihin*" means "the Pious Predecessors" or "the Righteous Predecessors" are often taken to be the first three generations of Muslims.

Accordingly, as the second step, a student of salah needs to read articles and books to ignite eagerness for worship in their heart. This allows them to visit the blessed realm of salah and fills them with awe of God by learning about the immense understandings and profundity of great guides. Said Nursi considered some works of *Risale-i Nur*, such as "Resurrection and Hereafter," significant, and he read them more than a hundred times. Should believers then not read several works related to the truth of Divinity, essentials of faith, and the meaning of worship at least a few times? The students of the Qur'an should certainly delve into the writings of spiritual masters like Imam Ghazali, Jalaluddin Rumi, and Bediüzzaman Said Nursi on salah. Additionally, exploring contemporary articles on the subject and engaging in discussions about it would be beneficial.

3. Persisting in both verbal and practical supplications, maintaining a resolute and consistent attitude towards achieving the desired goal, and advancing step by step with active patience are also crucial conditions. A love of salah may not spring into the heart of the seeker immediately; the person may not be able to feel the truth of salah in a few days, a few months, and even years. Therefore, it is very important to be insistent in striving for them, continue to ask God to bless us with them, and to do whatever is necessary that will lead us to the desired result.

If you aspire to be a paragon of salah, you should not neglect to utilize any factor that can help you reach those horizons. Whichever voice makes you fully vigilant and excites your heart, you should revisit it not just once but perhaps hundreds of times. You might find it beneficial to read a certain book tens of times, listen to a sermon repeatedly, or contemplate the words of a particular master. Always keep your target in mind throughout your daily life. You should never think of giving up by saying that it is not happening. You should never behave in a hurried fashion. You should not forget that on this path, you might flow like water in a stream for years, hitting many rocks along the way. However, with each challenge, you'll become a bit more refined, eventually reaching the ocean. To the extent of the depth of your intention and the loftiness of your endeavors, you will also take your place in the next world right behind "the Righteous Predecessors," each of whom was indeed a lover of salah.

10. The function of mosques

Mosques hold a unique significance in the hearts of Muslims. For this reason, their construction and maintenance bear great significance. The Prophet gave the glad tidings that God will build a house in Paradise for a person who builds a mosque in this world intending God's pleasure.[90] Upon his arrival in Medina, the Prophet ﷺ immediately initiated the construction of a mosque. It served not only as a place for administrative, civil, and security gatherings, but also for collective decision-making, consultative meetings on community and state affairs, and a space for believers to express their obedience, worship, and service to God in congregation. So much so that he worked like a construction worker with his Companions; sometimes he carried bricks on his back, sometimes he used a lever, pickax or spade… Free from every kind of bureaucratic understanding he dug in the ground, broke rocks… and worked as an ordinary person amongst the others. This example of his has been accepted as a *Sunnah* act among his followers from later generations. One of the first things the commanders of Muslim armies did when they conquered a new land was to establish a mosque, which would enable people to come together and fervently implore God with prayers, lift their hands to the heavens, and offer their servitude to Him.

In our time, unfortunately, mosques have lost most of their functions, merely becoming buildings where we can observe our servitude in an outward form. Actually, the Prophet attended to all his duties and responsibilities related to the military, justice, and administration in the mosque. This *Sunnah* has been continued by succeeding Muslim generations for a long time. In those times when all affairs were managed in the mosque, people would first bow their heads in salah in an air of accountability before God, then rise to fulfill their responsibilities. While they may have unintentionally erred, they found purification through seeking forgiveness from God in their next salah. The Messenger of God expresses this purifying quality of salah as follows in an authenticated narration:

الصَّلَوَاتُ الْخَمْسُ، وَالْجُمْعَةُ إِلَى الْجُمْعَةِ، وَرَمَضَانُ إِلَى رَمَضَانَ، مُكَفِّرَاتٌ مَا بَيْنَهُنَّ إِذَا اجْتُنِبَ الْكَبَائِرُ

---

[90] Bukhari, Salat 65; Muslim, Masajid 24, 25, Zuhd, 43–44.

The five daily prayers, and from one Friday prayer to the next, and from one Ramadan to the next, are all expiation for whatever sins come in between, so long as one avoids major sins.[91]

In another hadith, the Prophet ﷺ asked his Companions whether a person who bathes in a river passing by his door would have any impurity left on him. When they replied in the negative, the Prophet likened this to the five daily prayers, explaining that through them, God forgives all sins.[92]

We believe that when mosques functioned as they did in ancient times, people would carry out their duties with a clear conscience, inner dynamism and a sense of accountability before God, guiding their actions accordingly. They will leave behind things that belong to the "Era of Ignorance" and come one step closer to Islam. Maybe certain steps have been taken in this respect so far and some moves have been made, but the desired results are not obtained yet. It is hoped that by making decisions towards this end, mosques can cease to be places solely utilized for specific acts of worship and instead become venues where other duties for the good of society are also fulfilled. As the Qur'an expresses, those with unwavering faith in God are the ones who enable mosques to fulfill their true purpose and develop them both materially and spiritually. The Qur'an states the following:

إِنَّمَا يَعْمُرُ مَسَاجِدَ اللهِ مَنْ آمَنَ بِاللهِ وَالْيَوْمِ الْآخِرِ وَأَقَامَ الصَّلَاةَ وَآتَى الزَّكَاةَ وَلَمْ يَخْشَ إِلَّا اللهَ

> Only he will maintain God's houses of worship who believes in God and the Last Day, and establishes the Prescribed Prayer, and pays the Prescribed Purifying Alms, and stands in awe of none but God. It is hoped that such [illustrious] persons will be among the ones guided to achieve their expectations. (at-Tawbah 9:18)

The Ottoman Sultan Ahmed I is known for building his famous eponymous mosque (also known as Blue Mosque) in Istanbul. He was a pious man who expressed his love for the Prophet ﷺ with a poem in

---

91   Muslim, Tahara 10, 15, 16; Tirmidhi, Salat 46; Ibn Hanbal, Musnad 2/359.

92   Bukhari, Mawaqitu's-Salah 6; Muslim, Masajid 283–284.

which he expressed his desire to carry the Prophet's footprint (preserved in a museum in Istanbul) as a crown on his head. He was a person totally imbued with an Islamic consciousness. During the construction of this famous mosque, he filled his garment with sand and pebbles like a worker and then prayed, "O God, please accept this much of goodness from Your poor servant Ahmed; let this be provisions for him in the Afterlife!" Years later, it is told, one of Sultan Ahmed's descendants had a dream in which he saw Sultan Ahmed, who said that God Almighty had forgiven him by accepting those deeds and admitted him into Paradise.

Chapter 3

Preparation for Salah

1. Ablution (*wudu*)

A life wasted chasing one carnal desire after another is not what God is expecting from us; it is not where His pleasure can be sought. His pleasure is when we obey His command to appear at His presence at certain points in time, to offer our connection, love, reverence, gratitude, servitude, obedience, and readiness—readiness to receive His love, good pleasure, mercy and gifts. The foremost among these commands is the salah, observed five times on a daily basis.

Before observing salah, however, there is a required act of cleansing or purification, which is like a key, or password to enter a state of worship. Therefore, a person who neglects this purification will be unable to partake in salah.

لَا تَقُمْ فِيهِ أَبَدًا لَمَسْجِدٌ أُسِّسَ عَلَى التَّقْوَى مِنْ أَوَّلِ يَوْمٍ أَحَقُّ أَنْ تَقُومَ فِيهِ فِيهِ رِجَالٌ يُحِبُّونَ أَنْ يَتَطَهَّرُوا وَاللهُ يُحِبُّ الْمُطَّهِّرِينَ

> ...The mosque that was founded on piety and reverence for God from the very first days [in Medina] is worthy that you should stand in it for the Prayer. In it are men[1] who love to be purified [of all spiritual and moral blemishes]. God loves those who strive to purify themselves. (at-Tawbah 9:108)

---

1   The Arabic word "*rijalun*" normally means "men." But depending on the context and Arabic usage, it also includes women.

This verse was revealed about the people of Quba in Medina, in particular. But the meaning and implications are universal. The people of Quba, a town located on the outskirts of Medina, attached great importance to cleansing as a preparation for prayers and hence the ablution. Indeed, believers who are free from any physical impurities and uncleanliness exhibit their spiritual purity and cleanliness, as well as their ritual state of purity, through ablution. They earn in return the praise and pleasure of God. The believer who reflects this inner purity and cleanliness in the form of ablution is a person whom God loves. Such people make ablution solely for the sake of their belief in God. As an expression of having internalized the meaning of ablution, they may resonate with the experience of Caliph Ali: As mentioned earlier, while going to salah, as he was going to appear in the presence of God, a bitter smile and a bashful expression would appear in Ali's face, accompanied by a sense of awe that would permeate his body.

Ablution physically washes the body parts, cleansing them from any dirt and grime, physical impurities, and uncleanliness. With the spiritual meanings and effects it embodies, ablution not only purifies the body but also cleanses the mind and heart from negative traits, rendering them prepared and worthy to ascend to higher spiritual levels.

Then, the person's *sirr* (the spiritual faculty known as the *secret*) becomes a bright mirror in the face of the inspirational blessings bestowed by God, maintaining its purity. Such purification is akin to achieving half of the rewards of faith, affirming the truth of the hadith الطُّهُورُ شَطْرُ الْإِيمَانِ "Cleanliness is half of faith."[2] As for the other half of faith, it pertains to the creation of faith within the heart, a process entirely belonging to God Almighty. When a person initiates such an act of cleanliness with the intention to worship God, the dirt and grime within the spiritual heart will be erased, freeing the heart from sin, arrogance and hypocrisy, enabling the ability for faith to reside within the heart. As a result, God Almighty will kindle the light of faith in it.

The first exhortation on the way to salah

Wudu, or ablution, is the first directive, guidance, and exhortation on the path to salah. It is also the first act of preparation, serving as a

---

[2] Muslim, Tahara 1; Tirmidhi, Daawat 86.

means of spiritual readiness for worship and enabling one to derive maximum benefit from it.

Ablution is not obligatory for every deed and act of worship, but it is required for certain worships, with salah being the foremost among them. Ablution is obligatory for observing salah, making prostration on recitation (*tilawah*), or handling a *mushaf* (a printed copy of the Qur'an). Not to the same degree, but ablution for performing *tawaf* around the Ka'ba is *wajib* (necessary), and ablution for making a call to prayer or studying religious disciplines is *mandub* (recommended). Although religion does not strictly require it, ablution in such cases is a deed that earns merit for the individual. Moreover, we know that the Prophet ﷺ always preferred to be in a state of *wudu* and would not undertake any task without it. Therefore, it is *Sunnah* for a Muslim to maintain ablution constantly.

The Arabic word *wudu* carries meanings of beauty and cleanliness. Ablution also signifies the act where a person intending to worship purifies the heart from distractions other that thoughts of God, cultivates religious sentiments within, and cleanses the body parts, hands, arms, face, and feet. Consequently, the individual is purified and beautified properly both materially and spiritually, becoming prepared to petition to God.

One of the prerequisites of Salah is the removal of *hadath* (the state of non-ablution). This entails performing ablutions to cleanse oneself from the state of non-ablution, which is deemed impure for ritual worship. It may also involve performing *ghusl* (whole-body ablution) if necessary for the individual. Even though *wudu* and *ghusl* have many outward benefits such as ridding oneself of physical impurities and maintaining good health, they fundamentally serve as *ta'abbudi*, i.e., they are performed simply because they are commanded by God. This means, they are acts of purification imbued with religious significance, an intent to worship, performed solely for the sake of obeying Divine orders, which may hold additional wisdom beyond our understanding.

> O you who have believed, when you rise to [perform] prayer, wash your faces and your forearms to the elbows and wipe over your heads and wash your feet to the ankles. And if you are in a state of janabah [i.e. had a sexual intercourse or discharge], then purify yourselves. But if you are ill or on a journey or one of you comes from the place

of relieving himself or you have been intimate with women and do not find water, then seek clean earth and wipe over your faces and hands with it. Allah does not intend to make difficulty for you, but He intends to purify you and complete His favor upon you that you may be grateful. (al-Ma'idah 5:6)

The Qur'an teaches that under certain conditions, ritual purification can be achieved without water. If one can find no water, or if water is not available in sufficient quantities, or if it would be dangerous to use water, for instance if a person was wounded or very ill, clean earth may be used instead. This is called "*tayammum,*" after which one can observe salah.[3]

Observing salah mindfully

Wudu is the first exhortation and preparation on the path to salah. However, to be able to attain the desired gains from our worship depends on observing it mindfully as deep as one can. We can actually turn anything we do into a mindful action and thus even alter the nature of events we encounter, as long as we feel and think about that action with sincerity. Let me clarify this with an example.

When faced with misfortune, for instance, you will endure it one way or another. However, if you perceive it as an ordinary hardship to endure, you will confine all suffering and hardship to the narrow confines of that mistaken consideration. By solely focusing on the outward aspect of the misfortune and neglecting to reflect on underlying factors, you immediately confine it to that moment, thus narrowing the scope of your life; eventually your suffering becomes something you endured in vain.

However, from the very first moment you are confronted with misfortune, it is also possible for you to perceive it as a means of purification and an opportunity to earn merits. If you can look beyond the misfortune and see the One Who ordained it and understand that no action that occurs in this universe is aimless and without meaning, this

---

[3] *Tayammum* is performed with clean earth. One first strikes their hands lightly over the earth, dusts them off, rubs their face, and then strikes the earth again to rub hands and arms.

will instill in you a patience imbued resignation to Divine decree. You will turn immediately towards the Almighty God and appeal to Him, knowing that He sees everything and there are myriad wisdoms behind everything He permits. Yunus Emre expresses it as follows:

> *What comes to me from You is welcome:*
> *Be they robes or a coffin,*
> *Be it a fresh rose or a thorn,*
> *Graces and sufferings,*
> *Both are welcome.*

Even when you feel overwhelmed by the weight of adversity pressing down upon you, you may reflect, "Perhaps I needed to endure these trials to cleanse myself of sins and shortcomings and to attain a deeper level of spiritual strength; perhaps only such adversity could serve as atonement for my flaws. My God, I accept this hardship from You with resignation, knowing that You are forgiving." You endure not out of obligation, but with the conviction that it is from God Almighty, facing it with graceful acceptance. In this manner, you derive benefit even from adversity, infusing it with profound meaning through your profound reflections. Even if you do not articulate these sentiments, your serene demeanor and patient endurance will bring a sense of peace, transforming outwardly ugly misfortune into a conduit for forgiveness and mercy.

Likewise, in order to feel salah more profoundly, one needs to be full of the same heartfelt considerations starting with ablutions. It is essential to take ablution as a duty commanded by God, like a garb necessary for worship, and say, "My God, You have guided me to the fountain for ablution, and here I am complying with Your command." Only God knows and sees the actual significance of ablution, how it purifies us and beautifies us, and how it is reflected in the Realm of *Mithal* (the World of Representations and Ideal Forms). Additionally, with His permission, those in the High Assembly (*Mala' al-A'la*) in the heavens and the Guardian (*hafadha*) Angels witness it. Therefore, accepting purification as commanded by God and practicing it accordingly are manifestations of faith. The first step to benefit from the promises of ablution is to value it first and foremost for being a Divine command and then believe that it cleanses and purifies the person both physically and spiritually.

The Prophet ﷺ pointed out that the ablution is a cleanser, and it washes away spiritual impurities:

> When a believer washes his face while taking ablution, all of the sins he committed with his eyes go away with the water that drops from his cheeks. When he washes his hands, the burden of sin he committed with his hands drop down and disappear with the water of ablution. And when he washes his feet, all sins caused by his feet by walking to the forbidden flow away and expire with the last drop that falls from his toes. In this way, a servant who takes ablution properly will be completely purified of his sins.[4]

When a person cleanses their bodies, clothes, and the places of worship from material impurities through ablution, they also cleanse themselves from spiritual impurities, thus attaining the most suitable state for worship.

Every believer that stands in prayer makes ablution with an awareness of appearing in the Divine presence and rather gives importance to inward cleanliness. Along with outward purity, inward purity should also be maintained. If a contradiction or conflict persists between the two, and if inward impurity dominates and influences, and prevails, then the individual should be concerned about likely being a hypocrite (munafiq), as they are not maintaining the harmony, balance, and integrity between their inward and outward aspects. One may have washed the face and arms three times to remove physical dust, dirt and grime on the limbs; but if he or she is still standing in the presence of God with spiritual and moral impurities, without any remorse and repentance, and without earnestly seeking forgiveness and guidance to change for the better, it is a profoundly impious and preposterously impertinent attitude toward God. God Almighty values the heart more than the body and appearance; even if a person is outwardly clean, He might expel from His presence those jaded inside. Therefore, outward cleanliness in the faithful is assumed to be an aspect of inward cleanliness and purification as well.

In a hadith, the Messenger of God stated, "When one of you awakens from sleep, do not let him dip his hands into the vessel until he wash-

---

4   Muslim, Tahara 32; Tirmidhi, Tahara 2; Abu Dawud, Tahara 51.

es them three times. Verily, he does not know where his hand spent the night."[5] Today, scientists teach us that germs are especially prevalent in the moist regions of our bodies. It is always within the realm of possibility that our hands reach and touch such body parts, therefore collecting and spreading germs. During the night, people can touch any part of their body—armpits and/or private parts—but be unaware of it. Hence, whether the individual approaches it from a medical standpoint, viewing it as a hygienic practice, or simply follows it as an act of obedience to the Prophet's command, ablution remains a concise form of purification.

The dirt on one's hands can wash off pretty easily. As for the moral dirt, it can be washed off only by the grace and forgiveness of God. God can easily save anyone from their misdeeds. Therefore, a person who takes ablution five times a day wills and commits themselves to purify their body from material dirt and their inner being from moral filth and evil. Ablution becomes an expiation for all of these and also exalts the level of a believer.

Having *wudu* is akin to wearing appropriate attire and being impeccably dressed, preparing you for entering the sacred space of salah. Who knows, maybe if we witnessed how salah is reflected in the Realm of *Mithal*, we could understand better how splendid it seems in the realms beyond, depending on our immense or shallow considerations of it. In the same sense, maybe we could witness how the ablution made with enthusiasm for salah turns into a beautiful heavenly kaftan, while the ablution made as an ordinary act of washing the limbs remain just a shabby piece of clothing.

Detaching oneself from other engagements

Ablution not only ritually cleans one's body before praying but also helps detach one from all preoccupations and anything that might disengage one's mind and heart from the spirit of worship. It is for this reason that it is considered improper for a person to perform salah when they are in urgent need of using the bathroom. First of all, the person must rid themselves of the stress or feeling of discomfort and unease due to nature's call to enter the path of salah exclusively, with a sense of devo-

---

5   Bukhari, *Wudu*, 25; Muslim, Tahara 87-88.

tion. They need to start salah by having freed themselves of all distracting negative effects. Books of Islamic jurisprudence provide clear rulings on such matters, based on whether the individual's heart is preoccupied with other concerns during salah: if one is experiencing a call of nature, observing salah in that state is seen as a *makruh* (reprehensible). Because if the heart and mind are already preoccupied with a particular need or other matters, it becomes challenging for a person to concentrate on another task. In such a state, it is unlikely for a believer to pray in full consciousness, give salah its due reverence, and feel the worship profoundly.

Moreover, such behavior carries an implication of belittling the significance of salah, for salah is no trivial matter to be hastily dealt with. Salah is not meant to be hurriedly completed; rather, it is meant to illuminate that very moment and the individual's entire life. Due to these special qualities of salah, all scholars of *fiqh* (jurisprudence) deemed it appropriate to make the intention for *wudu* while going to relieve oneself. With this intention, every step taken to prepare for salah with a peaceful heart can be recorded as an act of worship. Undoubtedly, each stage, from preparing for *wudu* to starting and ending salah offers opportunities for the individual to earn rewards.

Wudu also serves a crucial role in setting the mood for worship and fostering concentration during salah. For a true believer it does not matter whether it is hot or cold, and they do their best to perform *wudu* perfectly. Regardless of the conditions, believers find a way to physical and spiritual purification in the manner of a wayfarer who tries to "ascend" to the heavens. As soon as the believer begins to wash their hands under the water, they will feel entering an atmosphere of worship, and illed with awe for the Majesty of God, will quickly abandon unnecessary, worldly chatter. With each subsequent limb washed, they progress further, stepping into a realm of light and vitality. If the believer recites the recommended prayers during ablution, reflecting on their meaning and turning to God with sincerity, they become completely infused with spirituality, entering a heightened state of metaphysical vigor and dynamism.

a. Cleaning of the teeth during ablution

Before beginning ablution, a believer should clean their teeth, which can be done using a *miswak*⁶ or toothbrush. Whether it is removing food remnants or eliminating bacteria from the gums and protecting the teeth, it does not matter; we do this first and foremost as a *sunnah*, a practice of the Prophet ﷺ.

Individuals are servants of God; even though they appear to be free in their thoughts and actions, there are limits to what they can do to themselves. They are prohibited from engaging in actions that fall outside the fold of prescribed or permitted acts by God. In this sense the person is an "'*abd*," an Arabic word mostly translated as "servant, slave," or more correctly "one who is subordinated to God, subordinated to Divine Will, and subordinated to obey and worship Him." A servant of God can only act within the permission of their Lord. For instance, no one can hurt themselves, let alone hurt others, even by causing a small wound to their own finger. You are forbidden to do so, and you must turn to God in genuine repentance if you were to do such a thing. Given the profound value Islam places on the human body and life, the preservation of teeth and preventing decay is a matter deserving serious attention. Consequently, even the smallest components of the human body hold significance; each is a distinct blessing with its own inherent value. While these blessings are bestowed without human intervention, their sustainability depends on an individual's will and the effort they invest in this regard. But what does this effort entail?

This effort simply entails thoroughly cleaning one's teeth at least a few times a day. God's Messenger states in a narration:

> Use the tooth stick, for the tooth stick purifies the mouth and is pleasing to the Lord. Jibril never came to me but he advised me to use the tooth stick, until I feared that it would be made obligatory for me and my Ummah. Were it not that I fear that it would be too difficult for my Ummah, I would have enjoined it upon them.⁷

It is also reported that God's Messenger used *miswak* so often that from time to time he wondered whether his teeth (or gums) might be-

---

6   The "*miswak*" is a teeth cleaning twig made from the Salvadora persica tree (known as *arak*).

7   Ibn Majah, Tahara 7.

come sore or damaged.⁸ Although this hadith was reported by more than forty Companions, some Muslims did not take the issue very seriously and did not give it its due importance. Cleaning teeth is given critical importance as a measure in preventive medicine today; it will continue to be so in the future. We know of no other saying which stresses the importance of the matter as much as this hadith does. In another hadith God's Messenger states the following:

إِنَّ أَفْوَاهَكُمْ طُرُقٌ لِلْقُرْآنِ، فَطَيِّبُوهَا بِالسِّوَاكِ

"Surely, your mouths are the paths of the Qur'an, so perfume [clean] them with the tooth stick."⁹

As Allah is beautiful, He also loves what is beautiful; He does not like what is unpleasant. So, you must keep your mouth clean so that God will be pleased with you. Otherwise, you will be called to account for it.

One final point here: Although we use the word *miswak* as the traditional toothbrush obtained from the branches of a certain tree and used for cleaning teeth, the word *siwak* mentioned in hadiths is "tooth cleaning in the absolute sense." While this can be done with a brush made from the branches of that tree, it can also be done with modern toothbrushes, even with our fingers, dental floss or anything else hygienic. Such dental care, when observed by a believer solely to attain God's good pleasure, indicates how important Islamic practices are regarding human health and life.

b. *The prayers recited during ablution*

Some scholars of *fiqh* acknowledge reciting *wudu* prayers as part of the adab, or etiquette of ablution. In *fiqh* terminology, adab encompasses deeds that are recommended, enhance the performance of other acts, bring rewards when performed, and are not considered sinful if abandoned. Actually, the prayers recited during ablution are not known to be directly reported from the Prophet ﷺ as they are; but they are derived

8   Ibid.

9   Ibid.

either from some Qur'anic verses or the Prophet's other blessed sayings by the Righteous Predecessors (*salaf al-salihin*), sometimes with additions, in shorter forms, or with variant versions. However, it is evident that these heartfelt supplications originate from the tongues of saintly servants of God, expressing their profound contemplations. Reciting these prayers transports individuals to different realms, imbues their hearts with sincere sentiments, and cultivates greater love and enthusiasm for worship.

When a servant begins ablution, they seek refuge in God from Satan—the one cast out of Divine presence and deprived of infinite mercy—and always start doing it with the name of the Infinitely Merciful, *Al-Rahman Al-Rahim*. As soon as the water touches and washes off the limbs, the individual starts reflecting over the greatness of the blessing of Islam and offers gratitude (*shukr*) to God, the One Who has made Islam a source of light and a means of purification from spiritual stains and Who has rendered water a means of physical purification.

While taking water to the mouth the person says, اَللَّهُمَّ أَعِنِّي عَلَى ذِكْرِكَ وَشُكْرِكَ وَحُسْنِ عِبَادَتِكَ "My God, I ask for Your help in reading the Qur'an, in always remembering You from the heart, in praising and glorifying You in a matter that befits You, and in observing servitude to You in the best way." اَللَّهُمَّ اسْقِنِي مِنْ حَوْضِ نَبِيِّكَ كَأْسًا لَا أَظْمَأُ بَعْدَهَا أَبَدًا "My God, allow me to drink to my heart's content out of the pond of the Prophet; let me drink such that I will never feel thirsty again," and fills with hope for a day they will be able to drink from the Kawthar[10] abundantly.

While inhaling water through the nose, to clean the nostrils, the individual aims to experience the fragrance of the heavenly realms beyond, even while in this world. They pray to continue sensing the fragrance of Paradise in the Afterlife too and to benefit from its blessings.

While washing the face the individual says, اَللَّهُمَّ بَيِّضْ وَجْهِي بِنُورِكَ يَوْمَ تَبْيَضُّ وُجُوهٌ وَتَسْوَدُّ وُجُوهٌ "My God, on the day You brighten the faces of Your friends while the faces of Your enemies become pitch-black, brighten my face as well and let it shine." As they pray so, they turn their inner gaze to the hills of Paradise.

Afterwards, with every limb they wash or wipe during ablution,

---

[10] Kawthar refers to a cool and refreshing drink, its river, or the Pond of Abundance in Paradise.

the individual voices another petition for an easy reckoning on the Day of Judgment, receiving their record of deeds from the right, their hair and skin to be protected from the Fire, to be sheltered under the shade of God's Sublime Throne on the day when there will be no other shelter, to be among those who only listen to beneficial words for a lifetime and who follow true wisdom, being freed from Hellfire, having steady feet on the day when many feet on the Bridge of Sirat will slip while walking towards Paradise and not failing there.

While completing the ablution, the individual says, "My God! Please reward my endeavors with abundant blessings, forgive my sins, and have mercy on me; accept my deeds, grant me a profitable trade without any losses," and asks to be one of the servants who continuously repent and who purify themselves from sins by making cleanliness an integral part of their character. A person who maintains these considerations in every step of ablution will gradually walk towards complete concentration.

Taking ablution properly despite difficulties

Once the Messenger of God asked his Companions: "Should I tell you something by which Allah effaces the sins and elevates ranks (in Paradise)?" The Companions replied in the affirmative, and he said, "Making *wudu* thoroughly in spite of difficult circumstances, walking with more paces to the mosque (even if it is far), and waiting for the next salah after observing one." Then the Prophet ﷺ added the following: "This is *ribat* [keeping loyal connection with God, like guarding the frontiers]."[11]

The Messenger of God referred to ablution in this hadith with the word "*isbagh*," and this term stands for fulfilling the requirements of ablution flawlessly, taking the full required amounts of water to the mouth and nose, and washing the hands, arms, face, and feet well. Another term used in the hadith is "*ala al-makarih*," and this means going to the water source without caring much whether the weather is cold or hot and making ablution perfectly in spite of all difficulties.

11   Muslim, Tahara 41; Tirmidhi, Tahara 39.

The matter of making ablution against all odds mentioned in this hadith always reminds me of what I witnessed in my hometown Erzurum, where people would make ablution from the mosque's frozen fountain and ice-cold water in the chilling winters. That sight still comes before my eyes, as if it had happened yesterday. The otherworldly state and manners of those sincere servants in the freezing cold are still so fresh in my memory. They reflect perfect faith in God: as if in a different otherworldly air, they roll up their sleeves and trousers, and come closer to the taps. In that moment, the air would be so cold that the water touching their fingers nearly turns to ice before reaching their elbow. The coldness of the weather and water combined causes every cell in their body to shiver even as they wash their hands. As their inner being resonates with this trembling, their sighs due to the freezing cold blend with the sound of flowing water, rising to Heaven and ascending to God as one:

اَللّٰهُمَّ أَعْطِنِي كِتَابِي بِيَمِينِي وَحَاسِبْنِي حِسَابًا يَسِيرًا

> My God! Please make my questioning easy for me on the day when You will call me to account for my life and give my record of deeds from my right as You do with Your righteous servants!

Believers in general are tested with everything. So, the men I saw then were aware that they were being tested by such difficulties, too. They had complete belief that all their efforts to concentrate, worship and turn to Him would fill the gaps in their record of servitude. With this conviction, they attached a particular value to ablution and saw it as a kernel that yields up to seventy kernels in one head. They add one deed of ablution in their record of good deeds, but they carry the hope that their harvest, their rewards, will be in many folds and much greater. And why should it not be? "That is God's bounty, which He grants to whom He wills."[12] The Messenger of God echoed this sentiment in the following hadith:

> Concerning a servant who takes ablution with proper compliance with the manners and opens his hands to the Heaven and says "I bear witness that there is no deity but Allah, He is One and He has

---

12 Al-Hadid 57:21, 168.

no partner. I bear witness again that Muhammad is His servant and Prophet," all eight gates of Paradise open for him and he enters from whichever he wishes.[13]

Not everyone who performs ablution will attain such great rewards, because not every believer will be as mindful on the way to salah and experience the immensity of ablution. However, attaining such reward is potentially valid and likely for everyone. Moreover, it is certain that the fortunate people for whom all gates of Paradise will be opened are going to be from among those who give ablution its due.

For the merits explained above, the Prophet ﷺ took separate ablution for each salah. Until the conquest of Mecca, he is not known to have prayed two times of salah with a single ablution, if at all. The Companions of the Prophet believed that being among those with bright faces, radiant foreheads, brilliant looks, immaculate limbs, and that having consciences as pure as the inner worlds of heavenly beings, depend on the salah and the preparatory deeds prior to salah. They always lived upon that belief. For instance, while taking ablution, Abu Hurairah would wash his arms up to almost the shoulders and his feet to his knees. When they asked him about the reason, he replied that he heard from the Messenger of God that his ummah will be called on the Day of Resurrection as their faces and limbs will shine because of the traces of ablution: إِنَّ أُمَّتِي يُدْعَوْنَ يَوْمَ الْقِيَامَةِ غُرًّا مُحَجَّلِينَ مِنْ آثَارِ الْوُضُوءِ Abu Hurairah added, "…and whoever can increase the area of his radiance should do so (i.e. by performing ablution regularly)."[14]

In another narration the Messenger of God stated that the adornment of the believer (in Paradise) will reach the places where the water of ablution reaches (on the body): تَبْلُغُ الْحِلْيَةُ مِنَ الْمُؤْمِنِ، حَيْثُ يَبْلُغُ الْوَضُوءُ[15]

Another hadith gives glad tidings about being among the foremost thanks to the signs on the limbs washed at ablutions and thus being spotted by the Prophet ﷺ. The Messenger of God ﷺ one day visited the Baqi cemetery and said, "I greet you O dwellers of the land of believers; In-

---

13   Ibn Hanbal, *Musnad* 1/19, 4/150.

14   Bukhari, Wudu 3; Muslim, Tahara 34-37.

15   Bukhari, Libas 90; Muslim, Tahara 40.

sha'Allah we will also join you one day." Later, he added that he really wished to see his brothers. When the Companions asked whether they were not his brothers already, the Prophet ﷺ replied: "You are my Companions (Ashab). My brothers [and sisters] have not come yet. They will come later on."

Upon this, when the Companions asked how he would recognize the members of his ummah who had not yet come, the Prophet ﷺ responded by asking if a man had horses with white markings among dark black horses, whether he would not recognize his horses. Then he said "my brothers [and sisters] are those who will come with faces radiant from their ablution and hands and feet shining. I will wait for them beside my Pool (of Kawthar)."[16]

Hence, ablution promises rewards both for this world and the next. Yet, there is a steep slope that must be climbed to attain the things it promises. Being able to pass over that slope is dependent on a person's freewill. Therefore, the duty that falls upon people is to make a willful endeavor to achieve concentration in worship. It may feel a bit difficult at the beginning and sometimes the conditions might be truly adverse. However, if you show patience and remain steadfast you gradually receive such a delight from ablution. You will begin to treasure it and regard it as the light of your eyes, in such a way that you would not exchange it for anything. Once you have started by saying *"Bismillah"* and climbed that steep slope through patience, you will savor such fulfillment and contentment that you will hope your travel between ablution and salah never ends.

Worship: too much or too little?

Inconsistency, or imbalance, between understanding and fulfillment of servitude to God can reveal itself in all shapes and forms when one goes to extremes in the observance of worship or non-observance thereof. On the one hand, it can be negligence of worship or its complete abandonment based on, for instance, self-proclaimed innocence and purity of heart (so much so that they do not need to worship); because they are too busy with worldly engagements; or they have too many family

---

16   Muslim, Tahara 39; Nasai, Tahara 110; Ibn Majah, Zuhd 36.

and business matters they are occupied with. Some people who take religious matters lightly claim that what really matters is having a good or pure heart, so there is no need for them to observe worship because they are already better than the pious. On the other extreme, there are the pedants with their own particularity and peculiarity about acts of worship. In this sense, for example, they waste too much water while making a "perfect" ablution or hopping and jumping weirdly in public for the sake of *istibra* (making sure that urine flow is ceased before making ablution). Neither of the two extremes can be found among the practice of the Prophet ﷺ, his Righteous Predecessors (*salaf al-salihin*), or the great scholars of the classic era.

Abu Said al-Khudri relates:

> The Messenger of God, peace and blessings be upon him, used to make ritual retreat (*i'tikaf*) in the middle ten days of Ramadan. One year, he made ritual retreat and came to the 21st night, which, ordinarily then, used to be the last night of his ritual retreat, whereafter he would leave his ritual retreat the next morning. Then the Messenger of God said: "Anyone who has made ritual retreat with me [for the middle ten nights], then let him [continue and] make ritual retreat with me for the last ten nights. For, indeed, I have been shown that Night [Laylat Al-Qadr, in it]. Then [the knowledge of its night of occurrence was taken from me, and] I was made to forget it. Yet, truly, I saw in a dream that I was making prostration in the mud the morning after Laylat Al-Qadr. So seek it out in the last ten nights. And seek it out on every odd night."
>
> Then the sky rained that night. The mosque had a thatched roof, so the roof leaked. Then with my own two eyes I saw the Messenger of God, peace and blessings be upon him, with traces of mud on his forehead the morning of the 21st.[17]

The Prophet ﷺ and the early Muslims did not carry a prayer mat with them to spread on the ground, for the earth was rendered a place of worship for them. It seems that they rather busied themselves with the inward essence and meaning of the matters rather than the outward

---

17   Bukhari, Fazlu Laylati'l-Qadr 2; Muslim, Siyam 213.

form or appearance. As they turned to God with a clear and pure heart, the inspirational blessings they received from Him were similarly pure and clear.

Those who are preoccupied unnecessarily with formality are most probably not so occupied with the inward aspect and they are not aware that their hearts have rusted up in time, either. It needs to be definitely known that no matter how oddly a person behaves about their istibra, or how much they are concerned about leaving a dry spot and therefore washing profusely or not wiping the limbs, the point here is that some individuals are living unaware of the true meaning and purpose of what they are doing, and that their actions will bear no value, likely be rejected and fail to obtain what they wanted.

Islam is a religion of ease; those who make it difficult are the ones who do not truly understand it. The Messenger of God ﷺ warns those who make religion difficult by extremism as follows:

> This is the religion of ease. Let nobody try to exceed religion by going to extremes (they cannot cope with that, and together with things they left missing); the religion will overcome them.[18]

Religion is something possible to practice; it has nothing to do with abandoning worship on claims of being already pure in heart or pedantic approaches like never prostrating oneself without finding a prayer rug, etc. Rather, a person's servitude to God is to the degree of the sincerity, affection, and devotion they possess and internalize. They must never engage in any artificial or impetuous acts to show that they have religious fervor. Otherwise, they will upset the innate balance. No matter how much they are busied with the outward aspect of the matter, if there is no integrity between the inside and outside, then they awkwardly wander around but return empty handed.

Accordingly, in a situation where even the Prophets put their forehead on the ground and trampled their pride, one should never adopt a conceited attitude to refuse prostrating. O reader, try to reach balance in your life of worship, do the *sujud* by putting your head on the ground, so that you come to the presence of Your Lord in humility and reverence. Then God Almighty will be your helper.

---

18   Tirmidhi, Salat 318; Abu Dawud, Salat 296.

As is the case with everything else, the Prophets brought a certain balance to societal life concerning worships as well. As long as we follow our Prophet ﷺ in his footsteps and observe our worships in the way he taught us, we will have kept a steady course and balanced life.

c. Blessings completed with ablution

A close scrutiny of human physiological anatomy reveals that God Almighty created the human being with mind-blowing systems each with a purpose. Imam Ghazali observed ages ago that there is no wonder like the human body.

If you try to change any of the delicate and well-arranged balances in the human body, you may harm, damage or destroy the whole system. For example, the circulatory system functions via the heartbeat, blood vessels and pressure, and pulse every moment. It pumps and conveys blood to all parts of the body through a network of blood vessels. It provides us with life. It functions for a lifetime in God's name while we are unaware. Sufis say that the rhythm of *"la ilaha illallah"* relates to a beating heart. When a person begins to chant *"la ilaha illallah,"* the heart experiences physiological alignment, joins this rhythm, and begins to say *"la ilaha illallah"* in harmony.

Capillaries are any of the fine branching blood vessels that carry blood to the remotest points of our body. Blood vessels can be compared to water channels and pipes; just as water pipes are calcified and blocked over the course of time, blood vessels, too, harden in time with the layers of fat that form on them, causing them to fail to fulfill their duty. The limbs to be affected from this condition most are the points remotest from the heart, like the tips of the fingers and toes and the farthest point of the brain. For those organs to be in good health, there must be proper blood circulation in the body. So, in comes here the function and contribution of ablution to this process.

The water of ablution contributes to the blood circulation system by stimulating capillary vessels at the remotest points. This is very important for the used blood to return to the heart, be cleansed in the lungs, then be sent back for those parts to retain their liveliness. All of these are blessings from God. With the verse which commands taking ablution, God Almighty states:

مَا يُرِيدُ اللهُ لِيَجْعَلَ عَلَيْكُمْ مِنْ حَرَجٍ وَلَكِنْ يُرِيدُ لِيُطَهِّرَكُمْ وَلِيُتِمَّ نِعْمَتَهُ عَلَيْكُمْ لَعَلَّكُمْ تَشْكُرُونَ

> Allah does not intend to make difficulty for you, but He intends to purify you and complete His favor upon you that you may be grateful. (al-Ma'idah 5:6)

What is meant by God wishing to complete His favor upon us? Everything He gave us is a Divine favor. However, completion of these favors is made dependent on individuals' free will. The first creation is a result of God's compelling willpower (*jabri* or Divine compulsion). God creates and decrees without asking anyone. However, continuity of His favors is conditional to human free will. For example, as doctors also emphasize today, one significant practice that helps maintain the elasticity of blood vessel systems is alternating between exposure to hot and cold water. Hot water helps them expand and cold water makes them contract. Therefore, a person who regularly performs ablution ensures that the vessels fulfill their function effectively by willfully aiding in their contraction and expansion as needed.

Both minor ablution and *ghusl* (complete body wash or major ablution) not only contribute to the circulatory system but also help stimulate the lymphatic system, which is an important factor in healing injuries and protecting the body against germs. Wiping the sides of the neck with wet hands is especially efficient in this stimulation. Also, sniffing water into nostrils and blowing it out help keep harmful bacteria away.

There is static electricity in the human body. It must be kept in balance for our body to stay healthy. Psychosomatic disorders put the body under pressure to a great degree. Polluted air, harmful substances or chemicals used in cookware, packaging and clothing are among other factors that upset the electrical balance in the human body. Water and soil are the prime elements in eliminating such imbalances and re-adjusting the static or body electricity. A person's regular ablution five times a day, and—in the absence of water—making *tayammum* with clean earth, regulates the electricity in the human body and discharges the excess. The Qur'an draws attention to this fact and commands us to make ablution when we rise for salah and to make major ablution whenever required. In the absence of water, the Qur'an commands us to make *tayammum*.

These practices are all part of God's continuous bestowal of His blessings and favors upon humanity.

Undoubtedly, life itself is a blessing, too. The perpetuity of this blessing, or rather, its attainment of eternity, relies on investing it in the pursuit of eternal endeavors. God Almighty has granted us the opportunity to turn our mortal life to an eternal one by means of our freewill. The protection of this blessing, i.e., life, is the reason some prohibitions are commanded by God. For example, substances like alcohol and other intoxicating beverages that are harmful to our health are prohibited in the Qur'an. This prohibition took place gradually over a span of years through various verses addressing specific issues.

Islam is a religion of ease. God Almighty never wants to put His servants into difficulty. The Qur'an (al-Baqarah 2:185) states: يُرِيدُ اللّٰهُ بِكُمُ الْيُسْرَ وَلَا يُرِيدُ بِكُمُ الْعُسْرَ "God wills ease for you, and He does not will hardship for you..." Therefore, the simple answer to the question "Why we are still required to make ablution even under difficult conditions?" is that God Almighty wills to complete His favor upon us and ablution is an important factor for the continuity of those blessings.

d. Degrees of purification in salah

Salah is a magnificent worship which includes four levels of purification. The *first level* is achieved by fulfilling the first two conditions of salah, through which we purify ourselves from impurity (*najasah*) and non-ablution (*hadath*) in preparation for salah. At this level, we ensure the cleanliness of both our clothing and body.

The *second level* involves preparing or grooming our body parts or limbs cleaned during ablution to abstain from sins: the eyes do not look at *haram*, the mouth does not speak evil, the hands do not do evil, and the feet do not take steps toward evil because we are stepping into the Divine presence in a moment.

At the *third level*, the level of cleanliness, the heart is detached and shielded against evil feelings and thoughts. A step further, the heart and mind of the person become fixed on or conditioned to seeking God's good pleasure.

God Almighty bestows on people a means of being honored by Him with the things He orders them; he renders their turning to Him

Preparation for Salah

as a means of His turning to them. In other words, if someone humbles themselves before God with salah, then God honors that person by turning to Him in response. Rabia al Adawiyya[19] explains this truth as follows:

> "Had it not been for God's turning to me, I would not wash myself for ablutions, do salah or fast, nor would I wake up for night vigils, assuming each to be one of *Mi'raj*. It is God's turning to me (His favor) that has made me become such."

What is mentioned by God's turning can be illustrated with an analogy: Why do sunflowers follow the sun, is it because of the sun's turning to them, or out of their own with no reason? Surely, sunflowers could not turn their faces to the sun, were it not for the sun's shining on them. Then the essential thing is the existence of the sun, which always turns (its rays) to them. In the same way, what really matters for a servant is the Eternal Sun's shining over and looking towards them. Without His guidance, a person lacks direction: They cannot discern the path to worship, identify the place of worship, recognize the direction of prayer, or avoid stumbling along the way. In reality, God has granted guidance to everybody, old and young, and has shown them the way to the mosque, worship and servitude to Him. Accordingly, we will look towards Him and He will look towards us... He will look towards us, and we will look towards Him. This is the very truth expressed by the Qur'anic verse, فَاذْكُرُونِي أَذْكُرْكُمْ "So remember Me and I shall remember you" (al-Baqarah 2:152). Namely, remember God in your times of ease, so that He remembers you in your hard times. You remember God in this world so that He remembers you when and where you need Him the most, in the grave, on the Great Gathering and Judgment, on the Bridge of Sirat, and when the sparks of Hell threaten you.

A servant must quest for Him like a moth attracted to light so that they can find Him one day. As such, salah provides the act of turning to

---

19   Rabia al Adawiyya (717–801 CE) was a female Muslim Sufi saint, considered by some to be the first true saint in the Sufi tradition.

God. Thus, believers who prepare for salah purify themselves through ablution and gain such a rejuvenated state; then they run to His presence. God Almighty will not be indifferent to this turning; rather, He will open wide all doors.

The *fourth level* represents the purification of the Prophets, marking the pinnacle of cleanliness. It entails the heart's complete detachment from everything except God, removing worldly matters from the heart even though they are not impermissible, allowing for God's self-disclosure within the heart. This is the level of cleanliness required from Prophet Muhammad ﷺ and all the other Prophets, which is the ultimate level of purification. In order to accomplish reaching this level, it is necessary to start from the beginning and follow the due sequence until the end. For example, it is not possible to be purified from things other than God, without subjecting one's heart to purification and getting rid of negative character traits and behaviors; because the heart cannot be connected to God without being freed from negative traits and being detached from things related to the world. Likewise, it is not possible to kindle a light in the heart without detaching one's limbs from sins. In other words, thanks to a person's being purified from sins in both the inward and outward sense, the light of faith will start shining in their heart.

Accordingly, it is not possible to reach the next level without going through these levels in sequence, one by one. Like climbing up the steps of a staircase, the believer will gradually ascend level by level, and attain God's good pleasure in the end.

The Prophets reached their levels by maintaining this balance with care. The Messenger of God, for example, was scrupulous about both ablution and salah; and in terms of purification of the heart, he would ask forgiveness from God a hundred times a day: إِنِّي لَأَسْتَغْفِرُ اللهَ فِي الْيَوْمِ مِائَةَ مَرَّةٍ.[20] Similarly, it is narrated that he prayed a few times in the morning and evening supplicating as, يَا مُقَلِّبَ الْقُلُوبِ ثَبِّتْ قَلْبِي عَلَى دِينِكَ "O Allah, Turner of hearts! Keep my heart firm upon Your religion."[21]

---

20   Muslim, Dhikr 41; Tirmidhi, Tafsiru's Surah, (47) 1; Ibn Majah, Adab 57.

21   Tirmidhi, Qadar 7, Daawat 89, 124; Ibn Majah, Dua 2.

2. The *adhan* – The call to payer

The *Adhan* constitutes the second step after ablution regarding concentration during salah. A believer steps towards being freed from unholy feelings and thoughts with ablution but gains further profundity with the *adhan*; the believer finds inner relief and feels the internal sweet breezes of Paradise beginning to flow with the *adhan*. The Prophet ﷺ stated that when the *adhan* for salah begins, Satan runs away, making repugnant noises out of the distress he feels.[22]

As *adhan* causes Satan and satanic souls to be seized by distress, such a call then is very important for a person to be freed from Satan and satanic thoughts and to observe salah in awe and in proper concentration. If the *adhan* is made, called in full consciousness of its meaning and significance, if it is called sincerely, from the bottom of the caller's heart, it has a significant effect on listeners. When it was time for salah, the Messenger of God would say to Bilal, his *muadhin* (caller to prayer), أَرِحْنَا بِهَا "Give us relief."[23] This can be paraphrased as, "Worldly affairs have burdened us. Please pour upon us the water of life, which brings spiritual refreshment and eternal solace, so that we may be relieved of the weight on our shoulders and liberated from the evil suggestions and whisperings of Satan that assail our souls."

Before the *adhan* was decreed, the Companions suggested other methods of calling to prayer such as blowing a pipe or tolling a bell; however, the Messenger of God did not accept any of these proposals. Given that it would be a call to salah, the task of calling had to be done with certain words that could express the spirit and kernel of salah; it had to be called in such a way that whenever people heard it, they feel a thrill and understand that they are being summoned to the Supreme presence. This call was not supposed to be with ordinary words, but with sacred words to be inspired by God. Eventually, God Almighty taught certain phrases through dreams and inspiration and granted a distinct beauty to the *adhan* through them. That is why scholars viewed the wording of the *adhan* as its pillars. In other words, just as acts like the opening *takbir*,

---

22 Bukhari, Adhan 4; Muslim, Salat 19.

23 Abu Dawud, Adhan 78; Ibn Hanbal, *Musnad* 5/364, 371.

the standing, recitation, and others are pillars of salah and conditions for its validity, so are the words of *adhan*. The words are the *adhan*'s pillars, without which there would be no real *adhan*.

Some individuals or groups claim now and again that a translation of the *adhan* will be just as good, but this will never be so. For instance, when one utters, "*Allahu Akbar*," their conscience is prompted to awaken to a profound truth. The word "*akbar*" can be translated as "the greatest." However, this does not mean that there are many other great beings and God is the greatest among them or compared to them. We merely translate the original meaning so because of an incapacity of words. If we wish to reflect the actual meaning, we can say the following: "The One who is great is solely and exclusively God. He is the Only One worthy of worship, the Only One Who deserves to be worshipped; the only One Who has the right to be worshipped. He is also the only One Who is deservedly and eternally sought after:[24] that is, unsolved problems can only be solved with Him, and seemingly insurmountable things can only be sorted out by referring to Him. Therefore, servitude is observed solely to Him." All these meanings are contained in and expressed by the phrase "*Allahu Akbar*."

A person bears witness to this truth in the *adhan* by saying أَشْهَدُ أَنْ لَا إِلَهَ إِلَّا اللهُ "I bear witness that there is no deity but Allah." Afterwards, a person declaring belief also adds the Prophet ﷺ to this testimonial by saying, أَشْهَدُ أَنَّ مُحَمَّدًا رَسُولُ اللهِ "And I also bear witness that Muhammad is God's servant and Messenger," because he is the person who conveyed this message to us. Then a "call" is made so that people run to observe salah to be relieved from various troubles: حَيَّ عَلَى الصَّلَاةِ. This call is repeated with the words حَيَّ عَلَى الْفَلَاحِ "Come on to salvation," because salvation is attainable only by turning to the One beyond Whom there is no one greater. The Qur'an (al-Mu'minun 23:1, 2) confirms the fact that salah is a means of salvation: قَدْ أَفْلَحَ الْمُؤْمِنُونَ ۞ الَّذِينَ هُمْ فِي صَلَاتِهِمْ خَاشِعُونَ "Prosperous indeed are the believers, those who observe their prayers in awe" (al-Mu'minun 23:1, 2). According to the Qur'an, the believers who pray and continue their prayers in humility, submission and

---

24   In the Turkish original text, the author uses "*Mabud-u bil-Hak*" for God's being the only One worthy of worship, and "*Maksud-u bil-Istihkak*" for His being the only One that is deservedly sought after.

awe before God's Majesty are the successful, the prosperous and the ones who will attain salvation.

The *adhan* comes to end by proclaiming God's greatness once more: اَللهُ أَكْبَرُ اَللهُ أَكْبَرُ، لَا إِلَهَ إِلَّا الله "...Allahu Akbar, Allahu Akbar, La ilaha illallah." After the completion of the *adhan*, believers are recommended to recite the following supplication:

اللَّهُمَّ رَبَّ هَذِهِ الدَّعْوَةِ التَّامَّةِ، وَالصَّلَاةِ الْقَائِمَةِ آتِ مُحَمَّدًا الْوَسِيلَةَ وَالْفَضِيلَةَ، وَابْعَثْهُ مَقَامًا مَحْمُودًا الَّذِي وَعَدْتَهُ

> O the Lord of this perfect call and the salah to be established! Render the level of our master Muhammad in Paradise higher and bless him with (further) virtue. Let him reach the exalted position You promised him.[25]

By saying so believers pray for the Prophet ﷺ, who not only brought the teaching of salah but also the *adhan*. The Prophet gives glad tidings that "whoever recites this prayer after the *adhan*, he [or she] will attain my intercession."[26] With this supplication, the believers petition for their salahs to serve as a means for them to be included in the fold of people whom the Prophet ﷺ intercedes for; believers also petition for him to reach *Maqam al-Mahmud*, the highest station of praise and honor, in the Hereafter. On the day of Resurrection there will be a banner named "*Liwa ul-Hamd*" (Banner of Praise), under which Prophet's ﷺ followers will be able to gather, as a result of such supplications done.

To conclude, the *adhan* is very important. It is *Sunnah* to repeat the words of *adhan* by reflecting their meaning while they are being called. The salaf, or the righteous guides of the early generations of Islam, all practiced and recommended that the listeners should not move around much nor engage in other activities while listening to the *adhan*. They also recommended that the listeners repeat the words of the *adhan* in tranquility and peace of heart. For maintaining concentration in salah, it is essential to be united beforehand with the *adhan* and the Divine inspirations it brings.

---

25   Bukhari 614 In-book reference: Book 10, Hadith 12 USC-MSA web (English) reference : Vol. 1, Book 11, Hadith 588.

26   Bukhari, Adhan 8, Tafsiru's Surah (17) 11; Tirmidhi, Salat 157; Abu Dawud, Salat 28.

The Messenger of God ﷺ did not ask people like Abu Bakr, Umar, and Uthman to call out the *adhan* although they were quite prominent among the Companions. Abu Bakr (r.a.), for instance, had a moving voice and people around would listen to him when he recited the Qur'an. However, the *adhan* requires a different voice, a different vocalization, so the Prophet gave this duty to Abu Mahzura, Ibn Ummi Maktum, and mostly to Bilal al-Habashi, perhaps because his voice touched the human soul. It is necessary to adorn the *adhan* with a tone that fits its beauty. It should not be called out flatly or raucously, but rather in a manner that allows people to perceive the power and impact of its words, along with the beauty of its chanting, so that they are well-prepared and focused for salah.

3. *Sunnah* prayers

Another important factor for maintaining concentration in salah is the *nafila* (*sunnah*) salahs. They are mostly observed before the obligatory (*fard*) prayers. Voluntary (*nafila*) prayers represent another step towards filling a person's heart with profound emotions and attaining a distinct sense of fulfillment. In essence, before embarking on the profound depths of closeness to God through obligatory prayers, souls are enveloped with *nafila* prayers by the gentle breezes of Divine Mercy. The concentration that has gradually deepened through ablution is revisited, examined, and further fortified. Through the performance of voluntary prayers, individuals make additional progress and draw closer to God.

All acts of worship other than *fard* and *wajib*[27] are termed as *nafila* (voluntary). Some of the *nafila* prayers are observed along with the five Daily Prayers, which are the *Sunnah* of the *Fajr*, the first and last *Sunnah*s of the *Dhuhr*, and the *Sunnah*s of the *Asr*, *Maghrib* and *Isha* prayers. These salahs are termed as the *rawatib sunnah*s. The *sunnah*s of the Friday Prayer can also be included into this category. *Rawatib Sunnah* is a term for any *nafila* salah observed in connection with a *fard* salah. God's

---

27 "*Fard*" and "*wajib*" are the terms that refer to the obligatory prayers. Hanafi school makes a technical distinction between these two; they call it *fard* when there is definitive evidence for the ruling of obligation, and *wajib* when the evidence is not as definitive.

Messenger stresses the importance of the *nafila*s in various hadiths in length. In one hadith about *rawatib sunnah*s, he states, مَنْ ثَابَرَ عَلَى ثِنْتَيْ عَشْرَةَ رَكْعَةً مِنَ السُّنَّةِ بَنَى اللهُ لَهُ بَيْتًا فِي الْجَنَّةِ "Whoever continues the twelve *rak'ah*s of salah observed as *Sunnah*, Allah will build a house in Paradise for him (or her)", and then explains the twelve as follows: "Four of them before *Dhuhr*, two after *Dhuhr*, two after *Maghrib*, two after *Isha*, and two before *Fajr*."[28] In other hadiths, the Prophet tells about the virtues of these *nafila*s separately. For instance, concerning the two-unit *sunnah* of the *Fajr*, he says, رَكْعَتَا الْفَجْرِ خَيْرٌ مِنَ الدُّنْيَا وَمَا فِيهَا "The two *rak'ah*s of *nafila* salah are better for you than the entire world and everything in it."[29]

Achieving such an outcome is possible for everyone, yet only God knows whether every individual who observes the *sunnah* of *Fajr* attains this level of benefit. However, striving to observe it is necessary for the sake of potentially attaining such benefits. In order to attain closeness in God's presence, you have to strive for it all the time. We can benefit from Divine bestowals and be honored with closeness to His presence only through the ways He showed us. Regarding the main path that guides us towards attaining all these blessings, flourishing our hearts and spirits, ensuring our salvation, and rendering us eligible for eternal realms, it is "the straight path," *sirat al-mustaqim*. A person who observes the pillars of this path and makes their way without falling into hopelessness will attain their objective sooner or later.

Indeed, practicing the requirements and manners of this path in their entirety is not easy; it is indeed a weighty task. God already points to that and decrees:

وَإِنَّهَا لَكَبِيرَةٌ إِلَّا عَلَى الْخَاشِعِينَ

Truly Salah is burdensome for all except the devout. (al-Baqarah 2:45)

There are numerous hadiths about the rewards and merits of *nafila* salahs. The Prophet ﷺ states:

مَنْ صَلَّى قَبْلَ الظُّهْرِ أَرْبَعًا وَبَعْدَهَا أَرْبَعًا حَرَّمَهُ اللهُ عَلَى النَّارِ

---

28 Tirmidhi, Salat 306; Ibn Majah, *Iqamah* 100.

29 Muslim, Salatu'l-Musafirin 96; Tirmidhi, Salat 307; Nasai, *Qiyam* 56.

Concerning the two *nafila*s of the *Dhuhr* prayer: "Whoever observes four before *Dhuhr* and four (*rak'ah*s of *nafila*) after *Dhuhr*, Allah makes that person forbidden to the Hellfire."[30]

Concerning the *Sunnah* before *Asr*: رَحِمَ اللهُ امْرَأً صَلَّى قَبْلَ الْعَصْرِ أَرْبَعًا "May Allah grant abundant mercy to those who observe the four-*rak'ah Sunnah* before *Asr*."[31]

Concerning the *Sunnah* of the *Maghrib* prayer: مَنْ صَلَّى بَعْدَ الْمَغْرِبِ رَكْعَتَيْنِ قَبْلَ أَنْ يَتَكَلَّمَ كُتِبَتَا فِي عِلِّيِّينَ "Whoever observes two *rak'ah*s of salah without speaking (i.e., right after the *fard* of the *Maghrib*), this salah will be raised to *illiyyun*," which is a lofty register.[32]

As for the *nafila* prayers apart from the *sunnah* prayers, they are known by different names such as *tahajjud*, *duha*, *awwabin*, *tarawikh*, *khusuf*, *istisqa*, *tahiyyatu'l masjid*, *istikhara*, *hajah*, and *tasbih*.

4. Iqamah

After having taken the steps of ablution, *adhan* and the *nafila-sunnah* prayers, the believers now make the final preparation with *iqamah*. When the *muadhin* with a moving voice calls it, the believers feel further enthusiasm one more time to be collectively standing and offering their servitude and reverence to God Almighty as they are about to meet further Divine manifestations through their obligatory prayer.

Incidentally, let me hasten to add that it is good if the voice and resonance you heard at *iqamah* serves as a basis for deepening our awe; otherwise, it is not anything desirable if the listener is preoccupied only with the melody of the call. This criterion also applies to all recitations of religious nature—hymns, chants or liturgies reflecting praise, thanksgiving, remembrance, supplication, forgiveness, or repentance. What really matters is that the voice goes deeper than the throat, in a way that the person's heart and conscience resonate with that voice.

30   Tirmidhi, Salat 317; Ibn Majah, Iqamah 108.

31   Tirmidhi, Salat 318; Abu Dawud, Salat 296.

32   Abdurrazzaq, *al-Musannaf* 3/70; Ibn Abi Shayba, *al-Musannaf* 2/16.

The *iqamah* is basically a repetition of the *adhan* but with an additional phrase to announce that the salah is starting: قَدْ قَامَتِ الصَّلَاةُ . After *iqamah*, the *fard* salah starts, which is a moment and state of being when believers are hoped to internally experience God's manifestations.

Chapter 4

The Components of Salah and Their Wisdom

The importance of the parts of something is proportional to the importance of its whole. A group or nation is advanced only as much as its members. Accordingly, the perfection of the whole depends on the perfection of the pieces which make up that whole. Salah is such a perfect whole that from the phase of visiting the washroom for the purification to its ending with the greetings of peace, each act we observe has its own unique value and meaning in its own place. Therefore, believers should do everything in salah consciously, as is prescribed. They must detach themselves from everything but God, in a sense, close their eyes and ears to all other things besides salah. They should not let other things cloud their imagination. As they immerse themselves in salah, and they are so imbued with it that every act they do in salah—recitations, prostration, rising, saying sacred phrases like *SubhanAllah* and the like—becomes a means of *tajalli*, the manifestations of the Divine.[1] This is exactly what is meant by awe and respect in salah. This state detaches a person from being heedless, uncaring, and indecent; it results in the worship becoming salah in the true sense.

Each component that constitutes salah has its distinct wisdom and therefore needs to be fulfilled meticulously. Imagine a gym and people training with a coach. The coach gives instructions to trainees about the movements and helps them execute the movements with the proper

---

1 *Tajalli* (manifestation) is being favored with God's special gifts. It also denotes that the Divine mysteries have become apparent in the heart of the seeker by means of the light of knowledge of God Almighty. Every traveler to the Ultimate Truth can feel this favor in the conscience according to their capacity and spiritual state.

technique. It is essential to comply with the technique so that trainees avoid possible injuries, with utmost care and diligence.

Let me add that it is wrong to compare salah to gymnastics and merely see it as another set of movements. With that being said, there are certain conditions or prerequisites for a valid prayer. They are indispensable components, and they are categorized into two: "the conditions of salah" and "the pillars of salah." The pillars of salah are the essential building blocks that constitute the worship. Each and every one of them must be performed as prescribed. As for the conditions for salah, although they are not the main acts, they are definitely required for the salah to be valid.

1. Conditions of prayer

a. Elimination of hadath

Hadath is any state of impurity which prevents a person from performing worship. They are basically spiritual impurities invisible to the eye. The "elimination of *hadath*" is done by performing ablution (*wudu*) before the prayer or by performing *ghusl* (major ablution, bathing) when in a state of major impurity, and *tayammum* (dry ablution) when the former ones are not possible.

In general, *hadath* refers to being ritually impure, and performing ablution is the means to cleanse oneself from that state of impurity. Although this purification has various benefits such as eliminating physical impurities and protecting body health, in its core is a sense of worship. This can be in the form of *wudu*, when one needs to perform salah, or *ghusl*, when one needs to take a full body bath. Those in a *junub*[2] state of major impurity cannot observe salah without taking complete body ablution. If the person in need of *ghusl* is not able to find water or are not able to use it, then they can meet this condition with *tayammum* with clean earth.

2   A state of major impurity, for both men and women, caused by seminal emission.

b. Purification from najasah

The condition of purification from *najasah* refers to being cleansed from material impurities. In order for a person to observe salah, they are supposed to clean their body, clothes, and the place of salah from things considered as dirty in Islam (e.g. human blood and urine, droppings and urine of animals like horses, sheep and the like...).

c. Satr al-awrah – covering the body

The human is an honored creature of God Almighty. God created humanity in the most perfect fashion and sent Prophets and scriptures to allow them to lead an honorable life. One of the means by which individuals can preserve their dignity and honor is through covering themselves.

يَا بَنِي آدَمَ خُذُوا زِينَتَكُمْ عِنْدَ كُلِّ مَسْجِدٍ وَكُلُوا وَاشْرَبُوا وَلَا تُسْرِفُوا إِنَّهُ لَا يُحِبُّ الْمُسْرِفِينَ

> "O children of Adam! Dress cleanly and beautifully for every act of worship; and eat and drink, but do not be wasteful. Indeed, He does not love the wasteful" (al-A'raf 7:31).

God Almighty commanded people to clothe themselves so that they can live as befits human beings. While covering the body brings value to a person in God's sight, it also brings them dignity in the eyes of all other beings, people being the first. Therefore, while it is obligatory to cover our private parts when we are near others. Covering the body is also among the essential requirements of worship like salah and *tawaf* (circumambulation) of the Ka'ba. The Prophet ﷺ ordered both male and female believers to be covered properly in salah. Concerning the women, it is stated that "salah by a grown-up woman without the headscarf is not acceptable."[3]

In addition to covering private parts, it is *Sunnah* for every believer to put on their best and cleanest clothes for worship, without going to excess. Pagan Arabs used to circumambulate the Ka'ba in stark nakedness. Tafsir scholars, including Ibn Abbas, commented that while the

---

3   Tirmidhi, Salat 277; Abu Dawud, Salat 85; Ibn Majah, *Tayammum* 132.

verse "O children of Adam! Dress cleanly and beautifully for every act of worship..." addressed these Arabs, it also commands covering properly during worship like salah and *tawaf*.

d. Istiqbal al-qiblah – turning to the qiblah

After having completed all preparations for salah, believers turn towards the Ka'ba standing for salah. They are commanded to do so except for the situations of valid excuse, where and when this is not possible. Turning to the *qiblah* is established by the Qur'an:

وَمِنْ حَيْثُ خَرَجْتَ فَوَلِّ وَجْهَكَ شَطْرَ الْمَسْجِدِ الْحَرَامِ وَحَيْثُ مَا كُنْتُمْ فَوَلُّوا وُجُوهَكُمْ شَطْرَهُ

> From wherever you go out (for journeying), turn your face towards the Sacred Mosque (in the Prayer). Wherever you may be, (O you who believe,) turn your faces towards it... (al-Baqarah 2:150)

The Ka'ba is an "ancient house" (Bayt al-Atiq), and all other mosques on earth are built in its direction. God Almighty says that the Prophet Ibrahim and his son Prophet Ismail constructed the Ka'ba, or Bayt Allah—House of God—which is the prayer direction for humanity until the end of the world, and the angels' place of circumambulation (*tawaf*) in the heavens up until Sidratul Muntaha.[4]

وَإِذْ جَعَلْنَا الْبَيْتَ مَثَابَةً لِلنَّاسِ وَأَمْنًا وَاتَّخِذُوا مِنْ مَقَامِ إِبْرَاهِيمَ مُصَلًّى وَعَهِدْنَا إِلَى إِبْرَاهِيمَ وَإِسْمَاعِيلَ أَنْ طَهِّرَا بَيْتِيَ لِلطَّائِفِينَ وَالْعَاكِفِينَ وَالرُّكَّعِ السُّجُودِ

> ...We made the House [the Ka'ba in Mecca] a resort for people, and a refuge of safety [a sanctuary, that is, a sign of the truth]. Stand in the Prayer [O believers, as you did in earlier times] in the Station of Abraham. And We imposed a duty on Abraham and Ishmael: "Purify My House for those who go around it as a rite of worship, and those who abide in devotion, and those who bow and prostrate [in the Prayer]." (al-Baqarah 2:125)

---

4   Sidratu'l-Muntaha, rendered as the Lote Tree of the Farthest Limit, denotes the limit, the final point, the furthest boundary of the realm of contingencies. Some have interpreted it as the final point which death-bound beings can reach. (Gülen, *Emerald Hills of the Heart Vol. 4*, "Sidratu'l-Muntaha," pp. 88-90)

The Ka'ba is at the center of Islam's most important mosque (the Masjid al-Haram in Mecca). As the most sacred site in Islam, it has a special place and significance in the eyes of Muslims. One day, the Messenger of God saw a smear of phlegm on the mosque wall facing the *qiblah*. His heart sank upon this sight; he scraped it off and then stated, "If anyone of you stands for prayer, he should not spit in front of him because in prayer he is speaking in private to Allah, as if He is in front of him."[5]

By turning to the Ka'ba, to the place of utmost sanctity, believers feel to be in the holy presence of God, as if having emptied all existing evilness, malevolence inside, repentantly asking forgiveness in tears and submitting themselves to Divine Grace and Mercy. And by taking a step further in consideration, the believer feels as if they are standing before God Almighty to give their account on Judgment Day. Salah performed with such conviction or consideration is one observed by distinguished servants of God. This is the state when the eyes and ears are closed to things other than God, when the heart comes nearly to a halt, and when the person wholly turns towards and stands before their Rabb along with the silent servitude of all creation. Namely, the person is virtually effaced and what remains is only Him. While saying *"La ilaha illallah,"* the individual feels this *tawhid* in the heart with its complete immensity. To attain this depth and completeness of heart, the most devout individuals, after uttering the opening *takbir*, exert themselves continually.

To summarize, upon beginning to observe salah, the believer should envision the Ka'ba in the mind's eye. Since the Ka'ba is the landmark of *tawaf* for the angels from the center of the earth up to Sidratu'l-Muntaha, believers should consider themselves to be in a blessed congregation, standing along with them in the Divine presence with the following thoughts: "I stand amidst a congregation where, as I gaze upon the Ka'ba, the members span from creatures crawling on the ground to individuals like myself and the blessed Prophets sent to guide them. Likewise, among this gathering are angels prostrating themselves alongside us before God. Facing the *qiblah* within this vast congregation, I fulfill my duty."

---

5   Bukhari, Adhan 34–36, 38–39, Mawaqit 8; Muslim, Masajid 52, 54.

e. Prayer times

One of the conditions is observing every salah within its due time span. It is an obligation to observe the five daily prayers within certain time segments of the day. The Qur'an says, "Verily, Salah is enjoined on the believers at fixed (prescribed) hours" (an-Nisa 4:103). Therefore, the due times, "prescribed hours" are conditional for the obligatory prayers. An obligatory prayer can be observed neither before the time is due nor after that time span has passed. It is not right for a person not to observe an obligatory salah in due time without a valid excuse. It is not right to knowingly delay it to be made up later, either. It will then be recorded as sin for the person who does so.

f. Intention

After having completed their inner and outer purification for salah the believer comes to God's presence with a consciousness in their heart, by which they know in what level they are and how they are supposed to behave there. This status also involves and indicates the worshiper's intention. For, intention is what is meant in the heart, by the heart, not what the tongue utters. The heart is supposed to totally turn to God. Things other than God should be removed from it. Once this has been maintained, it does not matter so much whether the tongue says it explicitly or not. Merely saying "here I intend to observe the *Sunnah* part of the *dhuhr* prayer" does not mean making proper intention by itself. The optimal way to intend prayer is by immediately clearing the mind and heart of all thoughts except those of God at the start of salah, and maintaining a steadfast awareness that the actions undertaken are solely for the sake of God. Even if the person said the intention with the tongue, they would not be truly regarded as observing the salah unless the heart is oriented to God in this manner. Therefore, some scholars like Imam Rabbani considered it objectionable to make the intention by tongue [only].[6] However, some believers may still tend to make their intention by the tongue. As they are following the opinion of some other scholars this should not be made or turned into a matter of disagreement and divisiveness.

---

6   Imam Rabbani, *Maktubat* 1/160 (186th Letter).

The quality of everyone's intention corresponds to their relationship with God Almighty. In this regard, it is feasible to discuss different intentions for different people. For beginners, who adhere to Islam and faith by imitation or simply by following what is said, the initial step of intention is to firmly establish the idea, both in mind and heart, that they are about to commence praying.

As for intention of the *hawas* (special, distinguished ones in knowledge) servants of God, the first step is to lock on salah with an exclusive concentration with all their feelings and thoughts. Above this, as for the intention of the most distinguished of the distinguished, it refers to clarifying and purifying the heart from all things other than God before and during the prayer, and maintaining this throughout the prayer. Any intention has only one object that is intended; there cannot be a second one. In salah, our intention is directed to God, and God only. If our seeking is truly directed towards Him, there cannot be two objects of supplication within a single intention. That is, if the person only meant to turn to Him and took Him as the sole aim, then it is necessary to remove all other aims—aims that are relativistic or absolute—out of one's heart and mind. If any other considerations come to their mind in the meantime, the people of this level, like Bediüzzaman and his first students, make a new opening *takbir*, thus forcing themselves until they manage to empty their heart from other things. However, it should not be forgotten that this endeavor is not supposed to be confined to mere form. If someone adopts a superficial attitude through imitation, it's unlikely to bring any real benefit to the individual.

With respect to a believer's inner journey, there are further levels of intention: at the level of *fana fillah* (total self-effacement in God) and *baqa billah* (subsistence by and with God) there is the state of even forgetting oneself entirely. For those who went beyond the sphere of the Divine Names and Attributes and virtually melted before *Subuhat al-Wajh* (Rays of the Divine Countenance), intention is being at a horizon where one cannot see, hear, and sense even themselves. According to the people of this level, if you are still able to feel yourself, then it means you are still busy with things other than God; and in their assessment of the situation, they become anxious if this is associating partners with God.

In short, the immensity or profundity of intention has its own varying degrees and levels. Depending on an individuals' degree of knowledge of God (*marifatullah*), they will establish and maintain their hearts' connection with God before starting salah accordingly, and in this state, they start off their prayer.

Intention is the spirit of our deeds

أَيُحِبُّ أَحَدُكُمْ أَنْ يَأْكُلَ لَحْمَ أَخِيهِ مَيْتًا فَكَرِهْتُمُوهُ

"Would any of you love to eat the flesh of his dead brother? You would abhor it!" (al-Hujuraat 49:12)

In the light of the verse above, Bediüzzaman explains word by word how horrible of an act backbiting is. He reminds that the letter أ (*hamza*) used in the beginning of and throughout the verse permeates each word, like light or spirit, with its inquisitive tone.[7] Intention is just like that. The believer's intention, representing their turning to God, entails recognizing that He alone is the true object of beseeching, supplication, and worship. This acknowledgment infuses every aspect of salah, permeating all its pillars. A worshipper should remain loyal to this intention in everything they recite in salah.

One can force their limits in this respect as much as they can, with scrupulous care, particularly with *nafila* salahs, for they are observed individually. However, it would not be right to do the same when praying with others, because this would mean making religion difficult. With that being said, when it comes to our *nafila* (optional, voluntary) prayers, there should be nothing wrong with doing our best to have sound intentions and maintain a consciousness of being in the presence of God.

Salah is the *mi'raj* of a believer. When God Almighty talks about the *mi'raj*, He states

إِنَّهُ هُوَ السَّمِيعُ الْبَصِيرُ

"Surely He is the One Who hears and sees" (al-Isra 17:1). Concerning the pronoun "He" mentioned in the verse, scholars state two possibilities: firstly, it can be referring to God Almighty, and secondly, it can alternatively be taken as referring to the Prophet ﷺ. If the pronoun

---

7   Nursi, *The Letters*, Twentieth Letter, Conclusion.

refers to God's Messenger, it means that he is being described with two Beautiful Names of God (the One who hears, the One who sees). Then an important truth is drawn attention to, that the Prophet ﷺ perceived everything presented to his sight and hearing during the *Mi'raj* with profound insight. In other words, he made the most of the experience and absorbed it to the fullest extent. He did not miss a second, not even a split second or millisecond. From the beginning to the end, everything was virtually sifted through his consciousness.

M. Lutfi Efendi of Alvar states, "salah makes the ship of religion sail on; salah is the master of all worship." As for Süleyman Çelebi, he expresses this meaning in his poetry that God rendered salah as a *mi'raj* for this ummah.[8] Given that salah is a *mi'raj*, a believer must take their hearing and sight under control. The ears and eyes must only perceive what is necessary to be heard and seen, as Mawlana Abd al-Rahman Jami put:

يَكِي خَوَاهْ، يَكِي خَوَانْ، يَكِي جُويْ، يَكِي بِينْ، يَكِي دَانْ، يَكِي گُويْ

> "Only ask for the One, call for the One, seek out the One, see the One, know the One, and tell about the One."[9]

Accordingly, during salah, believers must only see, know, hear, seek, call, and feel the One, and remain indifferent to everything else. They must try to attain this state in every element of prayer. Once a believer attains such a state, he or she should still seek even further, unsatisfied: "No, this is not how it should have been. I should have approached it in a manner that allowed me to forget myself completely, to not even sense my own presence. I should have transcended the awareness of my existence, reaching a state of near self-oblivion."

An exerted endeavor

Let me reiterate once more that all of these points explained above depend on a believer's level of commitment and devotion. It is not possible to attain such levels without trying, training, and putting your heart and soul into it.

---

8   Süleyman Çelebi, Mevlid, Vesiletü'n Necat, p. 118.

9   Molla Jami, "Yusuf and Zulayha," (Heft Evreng, 2/22 couplet 59).

Namely, if there is no pushing your souls to undertake it (*takalluf*) at the beginning, you cannot impose such a commitment (*taklif*) later on; you will not make your soul accept it. For this reason, a person who targets such horizons must strive for the ultimate degree. Junayd al-Baghdadi states, "I exerted myself for 60 years. And after 60 years, God granted it to me, and I started observing salah (in the real sense)." Those like us, who never experienced the real meaning of salah in life should compel themselves to pray properly, at least for some five or ten years.

Incidentally, the points we mentioned above should not be misunderstood; we are not arguing that salah we observe somewhat inattentively, carelessly or sloppily are by no means acceptable. That is not our job! On the contrary, it is our hope that our Creator, Who has infinite grace and mercy, will accept our salahs observed at that level too. It is our hope that He places us in Paradise even with such salahs, He renders them into a road companion for us in the Intermediate Realm (*Barzakh*), and He renders them into a steed to pass the Sirat Bridge with a blink of an eye, and he renders them into a source of light to brighten our darkest horizons. In this respect, we should never neglect salah nor take them lightly. On the other hand, we should not fail to set high aspirations. The act of worship we offer to our Lord of infinite grandeur must suit His Majesty and Greatness. Our worship should bear a meaning of thanksgiving in response to His favors and benevolence to us beyond measure. Therefore, a believer should seek to find the truth of salah for a lifetime.

Another important point about intention is that it should pervade all pillars and parts of salah with exuberance. One makes the intention with full concentration; then, since He is the only implored and beseeched One, the person should feel the intention at every pillar conscientiously and defy anything other than that. A believer during salah should not feel disturbed by any other consideration other than God, and have some kind of inner response or reaction to such. For example, while saying, اَلرَّحْمٰنِ الرَّحِيمِ "Ar-Rahman, Ar-Rahim," (al-Fatiha 1:3) if a person does not feel in the conscience various manifestations of His Infinite Mercy reaching up and encompassing everything, then they should be self-critical.

None of these are impossible to realize, as millions of people have experienced this level of devotion for ages. In the same way, millions of people are still eligible to experience them. مَنْ طَلَبَ وَجَدَّ وَجَدَ "If someone seeks to do something earnestly, they will surely find what they sought." If we think about this principle the other way around, if they did not find it, it means that they either did not pursue it enough or they did not show serious care while doing so.

2. The pillars of salah

Editor's note: The pillars of salah and doing them in the order are briefly given below. The objective here again is to understand their spiritual meaning and effect. Pillar of salah cannot be waived. Performing them in order is also essential. If a person deliberately changes the order, prostrates before bowing, for example, the prayer is invalidated. There are some differences of opinion among the *fuqaha* (scholars of jurisprudence) regarding details under these issues, which are discussed in detail in the books of *fiqh*. Yet, that is not the primary focal point of the line of arguments in this work.

a. The opening takbir

The opening *takbir* is the exaltation of God in the standing position at the onset of a prayer. It lets the heart gain integrity, transcend its limited material world to enter a different realm, and proclaim God's greatness virtually by counterbalancing the carnal self and its impositions. It marks the beginning of salah, and the person is actually in the prayer starting then.

The common characteristic of the powers sanctified like deities or leaders that are blindly followed are always their impression of grandeur, greatness, superiority, and highness. Therefore, a believer who begins salah by saying "*Allahu Akbar*" in a way declares having overcome all despots, tyrants and megalomaniacs and not recognizing any powers but God. Therefore, the person leaves behind everything that distracts and detaches them from God, lays their gaze to the openings of the divine realms, and begins to wait for things to be granted from there. They cannot commence salah with any other word but the *takbir*, "*Allahu Akbar*." The Prophet ﷺ said,

مِفْتَاحُ الصَّلَاةِ الطُّهُورُ، وَتَحْرِيمُهَا التَّكْبِيرُ، وَتَحْلِيلُهَا التَّسْلِيمُ

"The key to salah is the purification, its *tahrim* is the *takbir*, and its *tahlil* is the *taslim*."¹⁰ "*tahrim*" is prohibiting oneself from being busied with things other than salah, which is marked by the opening *takbir*. The thing that finishes salah and allows being busied with things out of salah is "*Taslim*," the greeting at the end. Therefore, it is obligatory to start salah with the *takbir*.

b. Qiyam – standing

A believer's obedient stance in God's presence serves as a reminder of how some creatures crawl on the ground or move on all fours with their bodies bent forward. However, God Almighty bestowed upon humans the ability to stand and walk in an upright position with ease. This is a blessing, among many others, granted to humanity, and not to animals, which have no other choice but to comply with the laws decreed in nature. If human beings try to count all their blessings, this would not be possible, as is pointed out by the Qur'an.¹¹ Therefore, people are not able to offer sufficient thanksgiving for what God blessed them with. Humanity is, first and foremost, honored with the best pattern of creation (*ahsan al-taqwim*) both inwardly and outwardly. God Almighty did not create them as lifeless beings and did not leave them without consciousness. Among the conscious beings, He endowed humanity with reason and freewill. As for a believer, God did not include them among unbelievers; on the contrary, through degrees of purification, God firstly blessed them with the honor of being human and then having belief. Moreover, He added more blessings one after the other along their advancement.

So, when a believer is in *qiyam* (standing), they can recall these blessings and imagine having been called to account before God on Judgment Day and asked to give an account of the breaths they took all throughout their lives.

---

10   Tirmidhi, Tahara 3, Salat 176; Abu Dawud, Tahara 30, Salat 74; Ibn Majah, Tahara 3, 30, Salat 75.

11   See Surah Ibrahim 14:34, "Were you to count the favors of Allah you shall never be able to encompass them" and Surah an-Nahl 16:18, "For, were you to count the favors of Allah, you will not be able to count them."

c. Qiraat— Qur'an recitation

After proclaiming God's greatness with the opening *takbir*, the person says أَعُوذُ بِاللهِ مِنَ الشَّيْطَانِ الرَّجِيمِ to take refuge in God against Satan the accursed. Because of the importance of salah to be established and the Qur'an to be recited, they wish God not to let Satan have any interference with their worship. This phrase is a confession of *ajz* (weakness, incapacity, incompetence) by the worshiper from the very beginning. Then the person recites the Basmala, (*bi-smillah ir-rahman ir-rahim*, "In the name of God Most Compassionate, Most Merciful), which expresses that everything that takes place and every movement made are and must be in the name of God. After confessing their powerlesness, the person petitions to God with an imploring heart and says, الْحَمْدُ لِلّٰهِ رَبِّ الْعَالَمِينَ "*Alhamdulillahi Rabbil alamin*," (all praise and thanks are for Allah, the Lord of all creations–realms). As he or she utters this phrase, they mean the following: "My God, You bestowed me all these organs and limbs that operate like splendid machines. Miniscule fragments and cells come together and make up my living body. Now, every part of me is like an individual worshipper; they observe servitude to You with their own movements, functions, and meanings they stand for. With my words I only serve as a spokesperson for their servitude. With the number of muscles and limbs that move during salah, I say 'all praise is due to You' as an expression of my gratitude and indebtedness."

This is followed by the next phrase: الرَّحْمَنِ الرَّحِيمِ by which the worshipper means, "Because of my weakness and poverty, You have laid this universe like a huge book of wisdom for me to read. Also, you endowed me with the willpower to read it and thus transform the rays I will gain from that reading into faith in my heart. You made it possible for me to go beyond the mysteries of the universe, to study and explore Divine Names, to look into and be conscious of Your Attributes, and thus to be aware of Your Holy Being."

Next, the worshipper says, مَالِكِ يَوْمِ الدِّينِ "You are the Master of the Day of Judgment." This in a way explains why God deserves so much praise (*hamd*) and thankfulness (*shukr*). By this, the person acknowledges and promulgates that God Almighty creates this huge universe, endows living beings of every kind with this and other worldly gifts, and that He is the Sole Master, Absolute Sovereign, and Supreme Judge of the Day of Reckoning, on which rewards and punishments are due.

Then, in order to acknowledge and declare that the only One worthy of worship is the One Who owns such attributes, might and majesty, and in order to be able to use their limbs and body parts for His sake, to have strength, ability and opportunities to serve and worship Him properly, the worshipper says, إِيَّاكَ نَعْبُدُ وَإِيَّاكَ نَسْتَعِينُ "You alone do we worship, and to You alone do we pray for help." By this, the worshipper has ascended to a further level of knowledge of and closeness to God, where it becomes possible to address God as "You." Because only with such a demand for help, one can handle the responsibility of servitude.

Finally, at that stage, the worshipper perceives as though they have been granted an opportunity and entitlement. Not to miss the opportunity, they immediately beseech God to guide them in all walks of life to a path which is absolutely true: اِهْدِنَا الصِّرَاطَ الْمُسْتَقِيمَ ۞ صِرَاطَ الَّذِينَ أَنْعَمْتَ عَلَيْهِمْ غَيْرِ الْمَغْضُوبِ عَلَيْهِمْ وَلاَ الضَّالِّينَ "Guide us to the Straight Path, the path of those whom You have favored, not of those who have incurred [Your] wrath [punishment and condemnation], nor of those who are astray." With all these and more in mind and heart, the person prays for guidance to their eyes, ears, tongue, lips, limbs and mind so that they will not succumb to and adopt false principles, beliefs, and conduct, which prevent them from true salvation and happiness. For, the person knows that there are many possibilities and probabilities of deviation and corruption concerning each of these body parts.

In a hadith the Messenger of God states, كُتِبَ عَلَى ابْنِ آدَمَ نَصِيبُهُ مِنَ الزِّنَى "Allah has written for the son of Adam his share of adultery which he commits inevitably..."[12] As explained in the rest of the hadith, the adultery of the eyes is to gaze at a forbidden thing; the adultery of the tongue or mouth is to talk in a licentious fashion; the adultery of ears is to listen to licentious things; the adultery of the feet is walking to licentiousness, and so forth. All of these are deviations into crooked paths. Here at this very point, as a response to the prayer of the worshipper with al-Fatiha, the Divine Mercy smiles at humanity, who is in so much in need of mercy and compassion: God Almighty becomes like the eye with which the person sees, the ears with which they hear, the tongue with which they speak; in the sense that God does not let that person

---

12 Bukhari, Isti'zan 12, Qadar 9; Muslim, Qadar 20–21.

take a wrong step, pursue a wrong affair, look in the wrong direction, or speak wrong things.

On the other hand, the person virtually speaks with God Almighty with the verses they recite. In a *hadith qudsi*, this truth is explained as follows:

> God Almighty stated, "I have divided *qiraat* (recitation) between My servant and Myself; one half belongs to Me and the other half belongs to him. My servant has been granted what he wished." When the servant says, "*Alhamdulillahi Rabbil alamin* [All praise be to God, the Lord of the worlds]!" God Almighty says, "My servant has praised Me." When the person says, "*Ar-Rahman'ir Rahim*," God says "My servant lauded Me." When he says, "Master of the Day of Judgment," God says, "My servant venerated Me and extolled Me." And when he says, "You alone do we worship and from You alone do we seek help," God says, "This is (a covenant) between Me and My servant. I have given My servant what he asked for." When the servant says, "Guide us to the Straight Path, the Path of those whom You have favored, not of those who have incurred (Your) wrath, nor of those who are astray," God Almighty says, "This, too, is My servant's; what he asked for has been granted to My servant".[13]

As such, Surah al-Fatiha is an expression of excitement of the human conscience. By reciting the Fatiha in salah, the servant on the one hand voices what is down in our conscience, and faces the outline of a community upon right guidance; on the other hand, one almost feels Divine Power supporting them from behind. Likewise, with the verses recited in addition to the Fatiha, the worshipper wanders in different horizons and meets different scenes. Sometimes, the servant goes into an ecstatic rapture, sometimes they weep and sob, and sometimes they feel strain and cannot find the strength to continue the recitation and bow to *ruku'* right away.

The Prophet would mostly recite long portions from the Qur'an. Companion Ibn Mas'ud relates one of his memories about it: "One night, I observed salah together with the Messenger of God. He prolonged the

---

13   Muslim, Salat 38; Tirmidhi, Tafsir 2; Nasai, Iftitah 23.

salah so much that the idea of doing a bad thing passed through my mind." When they asked what it was, he replied, "I thought of giving up the salah halfway and sitting down."[14]

Another hadith narrated by Companion Hudhayfa is as follows:

> One night I observed salah with the Prophet ﷺ. He started reciting surah al-Baqarah. I thought to myself, "he will bow to *ruku'* after completing some hundred verses." When he recited more than a hundred verses, I thought "he will probably recite the entire surah in one *rak'ah*," but he still carried on. I thought, "now he will bow to *ruku'* with this surah; then he started reciting the surah an-Nisa. He recited it too. Then he started surah Al' Imran, and recited it too. He was reciting slowly, when he came to a verse with *tasbih* (glorification), he was glorifying God and when he came to a verse of making a wish, he was making a wish, and when a verse about taking refuge in God came, he was taking refuge in God. Then he bowed to *ruku'* and started saying "I glorify my Exalted Lord from every kind of defect." His *ruku'* was as long as his recitation. Then he rose from *ruku'* by saying, "God hears the praise of one who praises Him; O our Lord, may praise and laudation be to You!" and stood for some time comparable to his *ruku'*. Then he prostrated himself and said, "I glorify my Lord, the Highest." His prostration too, was comparable to his standing.[15]

During special spiritual states he felt in salah, the Messenger of God would always implore God and make supplications. We cannot do this when we are leading the *fard* salah as the imam in congregation. However, in the *nafila* prayers we can and thus open up to our Lord at every aperture. Opening up to Him and asking from Him the cure and remedies for our moral ills and wounds will definitely result in a relief in our hearts.

Those unfortunate ones who cannot attain the true salah at all, although they think they observe it everyday, actually drift from the Divine Presence and therefore cannot know what it means to be oblivious of oneself and turn to Him wholeheartedly. Because they mistake salah as a

---

14   Bukhari, Tahajjud 9; Muslim, Salatu'l-musafirin 204.

15   Muslim, Salatu'l-Musafirin 203; Nasai, Tatbik 74; Ibn Hanbal, *Musnad* 5/384.

chore to carry out, a merely dry formality to be completed, and meaningless movement. In reality, when a real believer is going to observe salah, they feel relief and delight as if invited to a banquet or to take it even further, as if they are going to Paradise. And by means of the openings they sense, they immediately try to maintain an audience, a communion with God. May God Almighty enable us to feel all these meanings. For, unless we do so, we will not be able to shake of the heedlessness on us; we will not be able to rid ourselves from languor and listlessness; and we will not know how many *rak'ah*s we prayed or what we recited even though we are in salah.

d. Ruku'

أَلَمْ نَجْعَلْ لَهُ عَيْنَيْنِ ۞ وَلِسَانًا وَشَفَتَيْنِ ۞ وَهَدَيْنَاهُ النَّجْدَيْنِ ۞ فَلَا اقْتَحَمَ الْعَقَبَةَ

"Have We not made for him a pair of eyes, and a tongue and two lips, and shown him the two ways (one to follow, and one to avoid)? Yet he has not attempted the steep path." (al-Balad 90:8-11)

The worshipper imagines being brought before God to account for the blessings given, reflecting the meaning stated in the verse above. Then assuming that they have not properly used, benefited, and sometimes went out of the boundaries, they are concerned for likely reproaches, like "Although we granted every kind of blessing to you, guided you to the great and right road, you were still not able to overcome heedlessness, to give what needed to be given, and therefore, you failed to take the path of your Lord... now account for all of these...." Under the influence of such meanings, the person nearly feels unable to stand anymore and bows down.

Because of God's greatness and the blessings given, the person acknowledges so: 'O my Lord, it is true that You have bestowed me so much; as is the general case, the Great always keeps bestowing, but lesser ones may mishandle those bestowals. Here I am confessing my pettiness and defects before Your Exaltedness and glorifying You by saying سُبْحَانَ رَبِّيَ الْعَظِيم "*Subhana Rabbiya'l adheem*" in compliance with the command, فَسَبِّحْ بِاسْمِ رَبِّكَ الْعَظِيم "Glorify the Name of your Lord, the Supreme" (al-Waqi'ah 56:74, 96; al-Haqqah 69:52). I say, "I declare Your being absolutely above having any defects and partners; I knock on the door of Divine mercy with the glorification of angels." In this manner, the servant acknowledges, confesses, and declares that they are defective, as opposed to God Almighty, Who is free from all defects. When the Messenger of God bowed down to *ruku'*, he would pray as follows:

اللَّهُمَّ لَكَ رَكَعْتُ، وَبِكَ آمَنْتُ، وَلَكَ أَسْلَمْتُ، أَنْتَ رَبِّي خَشَعَ سَمْعِي وَبَصَرِي وَمُخِّي وَعَظْمِي وَعَصَبِي، وَمَا اسْتَقَلَّتْ بِهِ قَدَمِي، لِلَّهِ رَبِّ الْعَالَمِينَ

> O Allah, to You I have bowed, in You I believe, and to You I have submitted. You are my Lord. My ears, eyes, brain, marrows, bones, nerves, and everything my feet bear are in submission with God, Lord of the worlds.[16]

Likewise, the bowing position in *ruku'* is the worship of the creatures that walk with their body parallel to the ground. The believer remembers that too and with the prayer being made virtually says: "All praise is due to You my Lord! You did not create me like your creatures which walk with their body bent forward, but upright. Although I am bowing for acknowledging and declaring Your grandeur and greatness, I will be able to stand upright again. After having felt all of the above-mentioned meanings in the heart, the believer rises again and stands upright in expectation of Divine Mercy once more. They are ready for another pillar of salah, another great act of humility, obedience, and servitude, and that is prostration.

e. Prostration

A hadith relates that a man is called to account in the Great Gathering. Since his sins are more than his good deeds, he is decreed to be sent to Hell. As angels seize him to take him towards Hell, the servant looks back for a moment. Although God Almighty—who is not bound by time and space—already knows why, He says, "Ask My servant why he looked back." The servant replies, "O my Lord! I had never imagined this about You. I thought that even if I came to Your presence with sins as heavy as mountains You would forgive me and place me in Your Paradise. This was the opinion I held about You. But You are sending me to Hell!" Upon this, God Almighty decrees, "I treat My servant in accordance with his

---

16   Nasai, Iftitah 104; Ibn Hanbal, *Musnad* 2/268.

opinion about Me. I shall not prove my servant wrong in his hope. Take him to Paradise!"[17]

Thus, straightening up after bowing, returning to an upright position, as if by feeling a relief the servant says: سَمِعَ اللهُ لِمَنْ حَمِدَهُ "God hears the one who praises Him." And by standing upright, he says, رَبَّنَا لَكَ الْحَمْدُ "My Lord! All praise is due to You." With that he means, "You have created me as human. You have saved me with Your mercy from the dread of being called to account and granted me so many other blessings." Sometimes the believer does not find this sufficient and says like the Prophet did:

اللَّهُمَّ إِنِّى أَعُوذُ بِرِضَاكَ مِنْ سَخَطِكَ، وَبِمُعَافَاتِكَ مِنْ عُقُوبَتِكَ، وَأَعُوذُ بِكَ مِنْكَ، لاَ أُحْصِى ثَنَاءً عَلَيْكَ أَنْتَ كَمَا أَثْنَيْتَ عَلَى نَفْسِكَ

O Allah! Truly I seek refuge in Your good pleasure from Your anger, in Your exemption from Your punishment, and I seek refuge in You from You. I admit that I am unable to praise You as You have praised Yourself.[18]

رَبَّنَا لَكَ الْحَمْدُ مِلْءَ السَّمَوَاتِ وَالأَرْضِ، وَمِلْءَ مَا بَيْنَهُمَا وَمِلْءَ مَا شِئْتَ مِنْ شَىْءٍ بَعْدُ

O Allah, O our Lord, praises are due to You in a way to fill the heavens, the earth and all that is in between, and to fill everything else You like.[19]

By thinking that God's Mercy is with them, the worshipper is somewhat relieved from the anxieties about the toughness of being called to account, and breezes of hope begin to blow in their soul. Then as an expression of thankfulness to God again, the prostrating worshiper says three times: سُبْحَانَ رَبِّيَ الْأَعْلَى "Glory be to my Lord, Most High" in reverence to Him.

The Prophet would prostrate himself in compliance with the Qur'anic command فَاسْجُدْ لَهُ "Prostrate yourself for God" (al-Insan 76:26) and sometimes say, اللَّهُمَّ اغْفِرْ لِي ذَنْبِي كُلَّهُ، دِقَّهُ، وَجِلَّهُ، أَوَّلَهُ وَآخِرَهُ، سِرَّهُ

---

17   Bayhaqi, *Shuab ul-Iman* 2/9.

18   Muslim, Salat 222; Tirmidhi, Daavat 76, 113; Abu Dawud, Salat 152, 338.

19   Muslim, Salatu'l-Musafirin 201; Tirmidhi, Daavat 32; Abu Dawud, Salat 118.

وَعَلَانِيَتَهُ "My God! Forgive all of my sins, great or little, old or new, overt or covert!"[20] in utter self-effacement, and sometimes he would say: اللَّهُمَّ لَكَ سَجَدْتُ، وَبِكَ آمَنْتُ، وَلَكَ أَسْلَمْتُ، سَجَدَ وَجْهِيَ لِلَّذِي خَلَقَهُ فَصَوَّرَهُ، فَشَقَّ سَمْعَهُ وَبَصَرَهُ، تَبَارَكَ اللهُ أَحْسَنُ الْخَالِقِينَ "My God! I have prostrated myself for You, put my faith in You, submitted to You. My face, too, is prostrate for the One who created and shaped it, who endowed it with ears and eyes. Exalted is God, who creates what He does in the most beautiful form!"[21] and thus expressed his reverence.

In short, thanks to these prostrations the believer takes their due place behind the Prophet ﷺ who ascended with his worship to meet his Lord during the *Mi'raj*. They should observe salah with an intention to seek this exalted position. While fulfilling the command and duty given by God and seeking to gain what He promised, they will feel an immense delightful pleasure through all pillars of salah: not only being behind the Prophet ﷺ, having him in front of them, both as a guide and company; but greater than all, God's promises, having gained His good pleasure, and beholding His Beauty. May God let the joy of salah permeate throughout our souls and make us always be imbued with it! Also, may He enable all of us to achieve our own *mi'raj* through salah.

Insightful scholars (*muhaqqiqin al-ulama*) regard the prostration in salah as the utmost peak a human being can reach. They argue that "every other pillar is like a step to reach prostration." A person passes through different phases in salah, commencing with ablution and finalizing with standing before the Divine Presence. Through prostrations they acquire the closest state to their Lord, as is expressed in a hadith.[22] However, what is important at that state is what overflows in the heart and the profundity of the bond established with God through sincerity, obedience, servitude, and reverence. For instance, during every aspect of salah, a believer should fully immerse themselves in the experience, reflecting with sentiments like, "My Lord, had You not ordained this in religion, I wouldn't know how to serve You; endless praise and glorifica-

---

20   Muslim, Kitabu's Salah 246.

21   Muslim, Salat 216; Abu Dawud, Salat 147.

22   Muslim, Salat 215; Abu Dawud, Salat 148; Nasai, Mawaqit 35, Tatbiq 78.

tion to You!" During *ruku'*, they might think, "I'm unsure if my state adequately expresses my deep devotion (*ubudiyya*), but I strive to emulate the Prophet ﷺ and hope for acceptance." And during prostration, they might express, "If asked, my God, I would gladly bow my head lower than my feet just for Your sake."

Indeed, salah is one's journey in the shade of *Mi'raj* to the realms beyond this one and prostration is the most significant pillar of that journey. Therefore, a person should try to feel ultimate closeness to God and try to catch what it yields in the heart. Prostration is handed to humanity on a silver platter. It is "a night of union" of the lovers as the great Jalaluddin Rumi puts it. It is a favorable ground for each and every person to have their share of Divine inspirations, to the degree of their knowledge of God and of the worth they stand for.

Prostration is where a person will be oblivious to everything and everyone other than God by saying "*illallah*" (except for God, nothing but God) and savor the closeness with the Lord. Prostration is the title for perfect devotion to God Almighty which in a way suits His glory. Then what needs to be done in prostration, how and why they should be done should be considered accordingly.

f. Sitting in tashahhud and tahiyyat

The sitting in salah is after the second or the last *rak'ah*. It is called *tashahhud*, which literally means "testimony," or *tahiyyat*, i.e. "greeting." The sitting for *tahiyyat* is an expression of having used up all one has in their ascension to God. After having utilized all their energy in the body, all the cognitive power of their brain, excitement in the spirit, and alertness in the heart and senses, on the path to get closer to God, the worshipper then sits for the *tahiyyat*. *Tahiyyat* is a portrayal of the blessed journey of the *Mi'raj*, which took place when people were turning their faces from the Messenger. The gates of Heaven were opened for him as the dwellers therein warmly welcomed him in and he was honored by God Almighty into His Presence.

After a person has completed the previous pillars of salah, they reach *tahiyyat* in accordance with their own inner status and immensity of heart: Some sit for *tahiyyat* under the heaviness of being called to account, unable to get up. Some sit as if on the cushions of Paradise, freed from troubles. Or, some may have considerations like experiencing what is depicted in Surah an-Najm: appearing in Divine presence, acquiring a station between the categories of possibility (*imkan*) and necessity (*wujub*), and having the honor of speaking to the Lord. There, after having fulfilled salah with the entirety of its physical burden, the person will recite the episode of their *mi'raj*, depending on the immensity, profundity and alertness of their heart and feelings.

Tahiyyat is all about the *Mi'raj*. As such, it seems that it is very difficult for us to ascend to the Divine Presence on our own, unaided. No matter how much worship we can do, it is seemingly an impossible task to rise up to the Divine Presence without first turning to Prophet Muhammad ﷺ paying tribute to him, and then ensuring his intercession. For, the Prophet, as our predecessor, left a legacy and blazed a trail for us. This is why our *tahiyyat* to God, which is but our expression that we observe all of our worship – in all of its forms, bodily or financially – exclusively for Him, is followed by our greeting the Messenger when we say, "*Assalamu alayka ayyuhan Nabiyyu...*" This means that, while going to the presence of God Almighty despite our sins and faults, we imagine ourselves to be standing in prayer behind Prophet Muhammad ﷺ and to listen attentively to and comprehend the conversation between him and God during the *Mi'raj*:

التَّحِيَّاتُ لِلّٰهِ، وَالصَّلَوَاتُ، وَالطَّيِّبَاتُ

"All the compliments are for Allah, and all prayers and goodness."

السَّلَامُ عَلَيْكَ أَيُّهَا النَّبِيُّ وَرَحْمَةُ اللّٰهِ وَبَرَكَاتُهُ ،

"Peace be upon you, O Prophet, and Allah's mercy and blessings."

.السَّلَامُ عَلَيْنَا وَعَلَىٰ عِبَادِ اللّٰهِ الصَّالِحِينَ ،

"Peace be upon us and upon the righteous servants of Allah."

أَشْهَدُ أَنْ لَا إِلٰهَ إِلَّا اللّٰهُ وَأَشْهَدُ أَنَّ مُحَمَّداً عَبْدُهُ وَرَسُولُهُ

"I bear witness that there is none worthy of worship but Allah. And I bear witness that Muhammad is His servant and messenger."

In this prayer of *tashahhud*, the Messenger of God ﷺ firstly says that "*Tahiyyat, tayyibat* and *salawat* are for God." These words are very comprehensive with profound meanings. With these words, it is as if the Prophet ﷺ meant the following: "O Lord! All worship we do with all the atoms and cells of our body and with our charitable spending from what we earn are only for You and for seeking Your good pleasure. I come to you to express my pledge and my fidelity to You, and I greet You with those and the best of the words." To His beloved Messenger ﷺ who offered greetings to Him in this way, God honored him by greeting him back, saying "Peace be upon you, O Prophet, and Allah's mercy and blessings."

This conversation occurred in a place that was beyond human comprehension; a place which one cannot know if it really existed or not. Listening to this conversation eagerly and carefully, angels said "Peace be upon us and upon the righteous servants of Allah." In the end, the Archangel Jibril (Gabriel) contributed to that magnificent symphony with sweetness and harmony, as his words resonated in the heavens: "I bear witness that there is none worthy of worship but Allah. And I bear witness that Muhammad is His servant and messenger." Thus, Jibril declared to all heavenly beings that God is the Absolute One to be worshipped and the Eternally besought of all by right, and that Prophet Muhammad ﷺ is a Messenger with exalted glory, peace be upon him.

Then the *tahiyyat* is but a process of conceiving and contemplating this episode from the *Mi'raj*. It narrates the saga of a servant's Ascension to God by means of his servitude. After having been through all these pillars and their requirements in salah, the Messenger of God would recite the following prayer and finish his salah:

اَللّٰهُمَّ اغْفِرْ لِي مَا قَدَّمْتُ وَمَا أَخَّرْتُ، وَمَا أَسْرَرْتُ وَمَا أَعْلَنْتُ، وَمَا اَسْرَفْتُ وَمَا أَنْتَ أَعْلَمُ بِهِ مِنِّي، أَنْتَ الْمُقَدِّمُ وَأَنْتَ الْمُؤَخِّرُ لاَ إِلَهَ إِلاَّ أَنْتَ

> My God, forgive me for what I have done and for what I will do, for what I have concealed and what I have declared, and for that [in me] You know best about. You are the Hastener and the Postponer, there is no god but You, and there is no strength or power except in Allah.[23]

May God enable us to conceive and contemplate that event in the *tahiyyat* during our salah.

---

23   Muslim, Salatu'l-musafirin 201, Zikr 70; Tirmidhi, Daavat 32; Abu Dawud, Salat 121, Fadail 358.

3. Complementary components for salah

a. Ta'dil al-arkan inwardly and outwardly

Ta'dil al-arkan is fulfilling each act of salah as perfectly as one can. It is to fulfill these acts by giving their due and taking one's time. The salah must be performed without rushing it, but with enough time spent for each act and in between them. Your body must pause after each act with a full rest, satisfied, and calm. This is the physical condition the human body is supposed to take in salah, without which salah will not be complete.

Abu Hurairah narrates that while the Prophet ﷺ was in the mosque a man came in. After doing salah at one corner, he came near the Prophet, greeted him, and the Prophet ﷺ returned his greeting. When the man was about to sit, the Messenger of God ﷺ told him, "Go repeat your salah; your salah was not valid." The man went away, repeated his salah and came back. He greeted the Prophet, who greeted back, but told the man the same thing: "Go repeat your salah, your salah was not valid." At the second or third time the man said: "O Messenger of Allah! This is all I know, please teach me where it is mistaken." Upon this, the blessed Messenger, peace and blessings be upon him, stated:

> When you rise for salah, take your *takbir* and begin the salah. Then recite a portion from the Qur'an. Then bow down to *ruku'* and remain there until your joints come to rest (in another narration, until your joints let themselves and relax). Then raise your head back from *ruku'* and do not prostrate yourself until your body is upright. Then prostrate yourself and remain prostrate until your body parts come to rest. Then raise your head from prostration and sit until your body finds rest at the sitting position. Then prostrate yourself again and do not rise back until your body parts are settled... and observe all of your salahs this way.[24]

By taking this and similar narrations into account, most scholars of *fiqh*, including Imam Abu Yusuf of the Hanafi school regarded compliance with the manners of observance as *fard* (obligatory) for salah to

---

24   Bukhari, Adhan 95, 122, Istizan 18, Ayman 15; Muslim, Salat 45.

be valid. According to the opinion that determined the general *fatwa* (ruling) in the Hanafi school, compliance with the rules is *wajib* (necessary). Therefore, one must act in compliance with the manners of observance while observing salah. In my opinion, it is more sensible to take this opinion, which expresses compliance with the manners of observance as obligatory, as the basis of our acts when we observe salah. Let's not make it an issue of disagreement whether it is obligatory or not. The best course of action in case of such disagreements is to act in the most cautious and prudent way, which, here, is compliance with the manners of observance as obligatory.

Compliance requires fulfilling all pillars and principles of salah properly and trying to maintain them with enthusiasm without letting them lose their luster. For this reason, matters like making long recitations from the Qur'an and thus prolonging the standing, remaining in bowing and prostration for a good deal of time, are all very important, too. In a way what really matters is to fulfill the pillars properly despite seemingly laborious.

Proper compliance with these pillars will let the person attain different dimensions during salah. For this reason, the individual should revisit their salah once more, striving to deeply experience the standing, bowing, and prostration with their entire being.

Observing salah in an immaculate fashion in outward form and not leaving anything missing from its pillars, conditions, *Sunnah* acts, and even recommended acts and manners is surely a very important issue and nobody can dismiss it as simple. What really matters in a person's relationship with their Creator is the meaning, essence, and spirit; however, this meaning and essence are transported with words and physical actions, which are the outward forms. This is why performing the physical actions and reciting the words properly are important, so that the intended meaning can be conveyed. To reiterate, it is not possible to disregard the outward aspects of prayer, for external rulings are based on them. However, what really matters is the spirit of the prayer, which can be achieved by observing salah with a peace of mind and awareness.

Although no such terms are found in books of *fiqh*, for *khushu* and *khudu*—awareness of being in the Divine Presence and feeling due awe—I think they can be called "inward *ta'dil al-arkan*" (compliance with the inward manners of observance in salah). This means fulfilling the pillars by upholding the intended meaning of salah.

In one hadith, the Prophet ﷺ defines the concept of *"ihsan"* (perfect goodness) as "worshipping as if you were seeing God" and reminds that, "even though you do not see Him, He is seeing you!"[25] Salah must be observed with such an immense consciousness, with due care and awe in all conditions. Each salah should be observed in a different mode of being and state than the previous.

The content of salah is so vast that it allows people to contemplate deeply. There is a wide variety of ways to feel salah, from having the consciousness of being in the presence of God with deep enthusiasm and ardor, to feeling as if you are standing in prayer among the congregation behind the Prophet ﷺ, to seeing oneself directly among the ranks of angels, and to observing salah as if placing our forehead to the Sublime Throne, which is beyond our horizons.

The first condition for a person to succeed as such is to acknowledge salah as a *Mi'raj*, or a simulation of it, for it is not merely a series of physical acts like lying down or getting up... For a believer, every salah is a means of *Mi'raj* and what falls to him or her is to complete their *Mi'raj*, in as many varying levels as it may be.

The purpose of salah

There is divine grace and blessings in all worship observed for God Almighty. It is unthinkable for a person who turns to His door of mercy to remain deprived. However, one should not link the acts of worship to the spiritual delight and experiences they may bring. Sometimes there can be a condition known as a state of constriction, or *qabd*,[26] where you feel downhearted while observing salah. Judging hastily based on how that salah of yours looks from the outside can be misleading. However, this could actually be one of your most valuable salahs. Even when you're not experiencing material or spiritual blessings, you remain devoted and

---

25 Bukhari, Iman 37, Tafsir al-Surah (31) 2; Muslim, Iman 5, 7.

26 Contraction or compression. One of the stages of spiritual development, characterized by feeling of constriction, feeling down and/or sadness.

come to the presence of God Almighty. The fact that you receive no immediate reward in the form of inner contentment is not taking away from loyalty—this is nothing but sincere servitude.

Given that God Almighty stated, اُدْعُونِي أَسْتَجِبْ لَكُمْ "Pray to Me, (and) I will answer you" (al-Mu'min 40:60), we can be sure that He will answer every supplication to come out of our lips. We should then remind ourselves, "I should keep coming to His gate of Mercy"—not giving up on His mercy will be an expression of adherence and loyalty. Even if the person observes such servitude for a lifetime without feeling any sacred delight, then it will be counted as if that person spent an entire lifetime in sincere and genuine devotion.

Conversely, one should not worship to attain the status of a saint—such a spiritual elevation should not become our sole aim. For this reason, those who observe servitude for going to Paradise are criticized as *abd al-jannah*, "servants of Paradise" (not servants of God). Paradise cannot be a purpose for deeds and worship. Servitude is observed for obeying God's command and seeking His good pleasure. The actual reason for worship is Divine command; this is why we observe worship. Regarding the person who prays salah while trembling with fear of Hell and stands obediently before God, they are criticized as a "servant of Hell." So, how can one become a "servant of God?" One should engage in worship neither out of a desire for Paradise nor fear of Hell, but solely out of recognition of being a servant of God and in obedience to His commandments.

Even in a state of *qabd* when the person is devoid of feelings of physical or spiritual effulgence, one must definitely observe the salah. We can even argue that while a person crying during salah may indeed reflect a deep emotional state, it could sometimes be perceived as a negative experience or a trial for the individual. Even (something seemingly innocent such as) crying in salah can be dangerous for a person who cannot keep his heart under self-scrutiny in every moment. Although experiencing such emotional states during salah can be considered as pure blessings, consistently seeking them might cause individuals to overlook certain significant aspects of salah. It is essential to approach the presence of God solely focused on seeking His good pleasure.

Here, we pray to God, asking Him to allow us to attain the pinnacle of adherence to Him and sincerity of intention. Conversely, our situation may seem wretched in the eyes of others, but this holds little importance. What truly matters is being esteemed in the sight of God. In this regard, everyone should be troubled with concern and say:

اَللَّهُمَّ اجْعَلْنِي فِي عَيْنِي صَغِيرًا وَفِي عَيْنِكَ كَبِيرًا

> "O God, please make me little in my own sight, and as great as possible in Your Divine sight!"[27]

Another point is that God Almighty may bestow certain spiritual delights to those who observe worship. There are some great figures who completely erased from their hearts the vice called *ujb* (inward self admiration and putting trust in deeds with a feeling of self-satisfaction) and attained complete *tawhid*, thus they attribute all of the blessings they were honored with to the One Who gave it to them—they are in full consciousness that it was God only Who put these blessings like a garment on their back; they don't claim ownership over them. Therefore, they do not abstain from speaking of these blessings (*tahdis-i nimat*) from God. They consider promulgating that truth as an acknowledgement of blessings, as an expression of thankfulness to God. For example, the Messenger of God ﷺ states that when everybody is resurrected and gathered, he will be gathered as the owner of the Banner of Praise (*Liwa ul-Hamd*).[28] In another hadith, he says, "Allah gave me five things, which had not been given to any other Prophet before."[29]

These are expressions of gratitude and acknowledgment of blessings. It is like "Someone" has graciously provided me with a fine suit, so I proudly showcase His generous gift wherever I go. I declare it loudly, saying, "This suit enhances my appearance and adds another dimension to the beauty of my Lord's creation. However, this beauty does not stem from me, but from the One who bestowed it upon me and from the suit He gifted me." Hence, there is no harm in sharing the blessings of God in

---

27   Bazzar, *Musnad* 10/315; Daylami, *Musnad* 1/473.

28   Tirmidhi, Manaqib 1; Ibn Majah, Zuhd 37.

29   Bukhari, Tayammum 1, Salat 56; Muslim, Masajid 3, 5.

this manner; it can even be said that keeping such favors secret can even be seen as ingratitude.

The Prophet ﷺ made a similar acknowledgement of blessings and stated:

إِنَّ اللهَ عَزَّ وَجَلَّ جَعَلَ لِكُلِّ نَبِيٍّ شَهْوَةً، وَإِنَّ شَهْوَتِي فِي قِيَامِ هَذَا اللَّيْلِ

"God gave every Prophet a strong desire for something. My desire is for worshipping at night."[30]

However, he never observed salah for the sake of the spiritual delight he took from it. These statements allude to individuals who have a potential in perfecting their salah. It is essential to aspire to lofty goals and persistently strive until salah reaches that elevated state.

b. Salah in congregation

Observing salah in congregation is a very important *Sunnah* act which should never be neglected. The understanding of Imam Ahmad Ibn Hanbal about salah in congregation is noteworthy. He considered congregation as one of the obligatory conditions of salah. The respectable Tabiun (the Successors, generation of Muslims after the Companions) similarly had utmost care about praying in congregation. For example, the great Imam A'mash (Sulayman ibn Mihran)—from the Taba al-Tabiun (the generation after the Successors)—did not miss the first *takbir* of praying in congregation for 70 years, as Waki ibn Jarrah bore witness to it. For seventy years, he was not seen missing or making up a single *rak'ah* of salah, for he was never late for the prayer in congregation. Sa'id ibn al-Musayyib from the Tabiun was a very pious person—it is told that he never saw the back of someone else's neck during prayer because he was always in the first row of the congregation.

The Messenger of God gave much importance to congregational salah and encouraged it at every opportunity. He once said for hypocrites who habitually missed the prayers as a part of their efforts to dismantle the community: "Verily, the most burdensome of prayers upon the hypocrites are the night prayer and dawn prayer. If they knew the blessings that are in them, they would come to them even if they had to crawl. Cer-

---

30   Tabarani, *al-Mu'jam al-Kabir* 12/84.

tainly, I felt like ordering the prayer to be established and commanding a man to lead the people in prayer, then I would go with some men with firewood to the people who were absent from the prayer and I would burn their houses with fire."[31] This shows the importance he gave to congregational salah. Nevertheless, based on this hadith, scholars of *Fiqh* ruled that attendance to the congregation as either *fard*, *wajib*, or *sunnah mu'akkadah* (confirmed practices of the Prophet ﷺ who performed them continuously, or rarely left).

وَأَقِيمُوا الصَّلَاةَ وَآتُوا الزَّكَاةَ وَارْكَعُوا مَعَ الرَّاكِعِينَ

> "Establish the Prayer properly, and pay the *Zakat*; and bow with those who bow [in worship and obedience]." (al-Baqarah 2:43)

Based on Qur'anic verses and the ahadith like the ones mentioned above, and many other hadiths with similar meaning, Ahmad Ibn Hanbal gave the judgment that it is *fard al-ayn* (a direct obligation) to observe salah in congregation. While some scholars of the Shafi school regarded congregational salah as communal obligation (*fard al-kifayah*), Hanafi and Maliki scholars accepted it in unison as *sunnah mu'akkadah*, i.e. a strong *Sunnah*.

Prophet Muhammad ﷺ, the Pride of Humanity, stated that "Congregational salah is 27 times more meritorious than an individual one."[32] Rewards to be given in the Hereafter (like rewards of worship) are for all the participants (attendants in the congregation); rewards to be given to one person does not make others to be deprived of the same reward. By virtue of this mystery of illumination, the entirety of their collective reward is recorded in each individual's record of deeds (just as light may be reflected in different people's mirrors, without others' sharing causing it to diminish).

Individual devotions and achievements during spiritual journeying will receive due reward and response in an absolute sense. However, these hadiths teach us that those individual efforts will still remain in an individual level and never equal to the worship observed in congregation. While this principle holds true for acts of worship such as salah,

---

31   Bukhari, Adhan 29, 34, Ahkam 52; Muslim, Masajid 251–254.

32   Bukhari, Adhan 30; Muslim, Masajid 249.

fasting, Hajj and the like, it also applies to other services made for the sake of faith.

It is important to recognize that there is no guarantee for an individual to attain the promises Allah made for a collective group. Although a person works wonders on one's own for the sake of faith and the Qur'an, these will always remain as individual deeds, at an individual level. However, when individuals, who share the same values, feelings, and thoughts, participate in a deed they perform for the Hereafter (*ishtirak amal uhrawiyyah*), they will each receive a total reward as pertains to the entirety of their collective deed. We are living in an age of collective consciousness; we can undertake burdens heavier than mountains if we can act with collective consciousness.

Chapter 5

Prayer Times

A believer's life is best regulated in accordance with the times and sequence of salah. Salah encompasses every aspect of a believer's daily calendar. The daily agenda and activities should be programmed and oriented to salah accordingly. We see this programming within the statements in the Qur'an like "after the salah is over..." and "before such-and-such salah...." Observant Muslims who take such an approach tend to manage arrangements for the day in the same way, like, "after the morning prayer" or "before the evening prayer," etc.

Believers head to the *masjids* to attend prayers, desiring to receive the blessings of Divine Mercy. As they do so, they introspect their hearts first to attain full sincerity, and then they start looking for Divine favors through the observatory of the *masjid*. When asked, companions of the Prophet spoke about the feelings of awe and reverence they were imbued with in salah. They said, "We would sit and engage in conversation with the Prophet ﷺ; but when we started observing salah, we would not glance here nor there. We would become oblivious of one another, and our gazes would turn to other realms beyond our comprehension." As the Messenger of God ﷺ noted:

لَا يَزَالُ اللهُ عَزَّ وَجَلَّ مُقْبِلًا عَلَى الْعَبْدِ فِي صَلَاتِهِ مَا لَمْ يَلْتَفِتْ، فَإِذَا صَرَفَ وَجْهَهُ انْصَرَفَ عَنْهُ

> God looks at (and thus honors) His servant who observes salah; when the servant looks here and there and turns his face away from Him, God also ceases His (honoring) look.[1]

---

1 Abu Dawud, Salah, 164; Nasai, Sahw, 10.

Without a spiritual maturity as small as keeping one's eyes straight during the prayer, one cannot free themselves from corporeality and rise in the realms of the heart, even in the mosque. Without proper observance of at least the physical aspects of the prayer, they will bring in the confusion they are experiencing at home or in the street into the *masjid*. While performing the prayer outwardly, they may return home without earning its true rewards. Some insightful scholars of the classic period were very scrupulous on this issue and even remarked that during salah should a person recognize the other individual near him, his salah will be invalidated. The Messenger of God said:

ادْعُوا اللهَ وَأَنْتُمْ مُوقِنُونَ بِالْإِجَابَةِ، وَاعْلَمُوا أَنَّ اللهَ لاَ يَسْتَجِيبُ دُعَاءً مِنْ قَلْبٍ غَافِلٍ لاَهٍ

"Pray to Allah (knowing) that your prayers will surely be responded. Know that God does not accept the prayer of a (person with a) heedless heart distracted by other matters."[2]

Everybody protects their money and valuables against theft while going through a crowded marketplace. Accordingly, believers should mind their hearts on the way to the *masjid* after passing through streets where transgressions are prevalent. They should try to detach themselves from worldly distractions that may create distance from God, and instead, devote themselves to attaining complete focus and intentionality. Otherwise, in terms of establishing a relation with God, the person will not have given their heart the care they gave to their wallet, which will reflect accordingly their own worth in the sight of God. Believers should remember God alone at salah, directing their hearts, minds, and focus solely on Him with wholehearted devotion and orientation.

By faithfully observing the five daily prayers, one can effectively combat heedlessness that distracts and distances them from God, allowing their devotion to reign supreme throughout the day. Time, usually perceived as a nominal linear progression, will acquire genuine significance through this devoted servitude observed and will flow to the eternal realm like a fast stream; days and nights will follow one another and eventually will procure the heavenly fruits that will smile at the person in Paradise.

---

2   Tirmidhi, Daavat 65; Hakim, *Al-Mustadrak* 1/670.

Everything a person will encounter in the next world will be an expression of the relationship they established with God in this world. If one experiences a unique enthusiasm and zeal with every salah in this world, continuously deepening their faith and religious commitment, and if they emerge from each prayer with newfound insights and meanings, then God will surely reward each of these generously in the next world.

1. Salah observed at five different times

Both from the verses of the Qur'an and Tradition of the Prophet ﷺ (*Sunnah*) we understand that Allah has enjoined upon Muslims five obligatory prayers at specific times throughout the day and night: *Fajr* (dawn), *Dhuhr* (after midday), *Asr* (afternoon), *Maghrib* (after sunset), *Isha'* (nighttime). Now, let's examine some verses and Hadiths as references to understand how salah is comprehended and practiced.

a. The five daily prayers in the Qur'an

As an outcome of human nature, we tend to forget surprisingly fast. We forget what we have been blessed with due to our inattentiveness, carelessness, negligence and weaknesses. As the Almighty Creator knows us better than ourselves, He divided the 24-hour day into certain segments and portions. During these designated times and intervals, He calls upon us to come into His presence, to demonstrate our obedience to Him, and to recognize His blessings upon us with a consciousness of being held accountable. As long as a person maintains their closeness to God, an overwhelming feeling of reverence and admiration will prevail; as long as they remain detached and distant from Him, animal-like emotions, corporeality and worldliness can hardly leave them alone. So, for us to break this detachment and heedlessness, God Almighty decrees that, إِنَّ الصَّلَاةَ كَانَتْ عَلَى الْمُؤْمِنِينَ كِتَابًا مَوْقُوتًا "the Salah is prescribed for the believers at fixed times" (an-Nisa 4:103) and invites us to the prayers at these certain, prescribed, times.

The Qur'an refers to the times of salah in many verses. Here are a few:

وَأَقِمِ الصَّلَاةَ طَرَفَيِ النَّهَارِ وَزُلَفًا مِنَ اللَّيْلِ إِنَّ الْحَسَنَاتِ يُذْهِبْنَ السَّيِّئَاتِ ذَلِكَ ذِكْرَى لِلذَّاكِرِينَ

Establish the Prayer [O Messenger] at the beginning and the end of the day, and in the watches of the night near to the day. Surely good deeds wipe out evil deeds. This is advice, and a reminder for the mindful who reflect. (Hud 11:114)

أَقِمِ الصَّلَاةَ لِدُلُوكِ الشَّمْسِ إِلَى غَسَقِ اللَّيْلِ وَقُرْآنَ الْفَجْرِ إِنَّ قُرْآنَ الْفَجْرِ كَانَ مَشْهُودًا

Establish the Prayer in conformity with its conditions, from the declining of the sun to the darkness of the night, and [be ever observant of] the recitation of the Qur'an at dawn [the Dawn Prayer]. Surely the recitation of the Qur'an at dawn is witnessed [by the angels and the whole creation awakening to a new day]. (al-Isra, 17:78)

فَاصْبِرْ عَلَى مَا يَقُولُونَ وَسَبِّحْ بِحَمْدِ رَبِّكَ قَبْلَ طُلُوعِ الشَّمْسِ وَقَبْلَ غُرُوبِهَا وَمِنْ آنَاءِ اللَّيْلِ فَسَبِّحْ وَأَطْرَافَ النَّهَارِ لَعَلَّكَ تَرْضَى

Therefore, be patient [O Messenger] with whatever they say, and glorify your Lord with praise before sunrise and before sunset, and glorify Him during some hours of the night—as well as glorifying (Him) at the ends of the day—so that you may obtain God's good pleasure and be contented [with what God has decreed for you]. (Ta Ha 20:130)

فَسُبْحَانَ اللَّهِ حِينَ تُمْسُونَ وَحِينَ تُصْبِحُونَ ۞ وَلَهُ الْحَمْدُ فِي السَّمَاوَاتِ وَالْأَرْضِ وَعَشِيًّا وَحِينَ تُظْهِرُونَ

So glorify God when you enter the evening and when you enter the morning—and [proclaim that] all praise and gratitude in the heavens and on the earth are for Him – and in the afternoon, and when you enter the noon time. (ar-Rum 30:17, 18)

At the times of *maghrib*, *isha'*, and *fajr*, heavens overflow with angels and the earth with worshippers who call onto God with glorifications. During *dhuhr* and *asr*, the entire world unites to become as if one tongue in this collective sanctification and praise. While this is the case, what is expected of a servant is nothing but to join this extensive, wide-reaching symphony and harmony, aligning themselves with it rather than causing discord.

Nafi ibn al-Azraq, one of the people who learned about the Prophet's ﷺ understanding of tafsir from Ibn Abbas, asked Ibn Abbas, "Are the five Daily Prayers mentioned in the Qur'an?" Ibn Abbas confirmed this and referenced the verses, "*So glorify God when you enter the evening and when you enter the morning. And (proclaim that) all praise and gratitude in the heavens and on the earth are for Him and in the afternoon, and when you enter the noon time*" (ar-Rum 30: 17, 18) in response.[3] These verses show that the daily prayers are five and they must be observed one by one. In addition to Ibn Abbas, many other Companions derived the same meaning from these verses.

"But only four times are mentioned in this verse," one may doubt. As an answer we can explain that this number is alluded to more explicitly in the verse that states, "*Be ever mindful and protective of the prescribed Prayers, and the Middle Prayer, and stand in the presence of God in utmost devotion and obedience*" (al-Baqarah 2:238). In Arabic, the plural form is not used for things less than three. There is a separate plural form for "two things." Therefore, the term "*salawat*" in the original expression must be referring to at least three prayers. Additionally, the verse mentions one additional salah as the "middle" prayer. In order to be considered "middle" there must be equal number of things on both sides, which means a minimum of four. Thus, when we include the middle prayer with the other four, the total number becomes at least five. Although there are different opinions regarding which prayer constitutes the "middle prayer," the predominant view is that it refers to the *Asr* Prayer. An example supporting this is from the Battle of the Trench when the Prophet ﷺ could not observe *Asr* prayer on time, due to the intensity of enemy attacks. In response he said, "May God fill with fire the houses and graves of those who barred us from the middle prayer."[4]

Salah is so important that the Prophet ﷺ expressed deep regret for the salah he could not observe due to intense fighting during the Battle. While he had always prayed for the goodness and deliverance of humanity, this time he invoked a curse on them, because they had prevented

3   Abdurrazzaq, *Musannaf* 1:454; Tabarani, *Mu'jam al-Kabir* 10:247; Hakim, *Al-Mustadrak* 2:445.

4   Bukhari, Jihad 98, Maghazi 29, Daawat 58; Muslim, Masajid 202-206.

him and other Muslims from for observing their salah. But why did the Prophet of mercy act in this manner? Because salah held a distinct and special value in his eyes. That day, he had missed the "middle prayer," unable to divide the day as he should have to turn to God through salah, and one segment of *Mi'raj* had to be forsaken.

Salah is ordained to be performed five times a day so that believers can regularly come into the presence of God and accelerate their spiritual progress. Through these five daily prayers, they are called to account for their lives, enabling them to dispell *ghaflah* (heedlessness, carelessness, inattentiveness) and establish a relationship with God. By learning to sit in God's presence with reverence, their hearts become well-prepared to receive manifestations of Divine secrets, and their spiritual faculties become attuned to this purpose. Through this practice, grace and refinement are instilled in their spirits, allowing them to transcend their animalistic, material, and worldly inclinations.

Another point that is worth noting in the verses of ar-Rum 30:17, 18 is the reference to salah as "*tasbih*" (glorification) in فَسُبْحَانَ اللهِ (glorify God), which is one of the meanings of salah. By rule, "An unspecified reference alludes to the best example"; thus "*tasbih*" in this verse alludes to "salah." In our prayers, we try to find adequate words to convey God's greatness juxtaposed with our insignificance. We endeavor to express our reverence for Him through our words, actions, and demeanor, seeking to glorify and exalt Him. Indeed, the most fitting expressions to convey this sentiment are "*SubhanAllah,*" "*Alhamdulillah,*" and "*Allahu Akbar,*" each serving as integral components that together form a comprehensive acknowledgment within salah. Even before we begin the recitation of al-Fatiha, we start with the initial supplication of Subhanaka, we say, "O God, I declare that you are glorified above all attributes of deficiency and all of my praise is due to You." Likewise, at the beginning of al-Fatiha, we recite the verse, "Praise be to Allah, Lord of the worlds [all creations and realms]" and while rising from bowing (*ruku'*) we say, "O our Lord, all praises are due to You" and thus express our praises for Him. Likewise, we express our amazement and admiration for the mind-blowing operation of Divine Will and Power in the universe and proclaim the exaltation as "*Allahu Akbar.*" We say the *takbir* at every pillar we do. We say "*Allahu Akbar*" while moving one posture to another. In similar vein, we affirm our unwavering acceptance of Divine decrees and refrain from any objection by uttering "*SubhanAllah*." At times, we harmonize the manifestations of Divine Majesty (*Jalal*) and Divine Beauty and Clemency (*Jamal*), declaring, "O God, I glorify You with praise. My exalted God, I declare Your being free of defect or imperfection (*tanzih*)." In one hadith, delivering good news to us all, the Messenger of God said:

كَلِمَتَانِ خَفِيفَتَانِ عَلَى اللِّسَانِ ثَقِيلَتَانِ فِي الْمِيزَانِ حَبِيبَتَانِ إِلَى الرحمن سُبْحَانَ اللهِ وَبِحَمْدِهِ سُبْحَانَ اللهِ الْعَظِيمِ

> There are two phrases, which are light for the tongue, heavy on the balance (weighing deeds), and much dear to the All-Compassionate (Rahman): *SubhanAllahi wa bi hamdihi, SubhanAllah al-Azeem* [I glorify Allah with praise, I glorify Allah the Supreme].[5]

In short, salah is entirely formulated by God Almighty. Observing these five daily prayers adorned with sacred words will bring us the honor and rewards of glorifying, praising and exalting God every day. As a means of ascension (*mi'raj*), it will immediately transport us to His presence, both in heart and spirit.

b. The five daily prayers in hadith

Observance of the daily prayers in the five allotted times did not remain in the concise form as mentioned in the verses; rather God Almighty directly taught it to His Messenger ﷺ by sending the Archangel Jibril (Gabriel). In a hadith narrated by Ibn Abbas (r.a.), the Messenger of God stated this truth as follows:

> Jibril led me in salah near the House of God for two days. At the first, we observed *Dhuhr* prayer while shadows are like shoelace (i.e. right after the noon time when shadows are shortest). Then we observed the *Asr* Prayer when the shadow of everything is equal to its own length. We observed the *Maghrib* Prayer when the sun set and those who observe fast broke their fast; we observed the *Isha* Prayer when the brightness on the horizon completely disappeared, and we observed the *Fajr* Prayer at the dawn when eating and drinking

---

[5] Bukhari, Ayman 19, Tawhid 58; Muslim, Dhikr 31.

became haram for those who observe fasting. On the second day, we observed the *Dhuhr* prayer in the time when we observed the *Asr* prayer the day before; namely, when the shadow of everything reached its own size. We observed the *Asr* Prayer when the shadow of everything extended twice its own size. We observed the *Maghrib* Prayer at the same time we observed it a day before; and we observed the *Isha* prayer after the first third of the night had passed. As for the *Fajr* prayer, we observed it after the sky brightened a bit. Then Jibril turned to me and said the following: "O Muhammad, these are the prayer times of the Prophets before you. Your prayer times are the times that is between these two times."[6]

We clearly see the five daily prayers in the tradition of the Prophet ﷺ. Reliable sources of hadith like those of Bukhari and Muslim relate that after the Prophet ﷺ returned from the *Mi'raj*, unlike the fifty daily prayers given to other people, five daily prayers were rendered obligatory for his ummah, the Muslims. According to a hadith reported by Anas (r.a.), when the Prophet ﷺ made the *Mi'raj*, God ordered prayer to be fifty times a day. He then reduced it to five and then said, "These are five prayers and they are all (equal to) fifty (in reward), for My Word does not change."[7]

Similarly, in an authenticated narration, the Messenger of God ﷺ asked his Companions, "if any of you bathes five times a day in a river that passes in front of his door, will there be any impurity left on him?" The Companions answered, "this act will not leave any impurities on him." Upon this, the Prophet ﷺ stated, "This is the situation of the five Daily Prayers. God erases all wrongs by means of them."[8]

There is another hadith about the times of the five daily prayers as reported by Abu Musa al-Ashari:

> A man came to the Messenger of God and asked about the prayer times. Our Prophet ﷺ did not give any direct answer to him (in

6   Tirmidhi, Salat 1; Abu Dawud, Salat 2.

7   Bukhari, Salat 1; Muslim, Iman 263.

8   See Bukhari, Bad'u'l-Khalq 6, Manaqib al-Ansar 42; Muslim, Iman 259.

another narration he told the man to observe salah with them for two days). In the *fajr* time—when it was dark and recognizing another person was still not possible—he gave an order to his *muadhin* Bilal, who made the *iqamah* for *Fajr* prayer (in response, and they observed the salah). Then at the moment of the sun's shifting towards the west right after its zenith he gave an order again to Bilal, who then made the *iqamah* for the *Dhuhr* Prayer. With reference to this time, a person—who knew better than others—had said, "This is the middle of the day. Then at a time when the sun was still bright and high, the Prophet ﷺ ordered Bilal to make the *iqamah* for the *Asr* Prayer. When the sun set, he gave the same order for the *Maghrib* Prayer, and when the brightness on the horizon disappeared he did so for the *Isha* Prayer and the prayers were observed. The next day, he observed the *Fajr* Prayer with delay. So much so that when the salah was over we asked one another "has the sun risen?" We observed the *Dhuhr* Prayer at a time close to the time we had observed the *Asr* Prayer the day before. We observed the *Asr* Prayer when the sun lost its brightness and turned yellow, and we observed the *Maghrib* Prayer right before the brightness on the horizon disappeared. As for the *Isha*, we delayed it until the first one-third of the night passed. In the morning of next day, the Messenger of God called the man and told him "The Prayer times are those between these two times."[9]

In summary, just as salah has continued to our time to be observed as the Prophet ﷺ taught, so have the prayer times. Therefore, just as the five daily prayers are important for us, so is observing them within their due time. In other words, just as it is *fard* (an obligation) to observe salah, so is it to observe them within their due time. Likewise, just as it is haram to abandon salah, so is delaying it beyond its appointed times. Accordingly, every salah must be observed within the time limits taught by the Prophet ﷺ. When the Companions asked him about the most meritorious deed, he mentioned three things in response: "Salah observed within its due time, doing goodness and beneficence to one's parents, and en-

---

[9] Muslim, Masajid 178; Abu Dawud, Salat 2; Nasai, Mawaqit 15.

deavoring in the path of God."[10] Accordingly, we understand that these acts are equal in virtue.

2. The time of daily prayers, the Qur'an, and the universe

We witness, in the five daily prayers, interweaving of the Qur'an, the universe, the human being, and his or her worship. The "book" of the universe, the human as the epitome of the universe and its essence, and the Qur'an as their interpreter, all become interlaced in the salah. They virtually constitute the three facets of a single entity. The human being, as a servant, embodies a condensed representation of the entire universe. Through recitation of the Qur'an, they express their obedience to God, with the Qur'an serving as the interpretation of the universe. Surah al-Fatiha, the opening chapter that is recited at the beginning of each prayer unit, encapsulates the essence of the Qur'an. Therefore, by observing salah, a person presents to God the essence and summary of the worship of all things and beings in the universe.

To elaborate on this concept, the human being serves as the microcosm of the universe—a universe which reflects and manifests the Divine Names and Attributes. Hidden in the human are all the spheres and all the worlds folded (in their nature). In essence, the entirety of the universe is encapsulated within the individual, as if each aspect of the universe is inscribed or embedded within them, line by line, just as it is told that the Qur'an is written in *"ya sin."* Likewise, the sum of all Revelations is the Qur'an; Divine Scriptures such as the Torah, the Psalms, and the Gospels are concisely summed up in the Qur'an. Also, the suhufs (pages, short treatises), insight, and inspirations of the previous Prophets are also included in the Qur'an.

The entirety of the Qur'an is summarized in the opening chapter, Surah al-Fatiha. Many scholars of tafsir drew attention to the meanings and lessons the Fatiha conveys. They authored volumes of works in this respect and expressed unanimously that the Fatiha is the summary of the Qur'an in every way. Therefore, the Fatiha we recite in every salah becomes a tongue that expresses the meaning of the Qur'an. We express all sanctification, glorification, praise, and exaltation by means of it. We

---

10   Buhkari, Mawaqit 5, Jihad 1, Adab 1, Tawhid 48; Muslim, Iman 138-140.

try to offer our servitude to God by means of it. Surely, in order not to prove ourselves wrong, we fulfill these with our practical acts and virtually say: O God, we are not like hypocrites who do not carry out what they say. In order to confirm what we verbally expressed, we will worship and prostrate ourselves; we will seal our mouths with fasting; we will abandon the warmth and comfort of bed at night, hearing what is meant in the verse,

تَتَجَافَى جُنُوبُهُمْ عَنِ الْمَضَاجِعِ يَدْعُونَ رَبَّهُمْ خَوْفًا وَطَمَعًا وَمِمَّا رَزَقْنَاهُمْ يُنْفِقُونَ

"Their sides forsake their beds at night, calling out to their Lord in fear [of His punishment] and hope [for His forgiveness, grace, and good pleasure], and out of what We have provided for them [of wealth, knowledge, power, etc.], they spend [to provide sustenance for the needy and in God's cause, purely for the good pleasure of God and without placing others under obligation]" (as-Sajdah 32:16).

We will abide by such verses and show our acceptance with our sincere actions, because we hold that the tongue voices the heart and deeds are verification for the tongue. If there is purity in the heart, it will be revealed by the tongue; if what the tongue speaks is true, it will be reflected in the person's deeds. It is not possible to separate these three.

The human being, as the sum and speaker of creation, ascends to the presence of God with the *mi'raj* of salah. Salah is the sum of all worship. The Fatiha recited in salah is the sum of the Qur'an. The essence of the universe's purpose and servitude is condensed within human beings. It finds its wording and recitation in the Qur'an. Through reciting the Fatiha and the Qur'an in salah, humans fulfill the commanded worship with the prescribed acts and pillars. In doing so, they, as servants of God, stand before Him, offering universal servitude and reverence as prescribed and pleasing to Him. As to the meaning and wisdom of the prescribed times of the daily prayers, let's try to understand it with an analogy of a universal clock and its units, divisions and subdivisions: Just as a regular clock has arms that count seconds, minutes, and hours, imagine such a clock with arms that show time spans of a year, human life, and the universe's life. Each arm and its unit ticks on to the next notch when it is due; when one of these arms move on, the others move respectively. So, the universe is such a clock created and owned by God.

Time flows like a flood, with events and occurrences rushing onward, as this clock of existence continues its steady ticking. It has arms showing the day, week, month, and the year. Each of them ticks on to the next notch when their time is due. When we see the arms that show the year in that great clock, we have a feeling that there should also be some arms that indicate the human life, and as it moves along, the time span of the universe. So, all times will be definitely due. Then a day will come, and the mystery of the following verse will be manifest to all:

كُلُّ مَنْ عَلَيْهَا فَانٍ ۞ وَيَبْقَى وَجْهُ رَبِّكَ ذُو الْجَلَالِ وَالْإِكْرَامِ

> All that is on the earth is perishable; but there remains forever the "Face" of your Lord, the One of Majesty and Munificence. (ar-Rahman 55:26)

It is then that all clocks of the universe will have stopped ticking.

Nothing is immortal and everlasting. Everything and every being in the universe are bound to perish. However, on that day, the only that remains immortal is God; only He will speak, hear, and reign. Therefore, the human being will be able to continue to exist, in a way yet unknown to us, but to the degree of their relation and adherence to the Immortal and Everlasting Being, the High and Supreme, Lord Almighty alone. Since human beings came from God, they will inevitably return to Him.

In his Farewell Sermon, Prophet Muhammad ﷺ made an important declaration about time: "Time has completed its cycle and has returned to its (original) state when Allah created the heavens and the earth. The year is twelve months."[11] Although Arab polytheists of pre-Islamic Arabia had adopted the lunar calendar, they used to manipulate the dates by changing the order of the months.[12] The reason they did

---

11   Bukhari, Fitan 8; Muslim, Hajj 147.

12   This date manipulation was called *nasi'*. Every second or third year, the polytheists postponed the beginning of the year by one month. That, some called either "lunisolar intercalation" or simply "intercalation," doubled the month of the pilgrimage. As a result, polytheists gave the month of the pilgrimage and the following month the same name and kept on postponing the names and the sanctity of

this was to expand their business in safety by having their trade season in "sacred months" during which warring was forbidden. Over time this turned their calendar into a mess. This situation naturally caused confusion about the religious calendar too. Just as time flows in the realm of everyday existence, there exists a larger-scale order in the macro-realm, where a single cosmic clock ticks on synchronously as well. In the society where the Messenger of God lived, these two time codes were not concordant. This was one of the things Prophet Muhammad ﷺ pointed out as he was completing his mission as a Prophet during his Farewell Sermon. He promulgated that time "completed its cycle" and was then in its right tracks again. In essence, just as time in the macro realm operates cyclically, the time system in the micro realm reverted to its initial state and resumed its proper course thereafter. The obedience and worship observed within seconds and minutes at the prescribed times in this world correspond to the days and years of the macro realm. Thus, it's crucial to consider the designation of the time for the five daily prayers in relation to the alignment, harmonization, and regularity of the synchronicity between the time in both the normo and macro realms.

In the macro realm, time flows like an arrow flying, gradually reaching finer increments until it reaches us, manifesting as hours, minutes, seconds, and even milliseconds. Below the threshold of our sight and hearing, this timeline becomes so thin that we can only perceive it in milliseconds. For instance, the conventional wristwatches we use are incapable of measuring the speed at which electrons orbit the nucleus of an atom, nor can they measure the cycles of celestial bodies such as the moon and sun. Milliseconds serve as evidence of the passage of seconds, minutes, and hours, just as days, months, and years attest to the finite lifespans of humans and the universe. Therefore, when you observe the ticking of a second on your clock, you are essentially witnessing the entire solar system orbiting within the Milky Way, while also sensing the inexorable approach of life's appointed end. These perceptions prompt reflection on the eventual cessation of the universe's pulsations, bringing

---

all subsequent months in the year by one. That impious additions led the people into error and profaned that which God has declared to be inviolable, and sanctified that which God has declared to be profane. For more, see the tafsir of the verses in Surah at-Tawbah 9: 36-37.

everything to a conclusion. With this understanding, it becomes clearer what the prayer times of *Fajr, Dhuhr, Asr, Maghrib,* and *Isha* signify to us. That is what we'll explore next.

a. The time of fajr

At the break of dawn, as the night sky transitions into the bright hues of morning, we welcome the *Fajr* time with a sense of joy and anticipation, marking the beginning of a new day. The awakening of the day and the rise and emergence of the sun, reminds us of our own emergence, the start of our own embryonic stage and birth. It also reminds us of the first day of God's creation. As the sun rises, we find ourselves aligned with a timeline stretching from the personal to the universal, from our emergence in the mother's womb to the very first day of the creation of the universe. In this moment, we reflect on the day when He created us and the universe, solely to bestow upon us His grace, mercy, and countless blessings. Even though we may feel distant from Him, in this moment, we earnestly wish for His nearness and closeness to us. Therefore, we stand before His Divine presence to express our glorification, praise, and exaltation. The *Fajr* prayer, which is observed within this frame of mind and spirit, is such an appropriate act of worship at dawn.

Said Nursi voices his considerations about *Fajr* salah as follows:

> By nature we are weak, yet everything involves, affects, and saddens us. We have no power, yet are afflicted by calamities and enemies. We are extremely poor, yet have many needs. We are indolent and incapable, yet the burden of life is very heavy. Being human, we are connected with the rest of the world, yet what we love and are familiar with disappears, and the resulting grief causes us pain. Our mentality and senses inspire us toward glorious objectives and eternal gains, but we are unable, impatient, powerless, and have only a short lifetime. Given all of this, it will self-evidently be understood how essential a support for human spirit it is to present a petition through Prayer and supplication to the Court of an All-Powerful One of Majesty, an All-Compassionate One of Grace, at the time of *fajr*, and to seek help and success from Him. Such support is direly necessary to bear and endure the troubles and burdens waiting for us during daytime.[13]

---

13 Nursi, *The Words*, p. 60.

b. The time of dhuhr

Dhuhr occurs when the day reaches its peak, and everything has already started to develop and mature. It marks the time of the day which can be likened to the period in the lifetime of a tree when it starts bearing fruit; for a person, coming-of-age and the prime of youth. It marks the creation of Adam, our father and the first Prophet, amid the creation of the universe; the beginning of the era when the meaning of existence is to be understood; and the beginning of a time when the human willpower understood the essence and meanings of things and events. Considering all these in an order, *Dhuhr* signifies the prime of our own youth, the prime time of the day, the lifetime of the universe reaching its prime, and the rise of Adam to the honor of God's addressing him. In order to express our gratitude and praise to God for all of these, we appear in His presence in the *Dhuhr* time with a consciousness of obedience and say: "O God, Who has bestowed upon us His countless blessings since the day Prophet Adam was created up until the noon today! I have come to the *Dhuhr* prayer to praise You and extol the great acts of Yours. We do this again with Your sacred phrases, *Subhanallah, Alhamdulillah* and *Allahu Akbar...*" Indeed, human wisdom and consciousness compel us to present our devotion and reverence to God at this juncture and in this manner.

The time of *Dhuhr* reminds us of the time when daily pursuits are in their stage of maturity, full development and God's blessings are at their peak. When burdened by the weight of daily responsibilities, individuals often find solace in prayer. Seeking relief from life's challenges and expressing gratitude for the blessings bestowed upon them, they hasten to their prayers and bow down in prostration. They find a window of opportunity to take a breath of relief from worldly tasks and express their weakness, inability, impotence and poverty by declaring once again, "O Lord, how great You are, I am small, nothing!" To indicate their obedience before His greatness, they bow down for *ruku'* and then prostration. All of these provide a welcome breath of relief for the soul. Imagine the effect of a break after working hard or suffering in either extreme cold or heat!

إِنَّ شِدَّةَ الحَرِّ مِنْ فَيْحِ جَهَنَّمَ

The severity of heat is from the raging of Hellfire. [14]

---

14 Bukhari, Mawaqit 9–10, Badu'l Khalq 10; Muslim, Masajid, 180–184, 186.

Rushing to the *masjid* to attend the prayer, when the severity of heat is at its peak at noon, as the Prophet ﷺ describes in the hadith above, gives us coolness and solace as it will be when people will seek shelter with God under the Prophet's Banner of Praise (*Liwa ul-Hamd*) on the day of Resurrection and Judgment, "the day when no shade will be found." Approaching the *Dhuhr* prayer in this sense means temporarily forsaking physicality and worldliness but attending to the heart, lamenting in prayer and paying heed to the terms of the soul, which means to find true peace and bliss.

c. The time of asr

The *Asr*, or late afternoon time, marks the moment when the sun starts its descent. This segment serves as a reminder of the advancing years and seniority of humanity, symbolizing the period during which Prophet Muhammad ﷺ undertook his mission and eventually passed away. When observing the *Asr* prayer, we do it with the realization that everything is bound to set and inevitably disappear within a matter of hours. As we feel the effects of aging—aching limbs, joint pain, stooping posture, and graying hair—we understand that our souls, too, are transient and gradually approaching their decline. So, precisely at a moment when we might be susceptible to feelings of hopelessness and disappointment, the call to prayer (*adhan*) for *Asr* reaches our ears. In that moment, we feel the joy of having another opportunity to transform this fleeting time and transient life into something eternal, and we eagerly hasten to salah with that enthusiasm. Within the life span of humanity, *Asr* time also corresponds to the time of the Last Prophet, Muhammad ﷺ. He pointed out his being the late afternoon sun and made a comparison between his ummah and those of the past:[15] "The period of your stay as compared to the previous nations is like the period equal to the time between the *Asr* prayer and sunset."[16]

Therefore, "the Age of Bliss" is the herald of humanity's inclination towards its setting. Considering that God's Messenger ﷺ was the last of

---

15   Ibn Kathir, *Tafsir*, XII, p. 6549.

16   Bukhari, Mawaqitu's Salat 17.

the Prophets, humanity apparently must have a short life remaining. As the late afternoon sun is soon about to set, the time segment reminds us of our own aging, just as the Age of Bliss reminds of the aging and last period of humanity. No matter what, be it as an expression of sorrow or as a zest for passing to the Afterlife and attaining God's blessings in Paradise, we hasten to the presence of God and observe the *Asr* prayer. The Qur'an takes an oath by time in Surah al-Asr (103:1–3). In this profoundly significant moment, as we hasten to the presence of God with these contemplations and emotions, we strive to imbue our actions with an enduring quality rather than allowing them to fade away with time. The echoing exaltations of the *muadhin*, "Allahu Akbar," rejuvenate us and infuse new vitality into our inner selves.

d. The time of maghrib

Maghrib time is a moment of setting. The sun sets, the day ends, and we enter into a different segment of time. The Islamic day begins at sunset. The moment when the sun has completely set marks the end of the (previous) day and the start of a new day.

The conclusion of each 24-hour day reminds us of our own eventual demise; just as the day ends, so too will our lives come to an end. Our bodies then will be enshrouded and placed in our graves. Our loved ones will place a couple of stones to mark our graves and depart, leaving the deceased all alone. *Maghrib* also alludes to the earth's being in its throes of death. The setting of the sun is a reminder that everything will set one day and all systems will expire. It alludes to the verse,

إِذَا الشَّمْسُ كُوِّرَتْ ۞ وَإِذَا النُّجُومُ انْكَدَرَتْ ۞ وَإِذَا الْجِبَالُ سُيِّرَتْ

"When the sun is folded up [and darkened]; And when the stars fall [losing their luster]; And when the mountains are set moving…" (at-Takwir 81:1–3)

Such sharp reminders of one's own demise and the world's demise may become too heavy for some people to bear unless they take refuge in God's Grace and Mercy. Therefore, to console and comfort our heart that is downcast with this dread and in order to let our soul find relief, we run in hope to the *Maghrib* prayer, seeking Divine Grace and Mercy.

At *Maghrib* time, we are confronted with the choice between lamenting the setting of the sun and feeling despondent, or embracing the hope and enthusiasm of nurturing our eternal life in the hereafter. Amidst a backdrop of farewells and lamentations, the *adhan* signals a new beginning after the sun has set. It informs us that after death we will experience a new awakening, resurrection, and a vibrant life and existence. The *adhan* called out at this time connotes Sur (the Trumpet) that Israfil[17] will blow for the Resurrection and Reckoning after the end of the world; at a moment when everything has already expired, the call announces it is time for the Resurrection and Gathering before the Lord Almighty.

Prophet Ibrahim, peace be upon him, said:

لَا أُحِبُّ الْآفِلِينَ

"I do not love those that set…" (al-An'am 6:76)

We also say the same: we will not be content with those that set and that cannot be with us all the time. Thus, we turn to God, the Everlasting, Who is Immortal and Who does not perish. God is Ahad and Samad; that is, He is the Lord, the One Who possesses and disposes of all affairs; He is the One Whom all people come to with their needs; He is the One Whom everyone depends on to fulfill their needs, but Who at the same time is Complete and Self-Sufficient, needing and depending upon no one else; He is the One Who provides everything for His creatures, but He is not dependent on them for anything; He is the One Who creates existence out of non-existence; He is the One Who lets set those that set; He is the One Who decrees the demise of all that is destined to perish. Therefore, it is also Him Who will transform our non-existence into existence, Who will resurrect us to life after our demise, Who will grant us fresh love and ardor after all is erased from our minds and hearts, and Who will let our dead hearts gain life again.

e. The time of isha

The time of *Isha* is when the twilight of dusk has disappeared, when no sign of the sun is left, and the sky turns pitch dark. In that time, the cov-

---

17 Israfil is the archangel who will blow the trumpet to announce the Day of Resurrection, Gathering and Reckoning.

ering darkness leaves no clue for us to see how the previous day has existed. At dusk, we might see the last trace of the day lingering in the redness in the sky. However, when that disappears too, everything will be gone.

The time of *Isha* reminds us of the demise of everything, including human life. Death is a unique phenomenon: When a person passes away some people cry, some collapse, and some pass out at funerals or burials. However, with the passage of time, whether short or long, so many things and even memories related to the deceased are erased from people's minds. Some even develop a certain kind of emptiness, indifference to what that person meant or expressed. The deceased are as if "completely forgotten," as the Qur'anic verse goes (وَكُنْتُ نَسْيًا مَنْسِيًّا Maryam 19:23). Yes, there exist some people who truly remember their deceased parents, kids and kin, and commemorate, cry, pray or do events and charities on their behalf on certain days and periods. But the point is that as years pass it feels as if the person has never existed.

All that seems to have disappeared within the darkness reminds people of the impending termination of life in this world. Everything will have expired, and some people will feel devoid of any light in the grave. The only thing for a heart that is shaken and hit hard, is to run to his Lord and ask for comfort and consolation. The night and the heart will only be illuminated and brightened by revering God and prostrating before Him. Prayer at that time means that night might be the end of everything but at the same time it bears the glad tidings of a new birth, resurrection and attainment of unimaginable Divine gifts and blessings.

At the time of *Isha*, in the darkness of the night, the rendering of God's exalted name from minarets pours light onto the deceased, who expect favors from the living in the form of recitations of al-Fatiha, the Qur'an, supplications and invocations of Divine mercy and forgiveness. That will certainly brighten up their afterlife. In the dread of the grave where the deceased is alone, his or her bones squeezed, and distressed by the questions of Munkar and Nakir,[18] he or she will see that they are not left all alone, and their good deeds, especially their salah, will be their company. They will find Divine Providence and Mercy awaiting them, ever present, closest, and even accompanying, comforting, and rewarding them.

---

18   In Islamic eschatology, Munkar and Nakir are angels who test the faith of the dead in their graves.

f. The darkness of the night and tahajjud

The darkness of the night reminds us of a time when in the grave a person loses all his or her hopes as they cannot be heard anymore. It also makes us think of a time when the entire universe will be destroyed. In the dread of the grave, one may be overwhelmed as if they are seized by a nightmare, wishing to talk and shout but unable to do so. They find themselves unheard by any living being left behind, unable to move a muscle. In that state when it really dawns on them that that is the foretold fate for all mortals they begin to wait anxiously for what their previous life has procured for them.

How important it is, then, to offer sincere prayers and supplications at this time of the night and to illuminate it. Doing that, they realize that it is their salah which will fill up their grave with light and brighten their eternal life. Those who try to worship God as He wishes can deduce this from the following verse:

يَا أَيُّهَا الْمُزَّمِّلُ ۞ قُمِ اللَّيْلَ إِلَّا قَلِيلًا ۞ نِصْفَهُ أَوِ انْقُصْ مِنْهُ قَلِيلًا ۞ أَوْ زِدْ عَلَيْهِ وَرَتِّلِ الْقُرْآنَ تَرْتِيلًا

> O you enwrapped one, [under the heavy responsibility of Messengership]! Rise to keep vigil at night, except a little; half of it, or lessen it a little, or add to it [a little]; and pray and recite the Qur'an calmly and distinctly [with your mind and heart concentrated on it]. (al-Muzzammil 73:1-4)

The Surah itself expounds on it as,

إِنَّ نَاشِئَةَ اللَّيْلِ هِيَ أَشَدُّ وَطْئًا وَأَقْوَمُ قِيلًا ۞ إِنَّ لَكَ فِي النَّهَارِ سَبْحًا طَوِيلًا

> "Rising and praying at night impresses [mind and heart] most strongly and [makes] recitation more certain and upright. For by day, you do have extended preoccupations" (al-Muzzammil 73:6-7)

Hence, the Qur'an essentially outlines the Prophet's timing for petitioning God. The Qur'an insistently lays emphasis on night devotions and, in address to the Messenger of God again, states:

وَمِنَ اللَّيْلِ فَتَهَجَّدْ بِهِ نَافِلَةً لَكَ عَسَى أَنْ يَبْعَثَكَ رَبُّكَ مَقَامًا مَحْمُودًا

> And in some part of the night, rise from sleep and observe vigil therein (through the Prayer and recitation of the Qur'an) as addi-

tional worship for you; your Lord may well raise you to a glorious, praised station [of nearness to Him, and give you leave to intercede with Him, as He wills, on behalf of His servants, in the Hereafter]. (al-Isra 17:79)

To elucidate this verse, this "praised station" (*maqam al-mahmud*) cannot be obtained with carefree, frivolous pursuits, and prolonged rests in a warm bed. This can only be attained by means of salah and a few drops of tears you shed during your prayers. As for the Messenger of God, he responded to these commands with very serious, meticulous care. Even in the most delightful moments of his life that he could spend with his family he preferred to advance spiritually and thus sought the pleasure of God Almighty through that vista.

We learn from a hadith narrated by his wife, our mother Aisha, that the Prophet would stand in prayer and observe worship until his feet or legs swelled. In a reminder that God had already forgiven his past and present sins, she questioned why he was exerting himself so much. The Prophet responded saying, أَفَلاَ أَكُونُ عَبْدًا شَكُورًا "Should I not be a thankful servant?"[19]

While speaking about this situation in his poem *Qasida al-Burda*, Imam Busiri criticizes himself by saying, "I have strayed from the tradition of that glorious Messenger who would not go to bed before his feet were swollen and who would fill the darkness of the night with light"[20]; thus, Busiri reviles himself for spending too much time sleeping in his cozy bed.

By means of observing salah in the night, the believer establishes a relationship with God and gains the honor of being His friend. The Night prayer is an honor in and of itself. During that moment when everyone reunites with their beloveds, rising and approaching the Divine presence, engaging in an almost audience-like colloquy with Him, bestows upon the person an honor unparalleled by any other.

We have lost so much from our humanhood. We must reacquire the things that make us truly human. Relying on God and seeking refuge

---

19   Bukhari, Tahajjud 6; Muslim, Sifatu'l Munafiqin, 79–81.

20   Al Busiri, *Diwan al-Busiri*, p. 239.

in His mercy can indeed empower us to face great responsibilities and overcome challenges. It's like finding strength in something greater than ourselves, enabling us to accomplish seemingly impossible feats. With faith and trust, even the most daunting obstacles can be overcome, and small efforts can lead to remarkable outcomes, much like how a snowball can become an avalanche or a droplet of water can form a powerful waterfall.

It is impossible to achieve anything without relying on God. The future and fortune of Muslim communities today depend entirely on being true to His Message, the Qur'an. To the extent that we observe servitude to God by following the example of the Prophet ﷺ and by being under the guidance of the Qur'an, God will render us glorious and honorable. Otherwise, the doors we turn to will be slammed shut against us, our demands will be turned down, and new episodes of disgrace will follow those we have experienced over the past few centuries. Unlike the past honorable believers, who once upheld this blessed heritage for centuries, we will fall to the level of beggars. For God Almighty made our progress and prosperity conditional to our own attentiveness to Him, being true to our own souls, and transforming ourselves as He wills. With our prayers day and night, with our imploring hearts, we will try to invoke His Grace and Mercy to be so.

In fact, we are by nature rather weak, poor, and impotent beings. Yet our sphere of need is so large it could fill the skies. To the degree of our reliance on God we will find power, have our needs met, and be safe against enemies. It is indeed Salah that does, and will, give us such strength. By cutting sleep short and standing obediently in His presence during the darkness of the night, the person will be relieved of the burdens they carry inside like a scar. Moreover, this worship is so virtuous that it lets the soul breathe and improve its angelic side. And only that angelic side can discern the true joy of worshipping God.

Chapter 6

The Fruits of Salah

1. The fruits of salah regarding the individual

a. Giving peace and relief to the heart

Until now, we've discussed how salah serves as a process of purification. Initially, it involves the removal of physical impurities through ritual ablutions. Subsequently, it purifies the heart and spirit, preparing the individual to enter the Divine presence and offer reverence and servitude to God. In this respect, salah is an exceptional, special act of worship and it provides people with spiritual relief. While hearts find tranquility and contentment in salah, people are cognizant that they are about to gain something more significant, and that is God's good pleasure. Those who cannot feel and attain peace within salah, presumably, can hardly find peace in anything or anywhere else. I, most humbly, hold that humanity will attain true peace when they turn to daily prayers attentively and wholeheartedly.

For those whose hearts desire spiritual progress, the daily prayers provide an ascension five times a day and thus serve like a special staircase leading to God. The Messenger of God ﷺ referred to salah as "the light of my eye."[1] By this, he taught us that salah is something that fills us with relief and contentment, like an auspicious message coming from afar. At a time when the Messenger of God ascended to the Divine pres-

---

1 Nasai, *Ishratu'n Nisa* 1; Ibn Hanbal, *Musnad* 3/128, 199, 285.

ence, eagerly waiting for important news to come, salah was given to him as a "surprise" gift, prescribed upon him and his ummah.

Prophet Muhammad ﷺ made his heavenly ascension as a result of his journey in this materialistic world where he advanced his innate quality by means of his servitude to God and thus rose to the culmination of his spiritual potential. As a reward for his obedience, servitude and reverence, God took him into His presence during the *Mi'raj*. Having made use of his advanced spiritual qualities and the status he had already acquired, the Prophet ﷺ asked from God a means of deliverance for his followers, because they had been living disoriented without guidance on this earth before. God Almighty gave him the five daily prayers. Salah was inititally commanded to be 50 times a day; with consideration that this would be too hard on his ummah, it was later reduced to five. Additionally, glad tidings were given that if five are observed faithfully, the reward will be as if they prayed 50 times each day.

Indeed, when observed faithfully the five daily prayers are a "light of eye" for the Messenger of God ﷺ and his *ummah*. Just as parents who grieved by separation from their child find the "light of their eye" on receiving a piece of good news about the child, so does salah similarly fill believers with relief and let them reach a state of profound satisfaction.

Salah is a gift bestowed upon the Prophet ﷺ as a form of good news for him to celebrate during the *Mi'raj*. Consequently, consciously or unconsciously, every believer experiences a sense of sweet relief during salah. Despite how carefree we may be, we often find delight in salah, unmatched by anything else. The delight during salah is not a constant state we can experience all the time. Since such a delight could be considered as an immediate reward for the prayer, our compassionate Lord does not want us to exhaust all the reward for our servitude while still in this world—thus this delight is withheld from us at times. If we do happen to experience such a delight at any given time, it is important to remember that we do not observe salah for such spiritual rewards, but only for God's good pleasure. It is advisable to dismiss it in negation, as if we were pushing aside worldly matters, and instead affirm, "It is only You, my Lord, whom I seek," in the words of Yunus Emre.

Islam has rules that prescribes certain things and prohibits some other things. As believers, we regulate our lives within the frame of these commandments and prohibitions; we try to keep up with this upright course with our salah. Salah is a very comprehensive worship and arguable the heaviest responsibility as the Divine Names and Attributes are both reflected in it. It therefore has both a commanding and prohibiting character. However, as it establishes a bond between God and his servant it has a pleasant rewarding side as well. Sensing a flow of spiritual gifts from the Divine realm, a person feels during salah a contentment they cannot feel during other forms of worship. For this reason, believers eagerly run to observe salah when they are summoned for it. This practice five times a day becomes their way of finding a breath of relief out of the suffocating and distressing atmosphere of daily life. Mosques serve as a venue to take this breath, and the phrases of glorification, praise, and exaltation from there to the heavens become a means to invite God's Grace and Mercy. For this reason, a believer always lays eyes on lofty, superior horizons during salah. This journey commences with the opening *takbir* "*Allahu Akbar*" as the individual venerates God—our Gracious Lord we perceive within the heart as "hidden treasure" (*kanz-i makhfi*).

The person who enters the Divine presence with these sentiments unfurls and sails into the realm of the Unseen (*ghayb*) with every Qur'anic verse they recite. As the veils over their eyes and the veil of the mundane world are removed one by one, they begin to witness the vivid imagery of Paradise and Hell: the towering flames on one side and gardens of Paradise on the other. In such a scenario, any sane person will surely abandon the path leading to Hell and choose the path to Paradise. Similarly, through its essence and significance salah lifts the veil five times a day, allowing us to turn towards the spiritual realm.

Since salah bears those meanings, the heart finds satisfaction and relief within it. The Messenger of God therefore told his *muadhin* Bilal, "O Bilal, call *iqamah* for prayer: give us comfort by it."[2] instead of simply saying, "render the *adhan*."[3] Bilal al-Habashi would grasp the allusion perfectly; he would ascend to the roof of the mosque upon receiving the command and let the blessed city of Medina resound with the exaltations of "*Allahu Akbar*," a resonance that would endure eternally thereafter.

2   Abu Dawud, Adab 85.

3   Abu Dawud, Adab 78; Ibn Hanbal, *Musnad* 5:364, 371.

The people would run to worship, finding relief within, to fill their hearts with light, and to soar to the heavenly realms in alignment with their spiritual emotions and perceptions. Their motivation for coming to the mosque was not merely to shake off a burden or evade a responsibility—it was to observe salah, which serves as nourishment for the spirit and heart, allowing them to ascend even higher. We, too, should regard the call of the *muadhin* this way and head towards salah, to a mosque, with the same intention. While standing obediently in God's presence, we should be in complete awareness that we will attain peace and will try to replicate with our salah the *Mi'raj* the Prophet ﷺ actually realized.

What truly matters is observing salah in a state of consciousness, profundity, and sincerity. The early Muslims were good examples of that. For example, Umar ibn al-Khattab (r.a.) would mostly cry during salah because of what he felt during recitation; and Ali (r.a.) was once struck by an arrow, yet he remained so engrossed in his prayer that he did not feel or react to the injury until after his prayer had concluded. The deep spiritual engagement they experienced during salah completely enveloped them, preventing them from feeling or thinking about anything else.

Indeed, this deep immersion in prayer embodies the true essence of remembering and glorifying God in a manner befitting His greatness. Indeed, this is the essence of faith. With this profound understanding, individuals apply the word of God to their daily lives, endeavoring to lead lives imbued with angelic qualities. The Prophet ﷺ stated,

حُجِبَتِ النَّارُ بِالشَّهَوَاتِ، وَحُجِبَتِ الجَنَّةُ بِالْمَكَارِهِ

"Paradise is surrounded by hardships, and the Hellfire is surrounded by temptations."[4]

Therefore, one must forbear certain hardships to enter Paradise and resist against certain temptations in order to be saved from Hell.

Remembrance of God, being aware and conscious of Him at every moment and thus never being oblivious to Him in this sense, is a very exalted virtue. Right after delivering the Friday sermon and stepping down from pulpit, the preachers remind us of that virtue reciting the verse وَلَذِكْرُ اللهِ أَكْبَرُ "Remembrance of God is surely the greatest (of worship)"

---

4   Bukhari, Riqaq 28; Muslim, Jannah 1.

(al-Ankabut 29:45). Certainly, a sincere believer cannot fathom forgetting about God or enduring a state of obliviousness to His presence.

Inner peace and presence of heart

Consciously observing salah brings order to the chaos of a believer's life. It will bring balance and consistency to their disoriented heart, revive their broken feelings, and illuminate whatever is left in darkness in their soul. By observing salah five times a day with the consciousness that one is standing before God, accounting for their actions, a person becomes capable of seeing, thinking, and speaking correctly, along with gaining much more.

Real salah is the one observed in *khushu* (awe) of God. However, there are certain conditions to acquire *khushu*. The person has to have *hudhur al-qalb* (inner peace or inward presence; peace and presence of mind and heart) in salah; next they have to be aware of why and what they are doing during salah; then they have to trust in God and expect the manifestation of His infinitely profound Mercy with a positive and hopeful attitude; finally they have to come to the presence of God with humility and diffidently, aware of their imperfection.

Maintaining the intended movements and meanings during salah can bring about peace and a sense of presence in the heart. For example, a person bows down in *ruku'* after standing in the presence of God for some time, because of feeling unable to stand up any further. After *ruku'*, we prostrate ourselves in order to confess our pettiness before God. Right at the beginning of salah we say, "Praise be to Allah, Lord of the worlds…" in response to His mercy out of which He granted our tongue, lips, limbs, and everything fully functioning for us. Thanks to those body units, parts, and blessings, we are able to express ourselves. Likewise, consider the bone, joint, and skeletal structures of our body. Thanks to them we are able to move easily. The value of these blessings can truly be grasped by speaking with those who suffer from ailments, enduring great difficulty in moving their bodies or maintaining posture due to their pains and aches.

In the same way, we may recall during salah that we will walk on the Bridge of Sirat while the flames of Hell are towering below our feet and how people will prostrate themselves with the dread of this situation on the day of Resurrection and Reckoning. Then we say "My God, You are the One Whose decree prevails in this world and the Afterlife. This being so, why should I observe servitude to others? I worship You exclusively and ask help from only You to be saved from the dread of this world and the next." Thus, we implore, saying, "please do not let me be one of those who transgress from the path of servitude, fall to the path of misguidance, and are disgraced in both worlds!"

Hudhur al-qalb signifies remaining within these sentiments expressed during salah. The original Arabic word "*hudhur*" does not only mean "peace" but also "presence" or "being present." To put it simply, it means disengaging or becoming indifferent from the creation and worldly preoccupations, and instead bonding with the Divine Essence. You give your heart to Him and receive His mercy and good pleasure in return. If one's heart is preoccupied with worldly pursuits such as household affairs, property, and wealth, they are not acceptable offerings in the market of salah and its Reckoning. With *hudhur al-qalb*, where your heart and mind are present as one and ready at salah, your eyes will widen with awe as you become amazed and overwhelmed by the things you will see. While reciting the verses of the Qur'an you will discern that you are journeying within infinite dimensions of *marifa* (interior or mystical knowledge of self, God and the higher realities). Those verses will take you by the hand and guide you in terms of knowledge of God and inner richness; they will guide you along the heavens unknown to you. Then intuitively you will acquire knowledge of spiritual truth and ecstatically feel things about the knowledge of God, things you did not comprehend or experience before, but are pouring out onto you from different realms. And you will embark on a journey through inner and outer space and boundaries. As you travel among celestial bodies, you will perceive the entire earth like a heartbeat that proclaims God's name with the uproars it generates. Moving further from the world, the sun will captivate your attention as it courses through the Milky Way like a heart, chanting the name of God through its contracting, expanding, and releasing flares.

Together with your own heart's ticking, you will hear that all the systems in the outer space in their awe-inspiring forms declare and exalt the name of God. As you traverse between those systems like a space shuttle, you will weave a honeycomb of knowledge of God, and a profound reverence for God's Grandeur and Majesty will be instilled within you. Then you will proclaim the greatness of the One Who governs the vast realm of existence with the exaltation "*Allahu Akbar.*" You will bow down to *ruku'* with *Allahu Akbar*, prostrate yourself with *Allahu Akbar*, raise your body upright with *Allahu Akbar*, and then sit for the *tahiyyat* with *Allahu Akbar*.

Indeed, God Almighty is greater than everything. The servant bears witness to God's greatness with these words during salah, thus becoming the guardian of this testimony throughout the prayer. The Majesty of God sometimes fills the servant with utter astonishment and amazement. This feeling of amazement makes them become self oblivious, not knowing what to do. However, in a moment of clarity, they grow aware that God Almighty, Whom they invoke as "Rahman" and "Rahim" at the very beginning of salah will envelop them with His Compassion, Grace and Mercy, just as He does with everything else in the universe. To such an extent that they feel like the sole recipient of God's attention, sensing that they are the only ones whom God sees, hears, and responds to with every voice and breath. At a time of overwhelming fear and anxiety, coming across such hope is pure mercy for the servants. They embrace these sentiments, recognizing, "I have now reached this (spiritual) station and have been blessed with a more profound form of knowing God. Now I am enraptured with all the grace coming from Him." However, although they may be in this state of enrapture, that is still not a state of proximity with the Divine that could tolerate any discourtesy; mindful of their humility, the servant remains attentive to their conduct, acknowledging God as the Creator while recognizing their own status as created beings in absolute need of His Mercy.[5]

In short, a believer should always aspire to accomplish true salah. As far as they act with such intention and commitment, it is hoped that God, out of His Grace and Mercy, will reward them as if they accomplished so. Most of us endeavor to realize salah in the true sense and prostrate as if we were meeting the Beloved. Indeed, the true essence lies in experiencing the full magnitude of God's greatness within our consciousness at every moment, not solely during salah. Equally significant

---

5   For more about "amazement and stupor," see Gülen, *Emerald Hills of the Heart Vol. 1*, p.166–168.

is recognizing our own insignificance deep within our souls and offering our standing, bowing, and prostration to the Lord within that realization. Salah observed in this manner will provide our spirit and heart with a steadfast path.

إِنَّ الرَّجُلَ لَيَنْصَرِفُ وَمَا كُتِبَ لَهُ إِلَّا عُشْرُ صَلَاتِهِ تُسْعُهَا ثُمْنُهَا سُبْعُهَا سُدْسُهَا خُمْسُهَا رُبْعُهَا ثُلُثُهَا نِصْفُهَا

In the hadith above,[6] the Messenger of God ﷺ is teaching us that some people observe salah but only receive a tenth of its due reward, while some people receive a ninth, an eighth, a seventh, a sixth, a fifth, a quarter, a third, or half of it. Actually a believer is supposed to gain the full reward of salah; this can only be accomplished by observing it with a sound mind and consciousness of standing before His Presence. May God Almighty bless us with his forgiveness and mercy. May He let our feelings of reverence and awe for Him overflow endlessly, so that it permeates us! May He help us with windows of hope at times when we give in to hopelessness and are about to be drowned in a whirlpool of hopelessness. May He not deprive us of mannerliness, even for a moment, so that we do not commit any act of disrespect or impertinence before Him.

b. Attaining integrity with feelings

The human being is mostly greedy for readily available benefits, but indifferent to more beautiful things to be attained in the long run. The Qur'an expresses this truth with the verse, وَكَانَ الْإِنْسَانُ عَجُولاً "Man is prone to be very hasty" (al-Isra 17:11). Also another verse states, إِنَّ الْإِنْسَانَ خُلِقَ هَلُوعًا "Surely mankind has been created with a restless, impatient disposition" (al-Ma'arij 70:19). And the following verse continues to further describe human being as, إِذَا مَسَّهُ الشَّرُّ جَزُوعًا "Fretful when evil visits him..." (al-Ma'arij 70:20). Specifically, when some misfortune befalls them, they start lamenting, whining, and magnify their misfortune. They wish for others to share their sorrows. Their hasty and impatient reactions, driven by short-term self-interest, blind them to the fact that what they perceive as misfortune could actually be blessings in disguise. Some happenings may appear as bad on the surface, but there

---

6   Abu Dawud, Salat 127; Nasai, *Sunan al-Kubra* 1/211–212; Bayhaqi, *Sunan al-Kubra* 2:281.

could be a hidden good that arises out of the perceived misfortune. God Almighty, The All-Watchful Guardian, may inflict lesser hardships or misfortunes on people so that they continue to live on earth purified from sins, be alert against other greater misfortunes and protected from far serious consequences. Since the human being is an addict to prepayment and outright rewards they have no tolerance for misfortunes whatsoever. When God delivers them from such predicaments, they often forget to express gratitude and fail to recognize that it was indeed God Who saved and delivered them. The Qur'an also puts this as, وَإِذَا مَسَّهُ الْخَيْرُ مَنُوعًا "And withholding when touched with good..." (al-Ma'arij 70:21). They have an innate characteristic where they are unwilling to lose even a single dime, driven by greed, haste, and impatience, always seeking to turn one into a thousand.

These and similar dispositions, or character traits, are all inherent in human nature and can find a path to integrity with salah where they can begin to be utilized for the purposes they were intended for. They are provided as tools for individuals to enhance and progress towards character perfection. On the other hand, when mankind fails to establish a proper relationship with God they cannot know where to utilize and benefit them. When abused or misused in some way these core potentials make the person fall to the lowliest level, the lowest of the low (*asfal al-safilin*) (at-Tin 95:4-5), instead of taking them to the peak of spiritual progress and the Most High and Supreme Places in Paradise (*a'la-i illiyyin*) (al-Mutaffifin 83:18-21).

The other trait is determination. Since it relates to God and is oriented towards His Grace and Mercy, determination raises the person to the a'la-i illiyyin because this characteristic enables the person to remain steadfast upon what is right. When used properly, for example, in the face of the adverse waves of unbelief, the person determinedly says, "Once I have turned to You, my Lord, it is out of question for me to ever forsake You." The person thus shows steadfastness and determination and acts in accordance with the Divine decree, وَاعْبُدْ رَبَّكَ حَتَّى يَأْتِيَكَ الْيَقِينُ "And (continue to) worship your Lord until what is certain (death) comes to you" (al-Hijr 15-99). Thus determination becomes a laudable virtue and serves as a means for the person's ascending to the peak of spiritual progress and perfection.

The same holds true for another trait "ambition." The believer attains rewards of the afterlife thanks to ambition, a strong desire or determination to achieve something. This trait is ingrained in human nature by God in order to gain sublime virtues, deepen their servitude to God, and to never get enough of worship. With this and similar dispositions, the person says, "My God! Worshiping You is so sweet, please allow me to attain higher levels of it" thereby becoming eligible for the highest rank and degree in Paradise. If one lives detached from God, "ambition" starts to serve worldly desires and temptations. This constitutes its misuse and further distances the individual from God. With such misdirection, one cannot escape the vicious cycle and the entanglements of worldly pursuits.

Squandering these innate qualities for the fleeting pleasures of this world, which is not even worth a mosquito's wings in God's eyes, leads to nothing but a complete loss. After warning us against this terribly unfavorable situation, the Qur'an shows us the right course and states that those who observe salah will not be taken by this peril:

إِلَّا الْمُصَلِّينَ ۞ الَّذِينَ هُمْ عَلَى صَلَاتِهِمْ دَائِمُونَ

"Surely mankind has been created with a restless, impatient disposition: fretful when evil visits him, and forgetful when good visits him—Except those who are devoted to the Prayer. Those who are constant in their Prayer..." (al-Ma'arij 70:22-23). Hence, those who come before God in prayer five times a day are less likely to misuse these traits solely for worldly endeavors. Instead, they may harness them for their spiritual growth and aspirations in the Hereafter.

c. Accepting the Divine call

Salah serves as a means of relief and contentment for the servant, but fundamentally, it is the servant's affirmative response to God's call. With the *adhan*, the proclamation and exaltation of *Allahu Akbar* are heard from mosques five times a day and an invitation is made to all people. It's as if they are reminded, "God is the Greatest, and you are His servant. To attain what you seek, come into the presence of the Lord as instructed by Prophet Muhammad ﷺ," anticipating rewards through salah. When it is time for prayer, the believer responds affirmatively to this call, which is the call of Islam to Muslims to acknowledge its message revealed to the

Prophet ﷺ. Muslims abandon all work and other activities and stand to worship the One and Only. This action signifies, "My Lord, You summoned me to prayer five times a day, and here I am obediently responding. Even if You had called fifty times instead of five, I would still come and fulfill it as You willed." In return for their obedience, God Almighty rewards them as if they had observed salah fifty times a day.

For someone who doesn't practice or believe in Islam, the five calls to prayer throughout the day may not hold much significance. They can carry on with their usual activities, and the calls from mosques and other worshippers won't bring them any spiritual reward. On the other hand, to a believer, salah means a fruitful and prolific life. The good deeds they sow in this world's field yield a harvest in the Hereafter that multiplies manifold—tenfold, a hundredfold, seven hundredfold, or more. This abundance stems from their sincere intentions, which surpass the mere act itself. For this reason, as far as they retain a consciousness of servitude to God, every phase of their life will be accepted as to have passed within the scope of that servitude and worship.

As for how this sacred call relates to God Almighty, it is by means of salah that He invites us to His Grace and Mercy. Just as we warmly welcome guests at the door, ensuring they leave our reception happy and satisfied, God invites us to His Presence, Grace, and Mercy five times a day through the beautiful call to prayer. As an expression of the greatness of the *adhan*, the Qur'an states,

وَمَنْ أَحْسَنُ قَوْلًا مِمَّنْ دَعَا إِلَى اللهِ

"Who is better in speech than one who calls to God." (Fussilat 41:33)

As the Caller, God will not send people away empty-handed; out of His infinite beneficience, generosity, and mercy, He will provide nourishment for His servants' heart and spirits. He will lift the veil of the material world from their eyes, granting them insight into the otherworldly realms, and manifesting His blessings from there. Whether or not His servants are aware of it in those moments, God will honor them with a *mi'raj* (ascension). By responding positively to His call and entering the Divine presence through salah, individuals will find that salah becomes a special staircase, elevating them higher. So much so that at that ultimate point they reach, they will behold God. Just as the Messenger of God beheld his Lord during the *Mi'raj*, worshippers can feel the same truth in salah.

Prophet Muhammad ﷺ, the Truthful Messenger, once said, إِذَا أَتَاكُمْ كَرِيمُ قَوْمٍ فَأَكْرِمُوهُ "If there comes to you a man who is respected among his own people, then honor him [show him respect; treat him well]."[7] People with faithful hearts are regarded as the most respected of the living on earth. For, they do not associate partners with God, nor do they prostrate themselves before others; they only respond to God's invitation, as is the case with hearing the *adhan*. We wholeheartedly hope that God Almighty who let his beloved Prophet ﷺ speak this way will not deprive us and all those who responded to His call affirmatively, coming to His presence, from His generous treatment.

d. Speaking with the Lord

Salah means submitting to the Omnipotent Being, relying on Him, and expecting Him to resolve all troubles. When the Messenger of God faced with inundating difficulties and had not yet decided what steps to take, he would set about observing salah, stand obediently before God, and thus let his heart find satisfaction and peace. The way he did this is also commanded by God, as is stated in the verse,

يَا أَيُّهَا الَّذِينَ آمَنُوا اسْتَعِينُوا بِالصَّبْرِ وَالصَّلَاةِ إِنَّ اللهَ مَعَ الصَّابِرِينَ

> "O you who believe! Seek help through persevering patience and the Prayer." (al-Baqarah 2:153)

Indeed, many who profess belief in God turn to salah when faced with difficulties or a slew of unresolved problems, seeking relief and solutions. They come to God's presence through salah, acknowledging their helplessness and expressing their dependence on Him. Salah in that sense is a sublime station which elevates the person to the level to speak to God directly. In salah, the person establishes a connection with God via the heart and addresses Him by means of the acts, recitations and supplications, sometimes addressing Him and sometimes being addressed by Him. One *hadith qudsi* expresses the following:

---

7   Ibn Majah, Adab 19; Ibn Abi Shayba, *al-Musannaf* 5/234.

God divided the recitation in salah into two; one half belongs to God and the other to the servant. The servant's wish is granted. When the servant says, الْحَمْدُ لِلّهِ رَبِّ الْعَالَمِينَ "praise be to God, Lord of the worlds," the Almighty One of infinite glory and majesty states that His servant has praised Him. When the servant says الرَّحْمَنِ الرَّحِيمِ that He is Rahman and Rahim, God states that His servant has extolled Him and declared His supreme glory. When the servant says مَالِكِ يَوْمِ الدِّينِ "the Master of the Day of Judgment," God says that His servant has glorified Him. When the servant says إِيَّاكَ نَعْبُدُ وَإِيَّاكَ نَسْتَعِينُ, "You alone do We worship, and from You alone do we seek help," God states that it is a covenant between Him and His servant and that He has granted what His servant asked for. When the servant says, اِهْدِنَا الصِّرَاطَ الْمُسْتَقِيمَ ۞ صِرَاطَ الَّذِينَ أَنْعَمْتَ عَلَيْهِمْ غَيْرِ الْمَغْضُوبِ عَلَيْهِمْ وَلاَ الضَّالِّينَ "Guide us to the Straight Path, the Path of those whom You have favored, not of those who have incurred (Your) wrath (punishment and condemnation), nor of those who are astray" then God states, that this also belongs to His servant and that His servant's wish is granted.[8]

In summary, through salah, individuals ascend to a spiritual state where they feel as though they are face to face with their Lord, and they receive a reward commensurate with the depth of their heart, sincerity of their words, and genuineness of their acts. This is indeed what God Almighty promises.

e. Preventing illicit behaviors

Salah signifies that five times a day, individuals present themselves before God to give an account of their lives. In other words, they stand before God as if they have just died, awaiting Divine Judgment, seeking refuge in God against the misguidedness of Satan from the left, and feeling the joy of the angels who supported them from the right. This prayer shields from indecency, impropriety, and evil acts. By being free of moral and spiritual impurities, individuals gain the merit to stand before God. After such a prayer, there is no rational or logical justification for sinning and being tainted by transgressions. Committing sins then becomes inconceivable for the obedient servant.

8   Muslim, Salat 38, Tirmidhi, Tafsir 2; Nasai, Iftitah 23.

God Almighty states in the Qur'an, إِنَّ الصَّلَاةَ تَنْهَى عَنِ الْفَحْشَاءِ وَالْمُنْكَرِ "Surely, the Prayer restrains from all that is indecent and shameful, and all that is evil" (al-Ankabut 29:45). Indecent and shameful acts are burdens and hinder a person from realizing *mi'raj* and coming to God's presence. They are sins and God dislikes them. In line with the truth, "Each sin harbors a path that leads to unbelief,"[9] the person who sins gets far from God but closer to Satan. In other words, the more sins one commits, the further away from God they are. It's akin to losing the progress achieved through prayers due to sins, falling backwards because of trivial matters after ascending step by step. Accordingly, a believer who aims to draw closer to the Lord and prioritizes this goal must fear and steer clear of sin just as they fear and avoid falling into fire. The Prophet emphasized three virtues that indicate a person has truly experienced the delight of faith: the first is loving God and His Messenger above all else; the second is loving those whom you love purely for the sake of God; and the third is, fearing a return to disbelief as much as one fears being cast into fire after having been saved by God from unbelief and honored with Islam.[10]

Certainly, those who have tasted the delight of faith will regard the prospect of unbelief or anything leading to it with utmost dread, akin to the terror of being thrown into fire. They will do whatever is necessary to avoid reverting to disbelief.

Observing salah within this spirit and consciousness means that the person renews their covenant with God by standing submissively before Him, thus strengthening their bond with Him. This actually is an easy act. It might however be incredibly difficult for those who have never tasted the delight of it.

Observing salah is a means to gain closeness to God. On the other hand, abandoning it is a means to stray to associating partners with God and to unbelief. The Prophet stated that the only thing between a servant and associating partners with God is abandoning salah.[11] In another hadith, he stated that those who observe salah are under his protection:

9   Nursi, *The Gleams*, Second Gleam, First Point.

10 Bukhari, Iman 9, 14; Ikrah 1; Muslim, Iman 67.

11 Muslim, Iman 134; Tirmidhi, Iman 9; Abu Dawud, Sunnah 15.

The Fruits of Salah

مَنْ صَلَّى صَلاَتَنَا وَاسْتَقْبَلَ قِبْلَتَنَا، وَأَكَلَ ذَبِيحَتَنَا فَذَلِكَ الْمُسْلِمُ الَّذِي لَهُ ذِمَّةُ اللهِ وَذِمَّةُ رَسُولِهِ، فَلاَ تُخْفِرُوا اللهَ فِي ذِمَّتِهِ

That is, any person who observes salah and turns toward the qibla comes under the protection of God and His Messenger. Nobody should harm that person ever.[12] When a person recognizes the authority of a certain government, he or she enters under the protection of that government and enjoys the rights of its citizens. In a similar vein, a person's turning to the *qiblah* and observing salah is a sign of his or her acceptance into the protection of God and His Messenger. Wrongdoing committed against a person under this protection is regarded as crime against the Protector of that person.

To summarize, those who adopt salah, and other emblematic features of Islam (شَعَائِرَ)[13] for that matter, in their lives, come under a very significant protection, as they gain barriers against unbelief and associating partners with God.

f. A reminder of the essentials of faith

Salah is a composition of the pillars of faith (*arkan al-iman*). First of all, it establishes a relationship between God and the servant. By saying the exaltation "Allahu Akbar" and thus making the opening *takbir* for salah, the person seemingly throws everything that would bar them from God behind them; they would eagerly anticipate glimpses of spiritual realms and blessings to be bestowed from that sacred domain. Meanwhile, the individual surely understands that every utterance and sentiment during salah has the potential to ascend to God as pure offerings. The following Qur'anic verses express this truth:

أَلَمْ تَرَ كَيْفَ ضَرَبَ اللهُ مَثَلاً كَلِمَةً طَيِّبَةً كَشَجَرَةٍ طَيِّبَةٍ أَصْلُهَا ثَابِتٌ وَفَرْعُهَا فِي السَّمَاءِ

---

12 Buhari, Salat 28, Adaahi 14; Tirmizi, Iman 2; Nasai, Iman 9.

13 Mentioned in the Qur'an in several verses (al-Baqarah 2:158, 2:198, al-Hajj 22:32, 22:36), "emblems" refer to the distinctive signs and practices that symbolize the collective identity of Islam and the Muslim community, such as the *adhan*, the mosque, the Ka'ba, the salah, and others.

> Do you not see how God strikes a parable of a good word: [a good word is] like a good tree – its roots holding firm [in the ground] and its branches in heaven. (Ibrahim 14:24)

إِلَيْهِ يَصْعَدُ الْكَلِمُ الطَّيِّبُ وَالْعَمَلُ الصَّالِحُ يَرْفَعُهُ

> To Him ascends only the pure word [as the source of might and glory], and the good, righteous action [accompanying it] raises it… (al-Fatir 35:10)

By closing their eyes to things besides God, the servant becomes a watcher of the realm beyond and observes salah with this delight, because there is a different inner contentment in a person's admitting their own pettiness, poverty and humility before the grandeur of God and shivering in awe before Him.

Similarly, when saying, إِيَّاكَ نَعْبُدُ وَإِيَّاكَ نَسْتَعِينُ "You alone do We worship, and from You alone do we seek help…" the servants not only acknowledge His Being the One to be worshipped exclusively, but also their own inadequacy in serving Him as He deserves. With such an acknowledgment of impotence and poverty (*ajz* and *faqr*), the person takes refuge in Him and expresses in a sense "My Lord, I am observing servitude to You with the awareness of my poverty, inability, weaknesses, and impotence. Yes, I am a servant of Yours, indeed what an honorable servitude it is, as I am a servant to You alone."

God Almighty is the Ultimate Sovereign, and we all are servants at His door. We declare and confess this truth some 40 times a day when we sit for *tashahhud* in salah. We attest to the Eternal Sovereign as أَشْهَدُ أَنْ لاَ إِلَهَ إِلاَّ اللهُ "I bear witness that there is no deity but God" during the sitting in salah. Thus, we declare that God is the Sole One Worshipped, Eternally Besought, has no partners whatsoever in His dominion, authority, and rule. We then affirm our belief in the Prophets in salah. The declaration وَأَشْهَدُ أَنَّ مُحَمَّدًا عَبْدُهُ وَرَسُولُهُ that Prophet Muhammad ﷺ is both His servant and Messenger is also an affirmation of the missions of the Prophets of all times, from Prophet Adam to the Last Prophet, peace and blessings of God be upon them all. This affirmation leads us on a journey, sometimes reminiscent of Prophet Noah on the ark, sometimes of Moses on Mount Sinai, sometimes of Jesus the Messiah, whose spirit was breathed into his immaculate mother Mary by the spirit, and sometimes of the Last Prophet, Muhammad ﷺ, who embodied within him the qualities of all past prophets. Likewise, as we say اَلسَّلَامُ عَلَيْكَ أَيُّهَا النَّبِيُّ we feel as though we draw near our Prophet, sitting beside Him and saying, "O blessed Messenger, O whose depth of spirit and mission I cannot fully comprehend, but it suffices us to know you only by the Divine address and introduction of 'Muhammadun Rasulullah.' Here I offer my salutations to you, as numerous as all the atoms and particles that constitute my body. Please accept them."

Thanks to our belief in the Prophets, we do not see the past as a pit of darkness and we firmly believe that we will, God willing, pass through all future hardships and periods at the speed of lightning under their tutelage and guardianship.

In the same line of thought, feeling and conviction, we recall and reflect upon the belief in Angels. Thanks to our faith in their existence, we never feel alone no matter where we are. We think that they always accompany us like a faithful friend. They guide us towards the truth and build barriers against the paths of error. This belief we have instills a sense of serenity and peace within us; imbuing us with the conviction that the angels will welcome us in the next world like kings, forming a corridor to guide us into Paradise.

Likewise, when we say, مَالِكِ يَوْمِ الدِّينِ "Master of the Day of Judgment," we remember that God Almighty is our Master and Judge in this world and the next. On the Day of Judgment and Reckoning, no one will have the authority to challenge what He decrees as good or bad. And when we say, اهْدِنَا الصِّرَاطَ الْمُسْتَقِيمَ "Guide us to the Straight Path," we remember Islam as the manifest religion, the judgments, and contents of the Qur'an, and what they all demand from us.

All of these are reminded to us within salah, which is a precise composition of the pillars of faith. We may not fully know or comprehend what we are supposed to recall, feel and discern in the bowing, prostration, and sitting of salah; we may even find ourselves doing these physical moves within salah but with no idea as to what they mean. However, with salah God Almighty is offering us a formula of worship to respond to our inner desire for servitude, shaping it into specific forms, states and manners, such that He will be well pleased with us only if we adhere to it accordingly.

g. Expiating sins

If it is observed in an ideal sense—as it is stated in many sayings of the Prophet ﷺ—salah erases sins and purifies the person, because there is the act of making repentance (*tawbah*) into a consciousness at salah. In essence, while repentance through salah may not be a deliberate and conscious act, aligning oneself with the intended framework of salah and approaching the Divine presence with that integrity will instill a consciousness of repentance within a person. On the other hand, salah means utter repentance. *Tawbah* is so ingrained in all pillars of salah that it is virtually impossible to consider it independently from salah. Every form of repentance is not only in salah of course, yet each salah observed consciously is a repentance at the same time. However, for salah to have such an effect, it must first be observed with the intended depth of meaning.

I'd like to highlight a point inferred from relevant hadiths: if God Almighty so wills, He can forgive sins at every salah. However, the individual should feel remorse for their sins constantly, as this serves as a sincere invitation for forgiveness. This ensures that repentance fully permeates each day for the sins committed, prompting the servant to seek acceptance of repentance in every salah throughout the day. For those who spend every day in this way, observing salah with such consciousness should be another blessing. We do not know which salah we observe will serve as expiation for our sins. The wisdom behind this concealment is for us to approach every salah with the same devotion. This is similar to the wisdom behind why we do not know the exact time of the Night of Qadr and the exact time segment when prayers are accepted on Fridays: so that we keep seeking acceptance of prayers as much as we can. Similarly, the concept of salah serving as expiation for sins is kept secret to prompt individuals to seek expiation during every salah, approaching each prayer with the appropriate feelings and consciousness. Thus, the opportunity for expiation is available during any of the five daily salahs.

h. Coming closer to God

Salah is indeed the greatest means of closeness to God. It is not possible for a believer to gain closeness to their Lord with anything dearer or more lovable than salah. As reported in a hadith, the Prophet ﷺ said:

أَقْرَبُ مَا يَكُونُ الْعَبْدُ مِنْ رَبِّهِ وَهُوَ سَاجِدٌ، فَأَكْثِرُوا الدُّعَاءَ

> "A person is closest to his Lord at prostration; so pray there much (while prostrating)."[14]

If the person implores God fervently in prostration, in particular where and when no one but God sees and hears, such sincere devotions bring them closer to God. As individuals draw closer to God, Satan regrets missing out on such an honor and laments the damnation and loss he brought upon himself. He flees from this proximity, wailing in despair. The Messenger of God describes this situation as follows: "When the son of Adam recites a verse of prostration and does observe prostration, Satan retreats, weeps, and says "woe to me; son of Adam was commanded to prostrate himself, and he did; there is Paradise for him as reward. I was also commanded to prostrate myself, but I objected; and there is fire for me."[15]

Given that salah distances Satan from the believers this much and renders them this close to God, the believers should never abstain from performing their salah. In particular, they should prioritize prostration, seizing every opportunity to pray and prostrate. By doing so, they open themselves up to God, presenting their petitions to Him, and saying: "My God, nobody has listened to lamentations of my heart; nobody has been able to cure my troubles; so here I am presenting them to You." The sacred phrase recited at prostration, سُبْحَانَ رَبِّيَ الْأَعْلَى "Subhana Rabbiyal-A'la" (My Supreme Lord is All-Glorious) virtually conveys the meaning, "My Lord! I have wronged myself, indulged in pettiness and shameful deeds, and committed gross sins against Your commands and greatness. However, here I am now humbling myself before Your Grandeur, seeking refuge in Your Mercy, and placing my forehead on the ground out of repentance and humility. Please forgive me, because there is none but You Who can forgive. You are the Witness and Knower of all. Even though I am a sinner, I have not turned to anyone else but You

---

14   Muslim, Salat 215; Abu Dawud, Salat 148; Nasai, Mawaqit 35, Tatbi, 78.

15   Muslim, Iman 133; Ibn Majah, Iqamah 70; Ibn Hanbal, *Musnad* 2/442.

as my Lord; I have never prostrated or bowed myself before anyone else. Other human beings have involved in my acts, yet they have never witnessed me prostrating before anyone else but You. While Satan arrogantly refuses prostration and runs away in disobedience, I am obeying Your command just as is stated in the verse, فَفِرُّوا إِلَى اللهِ *So, flee to (refuge in) God* (adh-Dhariyat 51:50). Here I am fleeing to You. I am seeking refuge in You and coming under Your protection and shelter."

On account of the worth of salah, the duty shifts of the angels are in line with the times of salah throughout the day. In a hadith, the Messenger of God stated:

> There are angels who take turns in visiting you by night and by day, and they all assemble at the dawn (*Fajr*) and the afternoon (*Asr*) prayers. Those who have spent the night with you ascend to the heaven and their Lord, Who knows better about them, asks: "In what condition did you leave My servants?" They reply: "We left them while they were performing Salah and we went to them while they were performing Salah."[16]

Salah carries such profound meaning and significance; it is the worship of Angels, each pillar observed by specific groups of them in the heavens. Unlike other acts of worship where the archangel Gabriel served as the intermediary, salah was directly bestowed upon the Messenger of God during the *Mi'raj*, without intermediaries. Therefore, as mentioned earlier in this book, the Prophet ﷺ affirmed that when observed with such loyalty, rewards for salah are akin to praying fifty times.[17]

Also, despite humans' being so petty, prone to shortcomings, and susceptible to falling to the lowest of the low, salah promptly transports one to the presence of God Almighty and bestows upon them the honor of such an audience with Him. The servant virtually engages in a conversation with God in Salah. Sometimes the servant speaks, sometimes the Lord does, and sometimes Angels too attend this conversation. While

---

16 Buhari, Mawakitu's-Salat 16; Bad'ul-khalq 6; Tawhid 23, 33; Muslim, Masajid 210.

17 Bukhari, Bad'ul-khalq 6, Manaqibu'l-Ansar 42; Muslim, Iman 259.

coming to observe Salah, it is as if the person is saying, "My Lord, Who created me, Who took me to His presence despite my pettiness and unimportance, Who enabled me to address Him, and Who honored me with an address and audience by Him! I want to respond to you with my heart brimming with reverence for You. How can I offer due thanks in return for so many favors You have blessed me with? I am not able to find anything sufficient to say in return for so many blessings. Please provide me with such a tongue and way with which I can declare Your greatness and extol You in order to express my gratitude to You… Just as the way You declare Your greatness and extol Yourself."

God Almighty in a sense responds to this wish, "By means of Prophet Muhammad, I have given salah to you, as a special tongue and language from the *Mi'raj*; you will speak through the language of salah, and you will express your reverence for Me by the means of it. Every pillar of salah will become a tongue and you will express your gratitude through those tongues to Me…" After this response, the servant expresses thankfulness to God sometimes by standing, sometimes by bowing down, and sometimes by falling into prostration. After all of this, the person says, "My Lord, You blessed me with hundreds of joints like a wonderful machine and enabled me with the use of them to show You my reverence and awe of You. I feel a deep reverence not only for the wellness of my limbs but also for the chance You've granted me to demonstrate my servitude. This compels me to offer even greater praise and reverence. Please accept this as an extension of my genuine intent.

In short, salah, with the entirety of its pillars, voices the inner needs or concerns the person cannot express or is aching to express. God Almighty hears the voices coming from those tongues. Given that His servant has performed prostration and bowing as acts of servitude, God Almighty graciously fulfills their wishes in response. This serves as an ideal for human beings. It is our hope from God that He lets us feel the spiritual ascension (*mi'raj*) in salah and that—concerning the people who are actually alienated to worship, or who observe salah as a heavy burden, or who carry out salah only as a formality—He lets them feel the true meaning of salah.

2. The fruits of salah for society

Islam is a comprehensive religion for all times and nations. It is therefore a global call for people to maintain a unity before God. Islam, for Muslim individuals, also mandates the establishment of unity, closeness, affinity, and solidarity among themselves. It provides various ways and means to achieve this. The verse, إِنَّمَا الْمُؤْمِنُونَ إِخْوَةٌ "The believers are only brothers [and sisters] ..." (al-Hujurat 49:10) indicates this truth. Salah establishes a relationship between an individual and the Lord, as one of the most important essentials of Islam. It also maintains a dialogue, an interaction, between people in the best way. In this regard, it has a social and collective spirit.

The mosque, where a believer comes together with other fellow believers to pray five times a day, is not merely a place of worship. Historically, we see this with the Prophet ﷺ. Right after the Messenger of God ﷺ honored Medina with his arrival, he set about building a mosque where they could observe congregational worship and would provide a venue for both civilian and administrative councils to discuss public and community affairs. It was also where the public would attend study circles and receive education. Additionally, it was also where security and defense strategies were discussed and expeditions were organized.

This practice continued as an act of *Sunnah* after the Prophet's ﷺ passing. When we look into the early period of the Ottomans, we see that their practice was no different. For example, in the early Ottoman capital Bursa, many sultans convened the civilian, administrative, or military councils within the mosque complex and sometimes around the fountain inside the mosque. There were occasions when the military council convened on one side while the civilian council gathered on the other side, each addressing their own issues and devising strategies accordingly. Upon hearing the *adhan*, the council members would start to make ablutions from the fountain, observe salah with that purity, and after having been in the Divine presence, they would sit and continue to discuss state affairs. While coming to God's presence during salah and acknowledging His Majesty, they would simultaneously prepare for the worldly tasks they would undertake with a pure and clear heart. Knowing that matters were negotiated and decisions were made with the awareness that they would be held accountable before God, it is evident how pure, satisfactory, and well-placed their outcomes would be.

a. Maintaining equality among people

Islamic acts of worship help diminish societal disparities and contribute to achieving equality, a longstanding ideal for humanity. Salah, fasting, hajj, and *zakat* all serve these functions.

One of the purposes of the Islamic system of worship is to keep people sound in soul and body and thus to protect them against physical or spiritual diseases. Vainglory and conceit, flaws that are related to the soul, belong to weak individuals who have not attained maturity. Any person might fall prey to such diseases at any moment. Therefore, it is necessary to strive against such weaknesses for a lifetime. Sincerity, modesty, and humility are all aspects of virtue that make up for those human weaknesses. And the most comprehensive worship that bears all these meanings and the cardinal attributes within is salah.

Salah averts undesirable feelings in a person. It eliminates the barriers that prevent socializing with others in society and it establishes real harmony and equality between them. People who cannot come together equally under everyday circumstances stand side by side in congregational salah. Rich and poor, manager and worker, and lower rank and higher rank, all stand in the same line and rank side by side. Even when presidents or sultans, who walk outside with bodyguards and secret service agents in company, come to the mosque for salah, they share the same line and rank with ordinary citizens. In mosques, whether in the past or present, there has always been a striking absence of distinctions based on social status, wealth, or attire. The disparity that matters, evident in the hereafter, lies solely in one's level of God-consciousness and righteousness.

Islam embodies a profound social understanding that fosters equality within society. This principle is deeply embedded in salah and extends to and permeates throughout every phase of life. Therefore, believers must not look down upon others nor create distance between themselves and others. Just as they establish equality, solidarity, and unity during salah in the mosque, they are encouraged to do so across all levels and fields of social life.

b. Discipline in both individual and societal levels

Salah instills discipline in a believer's life, fostering a spirit of adherence and obedience to Divine will and commands. By observing salah five times a day, a believer divides the day into five fixed portions. Therefore, after standing in God's presence and attaining balance in life, with a heightened awareness of integrity and accountability, all other daily affairs are conducted in alignment with these principles and their influence.

When the person begins to follow the imam at the congregational salah, they entrus the imam with "speaking to the Lord" through the recitation of the Qur'an on their behalf. The imam's recitation becomes their collective appeal and the congregation only says "Amin" (Amen) to that, wishing for acceptance. In a hadith narrated by the Prophet's ﷺ companion Jabir, the Messenger of God stated مَنْ كَانَ لَهُ إِمَامٌ، فَقِرَاءَةُ الْإِمَامِ لَهُ قِرَاءَةٌ , meaning that whoever follows the imam [at congregational salah], the imam's recitation is his [their] recitation too.[18] When the imam bows for *ruku'* the persons bow too, and the same goes for prostration. This situation continues until the salah ends with the greetings of peace. In this regard, leading the worship is very significant in Islam. The Messenger of God always led his Companions as their imam and did not follow anybody else as imam throughout his life; the only exception was the final days of his life when his health did not allow him to attend the mosque and he assigned Abu Bakr as the imam to lead the prayers in his place. When the Prophet ﷺ felt a bit better and entered the mosque, Abu Bakr, noticing his arrival, immediately stepped back from the position of the imam and declined to lead the salah before him. Since Muhammad ﷺ served not only as a Prophet but also as the leader of the State, he held the position of the Imam, making it inappropriate for anyone to stand before him.

Though, obedience to an imam is not to be taken in a sense of blind compliance, adherence or conformity. If the leader errs or forgets, he must be guided to what is right. Once when the Prophet ﷺ was leading a four-*rak'ah* salah, he mistakenly finished it at the second *rak'ah*. According to Abu Hurairah, the Prophet ﷺ looked angry as he finished the salah. Perhaps, he was displeased with a certain vision he had. A Com-

---

18 Ibn Majah, Iqamah 13; Abdurrazzaq, *Al Musannaf* 2/136.

panion named Dhul Yadain then wanted to know if there was something new and kindly asked, "Have you forgotten or has the prayer been reduced?" The Messenger of God ﷺ turned to his Companions and asked whether they affirmed what Dhul Yadain said. They replied in the affirmative that he had done it as two.[19] Upon this, the Prophet told them that he would surely let them know had any change happened with salah. He also said "If there was any change to the prayer, I would surely inform you; but I am a human being like you and liable to forget like you. So if I do forget, remind me, and if anyone of you is doubtful about his prayer, he should follow what he thinks to be correct and complete his prayer accordingly, make *taslim*, and then offer two prostrations."[20] It seemed as though God Almighty intended to instill in the Companions a sense of reminder by allowing the Prophet ﷺ to forget the *rak'ah*s of salah, thereby inspiring them with how to handle such situations. In short, the imam for the congregational prayer steps forward and leads the prayer. If he makes a mistake unknowingly but noticeably, then you correct him. In this regard, salah is a very significant component for the collective to gain such discipline and is a well formulated model for how obedience, adherence, and submission should be understood and practiced.

c. Generosity

When we look at the developed societies of the world, we see that they own certain merits or attributes and stand out from other societies. The most ideal society will be one with a culture of modesty from the top level to the grassroots, whose members act with a feeling of adherence, conformity, and submission to Divine Will, who respect one another, and who help and donate to those in need with a consciousness of altruistic generosity. As such, salah is such an exalted act of worship that involves all these attributes or qualities within it. It is a formulated version of modesty and humility and a holy call that nurtures in people a feeling of benevolence, generosity, and magnanimity.

---

19   Bukhari, Salat 88, *Adhan* 69, Sahw 3, 4, 5, Adab 45, Ahbar 1; Muslim, Masajid 97, 99.

20   Bukhari, Salat 89; Muslim, Masajid 89.

During salah, the individual essentially practices generosity; foremost, they sacrifice their personal time. All times fly away but that person's time during salah earns or reaches eternity; time gains value with salah and becomes almost visible as a line of light between "possibility" (*imkan*) and necessity (*wujub*). If we explain this by means of an example, a man devotes nearly one-third of his time for the world and gives *zakat* for the sake of God out of the wealth he gained. He does not give this *zakat* from the principal capital earned, but from the harvest he garnered. However, salah is different; it is given purely out of the principal capital. When we consider the time one spends on ablution, going to the mosque, and the like, everyday the person devotes a significant portion of the 24-hour "lifetime capital" to God Almighty. This means that the individual is directly investing their time. Comparing this to giving *zakat* from the fruits harvested from a tree, the situation resembles directly giving the tree itself. With this generosity, the believer allows their time to attain eternity through salah.

People who pray, or who go to the mosque to pray, five times a day everyday are in a feeling of benevolence and generosity to the degree of giving even their capital for the sake of God, for they make a pledge that they can do this sincerely five times a day for a lifetime. Praise be to God Almighty that in our time, we witness many individuals—both young and senior, rich and poor, but all with humble hearts – prostrating themselves in sincerity and praying to foster a harmonious and peaceful human society, which is greatly beloved by God.

Chapter 7

The Friday Prayer

1. Significance of the Friday Prayer

The Friday Prayer is the same as any regular salah; it has the same components of standing, recitation, bowing, prostration, and sitting. This also means that the Friday Prayer is, like the regular salah, how worshippers fulfill their personal *"mi'raj,"* striving to ascend spiritually to the Divine Presence on the one hand. On the other hand, while in contemplation and imagination, they travel back in time fourteen hundred years to stand behind the Prophet ﷺ in prayer. Just as we divide the twenty-four-hour day into five segments and enlighten each of them with one of the five prayers, so do we put our week in order and sprinkle light over it by setting Friday as its milestone.

Friday is the most precious day among the God-given days. When Friday arrives, we turn to our Lord with all of our thoughts and feelings because of the extra blessings it will yield. With reference to the merits of Friday, the Messenger of God states:

Friday is the chief of days, the greatest day before Allah. It is greater before Allah then the Day of Adha and the Day of Fitr. It has five characteristics: Allah created Adam and sent down Adam to this earth on Friday. On it, there is a time during which a person does not ask Allah for anything but He will give it to him, so long as he does not ask for anything that is forbidden. On it, the Hour will begin. There is no angel who is close to Allah, no heaven, no earth, no wind, no mountain, and no sea that does not fear Friday.[1]

---

[1] Ibn Majah, Iqamah, 79; Ibn Hanbal, *Musnad*, 3/430.

In sync with the cycles of time which we call "days" in this world, there is a corresponding cycle in the macrocosm. In this realm, Friday is the day when humanity first appeared on earth, as the Prophet ﷺ stated. Therefore, when Fridays, Saturdays, Sundays or any other day of the week in this world are aligned with the days in the macrocosm, it is like finding the correct sequence of a combination lock. It is only then that a person attains the opportunity to complete their *mi'raj*—ascending to heavenly realms and returning to the world through the depths of their heart.

When these cyclical sequences do not align, people cannot benefit from the secrets emanating from the Divine effusion (*fayd al-aqdas*).[2] Prior traditions before Islam adhered to different days other than Friday and consequently failed to benefit from these manifestations. Muslims recognize and uphold this blessed day, due to its importance, and keep honoring it weekly in an enthusiastic manner. God willing, they will keep doing so until the end of the world.

The Friday Prayer holds a special significance among other salahs, being the most comprehensive. Believers are urged to recognize its value and strive to observe it despite any obstacles. This prayer marks the culmination of the week and elevates individuals to a position where they can draw closer to God. Through Friday Prayer, believers contemplate how to benefit from Divine Mercy. Essentially, after observing salah for six days, they ascend to a particular point on Friday to receive spiritual rewards from God; on this day, those who are consciously and spiritually aware and have given their hearts to God, fill their metaphorical sack with abundant heavenly blessings. Therefore, Friday symbolizes reaching a peak to receive divine rewards at the end of a week-long journey. The Messenger of God expressed this truth in the following hadith:

الصَّلَاةُ الْخَمْسُ، وَالْجُمْعَةُ إِلَى الْجُمْعَةِ، كَفَّارَةٌ لِمَا بَيْنَهُنَّ، مَا لَمْ تُغْشَ الْكَبَائِرُ

---

[2] For more about Divine effusions, in the sense of the overflow of all have been sent to human beings by God as either the Revelations, inspirations, manifestations, blessings or sensations, see Gülen, *Emerald Hills of the Heart Vol. 3*, "Fayd and Tajalli" (Effusion and Manifestation), pp. 57—64.

"The five prayers, Friday to Friday, and Ramadan to Ramadan will expiate the sins committed between them, as long as major sins are avoided."³

As mentioned in the hadith, the Prophet ﷺ divides the day (with five daily prayers), week (with the Friday prayer), and year (with Ramadan) into certain parts and segments and with this, he teaches that the salahs observed in those segments also bring blessings to the other parts that passed without salah.

يَا أَيُّهَا الَّذِينَ آمَنُوا إِذَا نُودِيَ لِلصَّلَاةِ مِنْ يَوْمِ الْجُمُعَةِ فَاسْعَوْا إِلَى ذِكْرِ اللهِ وَذَرُوا الْبَيْعَ ذَلِكُمْ خَيْرٌ لَكُمْ إِنْ كُنْتُمْ تَعْلَمُونَ

O you who believe! When the call is made for the Prayer on Friday, then move promptly to the remembrance of God (by listening to the sermon and doing the Prayer), and leave off business (and whatever else you may be preoccupied with). This is better for you, if you but knew. (al-Jumu'ah 62:9)

The Qur'anic verse mentioned above can be interpreted as follows: The One calling you is the Ultimate Being to be worshipped, the Everlasting Source of all. By calling you to the Friday Prayer, He intends to raise you and admit you to His presence. Just as the host of a significant event signs their invitation card, He symbolically signs this invitation with the sacred phrase *"Allahu Akbar."*

The phrase إِذَا نُودِيَ "when the call is made..." in the verse refers to the *adhan*. The common Muslim call to prayer recited from minarets and ascending to the heavens five times a day is the *adhan*. The term ذِكْرِ *dhikr* (remembrance) refers to salah, which commences with the sermon (*khutbah*). During the Prophet's time, the *muadhin* would call the *adhan* while the imam was on the pulpit (*minbar*); then he would declare the *iqamah*, the final call before the obligatory prayer, and the salah would begin. This practice continued during the reign of the first two caliphs. However, as the Muslim population and cities expanded, the *adhan*'s sound did not reach everywhere and could not be heard by all. To address this, Caliph Uthman introduced a third *adhan* to be called outside to ensure everyone could hear it. This decision was unanimously

---

3   Muslim, Tahara 233.

accepted by scholars (*'ijma*). The *adhan* that was called during the *khutbah* has not been abandoned due to the third *adhan*—it has been kept as a *sunnah* act to continue the practice of the Prophet ﷺ.

The phrase فَاسْعَوْا إِلَى ذِكْرِ اللهِ in the verse above that literally means "run" to remembrance of God was understood as "move promptly." The companion Abdullah ibn Masud says, "Had this meant running in the literal sense, by God, I would break into a run in a way to cause my cloak fall down from my shoulders."[4] The Companions understood this command as "walking briskly" to the mosque. After all, keeping solemn and serene while going to salah is essential. Perhaps you feel the urge to sprint in your heart, yet you will temper that enthusiasm with the dignity befitting a believer, proceeding calmly and steadily. If you happen to be slightly late and miss the beginning with the imam, you will join the congregation and then you will complete the remaining *rak'ah*s you missed in compliance with the following hadith:

إِذَا أُقِيمَتِ الصَّلاَةُ فَلاَ تَأْتُوهَا تَسْعَوْنَ، وَأْتُوهَا تَمْشُونَ، عَلَيْكُمُ السَّكِينَةُ، فَمَا أَدْرَكْتُمْ فَصَلُّوا، وَمَا فَاتَكُمْ فَأَتِمُّوا

> "When *iqamah* is pronounced for salah, do not go running to it. Come walking, do not give up dignity. Observe what you catch up with; complete later what you missed."[5]

Whenever the *adhan* was called, the Companions of the Prophet would go to salah with desire and enthusiasm. The *adhan* would virtually sprinkle their hearts with refreshing water and provide them with a brief relief from the suffocating conditions of the worldly engagements. These feelings and actions, such as experiencing inner relief and contentment through salah and promptly responding to the call without missing it, are truly distinctive traits of an observant Muslim: when they are summoned by a Divine call, they react affirmatively without delay. The Qur'an captures this exact sentiment in the verse quoted above, as well.

Another point that catches attention in the same verse is the command to ذَرُوا الْبَيْعَ "leave off business." One of the most compelling pursuits for individuals is to seek profit and increase their earnings through

---

[4] Ibn Abi Shayba, *al-Musannaf* 1/482; Abdurrazzaq, *al-Musannaf* 3/207.

[5] Bukhari, Jumuah, 18; Muslim, Masajid, 151.

business or work. However, when the *adhan* is called, people are expected to listen to the *adhan* attentively, heed the call, and proceed to the mosque for prayer: a trader will abandon their lucrative trade; a clerk will leave their desk; and a laborer will step away from their workbench to join the prayer in the mosque.

The expression at the end of the same verse above, "This is better for you, if you but knew" gives the following message: for the sake of making God pleased and attaining otherworldly gains and happiness, it is better for you to leave every kind of business and go to the Friday Prayer, which is one of the supreme blessings on the feast the Prophet ﷺ laid before you. In essence, if you deeply understand the significance of the Qur'an's commands and feel the profound impact of salah on your conscience, then there's little need to elaborate on the importance of the Friday Prayer. You inherently recognize which choice holds greater value and benefit. Thus, upon hearing the call to prayer, you will promptly cease your business activities and, with the dignity and solemnity befitting a believer, make your way to the mosque. The next verse of the same Surah continues as follows:

فَإِذَا قُضِيَتِ الصَّلَاةُ فَانْتَشِرُوا فِي الْأَرْضِ وَابْتَغُوا مِنْ فَضْلِ اللهِ وَاذْكُرُوا اللهَ كَثِيرًا لَعَلَّكُمْ تُفْلِحُونَ

> And when the Prayer is done, then disperse in the land and seek (your portion) of God's bounty, and mention God much (both by doing the Prayer and on other occasions), so that you may prosper (in both worlds). (al-Jumu'ah 62:10)

Concerning what "God's bounty" (فَضْلِ اللهِ) here is, Ibn Abbas made the following comment: "This verse does not exhort believers to run after worldly pursuits. What is meant by 'God's bounty' is visiting the sick, attending funerals, and visiting a fellow believer for the sake of God."[6] However, we can perhaps consider the meaning a bit more broadly to mean the following: "Prioritize the observance of Salah, allowing it to purify and clarify your inner being. Then, disperse across the earth with a sense of duty, benefiting from both worldly and spiritual blessings bestowed by God. Strive to lead a purposeful and prosperous life, fostering orderliness and achieving success."

---

6   Bagawi, *Maalimu't Tanzil* 4/345; Suyuti, *Durru'l Mansur* 8/165.

The subsequent verse in the same Surah is as follows:

وَإِذَا رَأَوْا تِجَارَةً أَوْ لَهْوًا انْفَضُّوا إِلَيْهَا وَتَرَكُوكَ قَائِمًا قُلْ مَا عِنْدَ اللهِ خَيْرٌ مِنَ اللَّهْوِ وَمِنَ التِّجَارَةِ وَاللهُ خَيْرُ الرَّازِقِينَ

Yet (it happened that) when they saw (an opportunity for) business or pastime, they broke away for it and left you standing (while preaching the sermon). Say: "What is with God is better (for you) than pastimes and business. God is the Best to be sought as the provider with the ultimate rank of providing." (al-Jumu'ah 62:11)

This verse refers to a specific occurrence during the time of the Prophet ﷺ. Once, the Messenger of God ﷺ was delivering the sermon from the *minbar*. During this period, Medina was experiencing hunger and high prices, and the sound of drums heralded the return of a trade caravan from Damascus. Upon hearing this, some individuals in the mosque ceased paying attention to the Prophet ﷺ and rushed towards the caravan. At that time, they were unfamiliar with the proper etiquette for listening to the sermon and attending the Friday prayer. It is reported by Companions such as Salman al-Farisi, Ibn Masud, and Bilal al-Habashi that only twelve men and one woman remained in the mosque during this incident. The Messenger of God was much displeased with the situation and stated, "For the sake of God in whose grasp Muhammad's soul is, had all of you gone, a flood of fire would fill the valley and take you away." And in another narration: "Had it not been for those who remained, you would have suffered a hail of stones from the sky."[7]

The reason many people rushed out was to purchase daily necessities, before they were sold out. But it was highly inappropriate to abandon God's Messenger during the Friday sermon. There is a stern admonition against the Companions for this action. Only a few blessed individuals were mindful of this, and by not leaving God's Messenger alone, they averted a potential calamity. It is also reported that following this incident, the Companions listened to the Prophet ﷺ with such attentiveness that it seemed as if they were rooted to the spot. From then on, they listened to the sermon with such decorum that their demeanor

---

7   Abu Ya'la, *al-Musnad* 3/468; As-Sa'labi, *al-Kashf wa'l Bayan* 9/317; Bagawi, *Maalimu't Tanzil* 4/345.

resembled that of salah. In the words of Said ibn Jubayr, "listening to the sermon at the time of the Prophet ﷺ was considered an equivalent of observing two rakahs of salah."[8]

In essence, Friday, as the master of days, remains fixed in its original place within universal time, retaining its special significance, while the rest of the days of the week position accordingly. Other days like Eid and Arafa fluctuate and occur at different times. Therefore, believers often prioritize Friday over other days, showing more care and dedication. Yet, despite its weekly occurrence, some individuals struggle to attend Friday prayers regularly. Instead, they prioritize attending Eid prayers, finding solace in them only twice a year. However, it's crucial to note that Eid prayers can never match the significance of Friday prayers. The Companions understood this well and gave much greater importance to Friday prayers over Eid prayers. They were mindful of the Prophet's statement:

مَنْ تَرَكَ ثَلَاثَ جُمَعٍ تَهَاوُنًا بِهَا، طَبَعَ اللَّهُ عَلَى قَلْبِهِ

"Whoever misses three consecutive Friday prayers without a valid excuse, God seals their heart."[9]

This signifies that neglecting Friday prayers leads to a decline in one's love for worship, affecting not only Friday prayers but also all five daily prayers. Consequently, such individuals struggle to nurture their love for God in their hearts and fail to appreciate the guidance of Prophet Muhammad ﷺ and their position behind him. Furthermore, if they do attend prayers, it feels as if they are compelled rather than willingly attending, akin to being dragged into the mosque with a rope around their neck.

Another hadith emphasizes the admonition and caution for those who neglect or abandon Friday prayers, stating that individuals will either cease abandoning the Friday Prayer or God will seal their hearts, after which they will become among the heedless masses, devoid of sense and emotions.[10]

8   Qurtubi, *al-Jami li'l Ahkami'l Qur'an* 18/114.

9   Abu Dawud, Salat, 209; Nasai, Jumu'ah 2.

10 Muslim, Jumuah 40; Nasai, Jumu'ah 2.

This highlights the immense significance of Friday. These hadiths underscore the profound care demonstrated by Prophet Muhammad ﷺ, or more precisely, the weight of God's message to him regarding this matter.

2. The Friday Prayer encompasses comprehensive worship

Arabic speakers commonly refer to the days of the week as the first day, the second day, and so forth. However, Friday is designated as "Jumu'ah," which translates to the day of "gathering" or "assembly." This term signifies the collective focus of public consciousness on a specific point in time, allowing for greater benefit from God's blessings. In pre-Islamic Arabia, Friday was known as "aruba." Regardless of its previous names, the essence of Friday remains a day of gathering; it's a day dedicated to the weekly introspection and self-accountability before God, as well as a time for God's weekly assessment of His followers. After fulfilling our personal obligation of the five daily prayers, Friday serves as an occasion for collective presence in the Divine realm to assess ourselves, reaffirm our commitment to obey God's commands, and remain steadfast in our devotion to His Lordship.

Surely, when we respond to the call on Fridays and forsake our worldly pursuits, we come to the prayer with expectation of reaching the pinnacle of our servitude for the week. For, it is believed that angels also join the congregation in the Friday salah. As a result, alongside the congregation's supplications, those of the angels' ascend to God, too. Among these innocent beings, our humble supplications, however insignificant they may be, gain greater eligibility for acceptance.

The Friday Prayer transcends individual worship; it represents a collective turning of public conscience towards God. It's akin to a single person realizing their inability to adequately express gratitude for Divine blessings and thus pleading, "My Lord, as an individual, I cannot fully respond to Your countless blessings. As You have said, وَإِنْ تَعُدُّوا نِعْمَةَ اللّٰهِ لَا تُحْصُوهَا 'Should you attempt to count God's blessings, you could not compute them,' my own conscience alone is insufficient for that task. Therefore, I join others in congregation to offer our combined servitude and gratitude to You. Please do not merely consider my feeble voice, O Lord! Rather, consider how the entire congregation resounds with 'Al-

lahu Akbar' as we stand before You, bow down, prostrate ourselves, and praise and glorify You with '*SubhanAllah.*' Within this collective voice of the congregation, I seek to express my gratitude in response to Your infinite blessings."

Friday is the focal point of the manifestation of the Divine Names, which encapsulates in the form of a catalogue of everything that is created as a Divine work in the macrocosm. This means that everything in that catalogue or index is, as it were, preserved like a concentrated substance; when needed, they are diluted to transform and fulfill far-fetching duties. In this regard, Friday embodies a significance that unites all the days of creation, acting as a condensed representation of the entire week. While it delineates the days of the week, it also delineates months and years, filling the entirety of a year, a human lifetime, and all periods of time with light. Furthermore, on Fridays, we experience the same enthusiasm and delight as the angels who continuously stand, bow, and prostrate before God for a lifetime.

3. Conditions of the Friday prayer

The Friday prayer is undoubtedly very important for Muslims and for such a significant, exalted, and obligatory prayer to be valid and accepted in the sight of God certain conditions need to be met.

First and foremost, the Friday prayer is a congregational worship and is not intended to be observed alone. It is specifically performed in congregation and consists of two *rak'ahs fard* prayer, just like the morning (*fajr*) prayer. It is offered immediately after the sermon (*khutbah*), which the congregation should attentively listen to. Additionally, when attending the prayer, it is customary to dress in our finest clothes and put on a pleasant fragrance, thus, we offer our prayers in an atmosphere that honors the sanctity of Friday.

Friday is the last of the six days of creation of all existence. In the macrocosm, days are not 24-hour cycles; each day refers to an epoch or an age. These are the periods that passed from the creation of the heavens and the earth till the moment when the earth became suitable for continuation of human life; these are named in God's sight as six days: إِنَّ رَبَّكُمُ اللّٰهُ الَّذِي خَلَقَ السَّمَاوَاتِ وَالْأَرْضَ فِي سِتَّةِ أَيَّامٍ "Indeed your Lord is God, Who has created the heavens and the earth in six days..." (al-A'raf

7:54). Companion Abu Hurairah narrates a hadith about these days or periods as follows:

خَلَقَ اللَّهُ عَزَّ وَجَلَّ التُّرْبَةَ يَوْمَ السَّبْتِ وَخَلَقَ فِيهَا الْجِبَالَ يَوْمَ الْأَحَدِ وَخَلَقَ الشَّجَرَ يَوْمَ الِاثْنَيْنِ وَخَلَقَ الْمَكْرُوهَ يَوْمَ الثُّلَاثَاءِ وَخَلَقَ النُّورَ يَوْمَ الْأَرْبِعَاءِ وَبَثَّ فِيهَا الدَّوَابَّ يَوْمَ الْخَمِيسِ وَخَلَقَ آدَمَ عَلَيْهِ السَّلَامُ بَعْدَ الْعَصْرِ مِنْ يَوْمِ الْجُمُعَةِ فِي آخِرِ الْخَلْقِ وَفِي آخِرِ سَاعَةٍ مِنْ سَاعَاتِ الْجُمُعَةِ فِيمَا بَيْنَ الْعَصْرِ إِلَى اللَّيْلِ

> One day the Messenger of God held me by the hand and said the following: "God created soil on Saturday. He created the mountains on Sunday. He created the trees on Monday. He created the things necessary for life on Tuesday. He created light on Wednesday and He let animals spread on Thursday. He created Adam, peace be upon him, in the *Asr* time on Friday, in the last hour of the hours of Friday, i. e. between afternoon and night, as the last creation."[11]

Some People of the Book remarked that everything was over on Friday and God rested on the next day; it is a gross mistake to ascribe tiredness to God.

Another condition for the Friday prayer is the specific time of the prayer, which is the time of *zawal* (right after the sun begins to decline from its zenith, the same as *dhuhr*). Namely, the prayer time corresponds in human life to the time, or period, of human maturity. God Almighty assigned the post-zenith time for this salah, and observing this worship is a means of seeing Him. The Messenger of God illustrates this with an example and stated, "Do you have any doubt in seeing the sun when there are no clouds?" The people replied in the negative. The Prophet said, "You will see Allah (your Lord) in the same way."[12]

Another condition concerns the location for the Friday prayer: it must be held in a specific residential area for proper observance. As for the daily prayers in general, the Prophet states: وَجُعِلَتْ لِي الْأَرْضُ مَسْجِدًا وَطَهُورًا، فَأَيُّمَا رَجُلٍ مِنْ أُمَّتِي أَدْرَكَتْهُ الصَّلَاةُ فَلْيُصَلِّ "The earth is rendered to me clean, pure, and a place of worship (*masjid*). Whoever enters a salah

---

11 Muslim, Sifatu'l Munafiqin 27; Ibn Hanbal, Musnad, 2/327.

12 Bukhari, Adhan 129, Riqaq 52, Tawhid 24; Muslim, Zuhd 16.

time, he observes the salah wherever he may be."[13] However, this is not the case with the Friday Prayer. You cannot observe it in the wilderness; you simply need more than putting a stick on the ground as barrier before you, which you may do with other prayers. The Friday prayer can only be observed in urban or civilized areas, where people have already grasped the meaning of community, consensus or the collective conscience and have therefore become able to decide and act together.

The Messenger of God also emphasized specific considerations for the Friday Prayer. For instance, during one sermon delivered from the *minbar*, he addressed the issue of the congregation's discomfort. Many attendees, having engaged in strenuous manual labor, would arrive at the mosque wearing woolen garments on hot days, resulting in a pervasive odor of sweat and wool that disturbed many worshippers. Upon this, the Messenger of God counseled his Companions to take a shower before coming to the mosque, clean their teeth with *miswak*, put on the best fragrance they could find, and have separate clothing for the Friday prayer. He said:

الغُسْلُ يَوْمَ الجُمُعَةِ وَاجِبٌ عَلَى كُلِّ مُحْتَلِمٍ، وَأَنْ يَسْتَنَّ، وَأَنْ يَمَسَّ طِيبًا إِنْ وَجَدَ

> "*Ghusl* (taking shower in compliance with ritual conditions) is *wajib* (necessary) upon every person who has come of age. So are using *miswak* [tooth stick] and wearing fragrance if available."[14]

Scholars have discussed this issue extensively. Some of them took what the Prophet ﷺ said as it is and ruled that it is *wajib* to take a ritual shower before coming to the Friday prayer. Others pointed out that this does not express a responsibility and asserted that it is a *Sunnah* act. Related to the topic here, Bukhari and Muslim narrate an interaction between the Caliph Umar ibn al-Khattab and another Companion. While Umar was giving the Friday *khutbah* on the *minbar*, one of the companions of the Prophet, who was one of the foremost *Muhajirun* (emigrants), entered the mosque. Caliph Umar abruptly stopped the sermon and asked, "What is the time now?" in the sense that "Where have you been until now? Were you not supposed to come to the mosque right away

---

13 Bukhari, Tayammum 1, Salat 56; Muslim, Masajid 3, 4, 5.

14 Bukhari, Jumuah 2–5, 12, 26; Muslim, Jumuah 1–12.

when the *adhan* was rendered?" The Companion replied, "O Caliph of the Messenger of God! I was busy and could not go back to my house till I heard the *adhan*. I did not do anything other than the ablution." So he ran home on hearing the *adhan* to make *wudu* (ablution) and was not busied with any other pursuits then. Alongside acknowledging his mistake, he provided a valid excuse and managed to perform the Prayer with a slight delay. Thereupon Umar said to him, "Did you perform only the ablution although you know that Allah's Messenger ﷺ ordered us to take a bath (on Fridays)?" Umar was saying that his sufficing with ablution is also a shortcoming because the Prophet ﷺ ordered Muslims to make *ghusl*.[15]

The Companion being addressed knew well it was neither obligatory to take *ghusl* on Friday nor it was among the conditions of the Friday Prayer. As he knew that the saying of the Prophet ﷺ did not state an absolute requirement, he only regarded it as a virtuous act. Therefore, he had come to the Friday Prayer with the regular ablution only. However, the blessed Companions would warn one another even about the details of the matters of religion and would bring them to account. But they did so with honest feelings, not because of any personal grudge. This was why they were accepting of each other, prepared to handle whatever might arise without taking offense. For this reason they could easily warn each other about their faults. Realizing this requires being natural and being distant from affectation in words and actions. This is not something contemporary societies can bear. Mentioning someone's fault today is virtually impossible, as many individuals consider themselves faultless. Consequently, even when approaching them with gentleness, you're often met with immediate defensiveness and resistance. Maybe we too are in the same situation. Although we often proclaim our willingness to acknowledge our personal faults, there are times when we exhibit stubbornness and refuse to admit them under any circumstances.

Our time is the era of arrogance and pride. It is not possible to speak to people's face about their shortcomings. It seems to me that even if the Pride of Humanity ascended the *minbar* and counseled people about their shortcomings today, some individuals might express discom-

---

[15] Bukhari, Jumuah 2; Muslim, Jumuah 3–4.

fort with his words for they touched their sore points. It is a difficult matter. If only we had friends whom we authorize to tell our faults to our face without hesitation; then we would be able to warn one another against our faults and shortcomings right away so that we could supervise and reform ourselves. What a pity!

As for the Companions, they collectively exercised such self control. Sometimes the Caliph would question a Companion for coming to the prayer without taking *ghusl*. Sometimes a Companion would stand up and demand an explanation from the Caliph, as in the case of the Caliph Umar again: a Companion was demanding an explanation, but nobody was annoyed on account of such questioning when he had asked Umar, "How did you find the extra cloth for the shirt on your back? I could not do that with the cloth that fell to my share!" Interestingly, just as the Caliph would reasonably explain from where he found the extra cloth and thus eliminate the suspicions from the believers' hearts, so would the Companion admit his faults and could give valid reasons and explain the case, as seen above.

4. The first Friday Prayer ever

Coming together with other people, socializing with them, and sharing their joys and sorrows, are all a requirement of civilized life. In the same way, the local Muslims of Medina had discussed among themselves to determine a certain day of the week to worship together, offer thanks to God collectively, just as the Jewish and Christians observed for themselves. They had this discussion even before the *Muhajirun* – the persecuted Muslims of Mecca—immigrated to Medina. Then, they gathered in the house of Asad ibn Zurara on a certain day and Asad led them in the congregational salah. Years later, Ka'b ibn Malik—who is reputed for having a tongue as sharp and effective as a sword—would fondly remember this gathering in his old age as he was guided by his grandson to the mosque because of his poor vision. On hearing the Friday *adhan*, he would remember those bygone days and say, "May God have mercy on Asad ibn Zurara. After we embraced Islam in Medina by means of Mus'ab—I do not know whether he had received any instructions from the Prophet—he set about gathering people through Medina and assembled 40 people [or 12 according to another narration]. Then he led us in the Friday Prayer. Afterwards he slaughtered a young goat and gave a feast to us. Thus, Asad ibn Zurara was the first person to announce the Friday Prayer. May God have mercy on him until the end of his life."[16] Later on, when a written order came from the Prophet ﷺ, the Muslims then began to observe the Friday Prayers in congregation behind Mus'ab ibn Umayr.

We understand the following from all of these: gathering together at least once a week, worshiping collectively, and conversing with other pure souls are all a social issue and an essential need. Even in the early periods when Islam was newly flourishing, conscious Muslims had realized this situation and believed in the necessity of the Friday prayer. They observed the Friday Prayer even before such a command came from the Prophet ﷺ.

According to Ibn Hajar, the Messenger of God ﷺ was made responsible for Friday prayer even while in Mecca.[17] This great scholar probably has a solid foundation for this argument. Otherwise, it does not seem to be very likely, for the necessary conditions for the Friday Prayer were not available in Mecca back then. Namely, under the given circumstances in Mecca, the Prophet ﷺ would obviously not be able to observe Friday Prayer. According to what is known in this regard, the Prophet ﷺ did not observe even a single Friday prayer in Mecca. The Friday Prayer is a congregational prayer. It requires an imam who has devoted his heart to God and who leads people in all their affairs, and it requires a congregation consisted of individuals who obey the imam and uphold what is right. Since these were not available then in Mecca, the Messenger of God ﷺ was not held responsible for Friday Prayer there. However, when he received the command for emigration and set out, he first came to the town of Quba on the way to Medina. Within the first four or five days of his arrival, he personally had the Quba Mosque built. When they departed from there and arrived at the valley of the Salim ibn Awf tribe, the Archangel Jibril brought him the revelation and they thus started to observe the Friday Prayer there. Due to the presence of an established community, the Messenger of God ﷺ had the opportunity

---

16 Abu Dawud, Salat 209; Ibn Maja, Iqamahtu's Salat 78.

17 See Ibn Hajar al-Haythami, *Tuhfatu'l Muhtaj* 2/405.

to institute the Friday Prayer, which is considered one of the distinctive marks of Islam (شَعَائِرُ). Likewise, he had entered the area of the city-state he was going to establish, where he become the imam and the congregation would listen to him.

No sooner did the believers enter Medina with the joy, peace and glad tidings of the Friday Prayer, than their first task with the Prophet was to build a mosque at a convenient site they purchased from old ruins. Afterwards the Friday prayers were observed there. Today no matter whether we refer to that place as the Prophet's Mosque or Rawda al-Tahira (The Garden of Paradise), we will never have expressed the true quality of that place by mere terms, because the ground of the place where the Messenger of God ﷺ rests after his passing can never be compared to any other ground on earth. We cannot know whether it came from Paradise or was created with a special quality from the light of God. But the Messenger included his mosque in Medina together with Masjid al-Haram in Mecca and Masjid al-Aqsa in Jerusalem, as the three mosques to make a journey to and visit.[18] Masjid al-Nabawi (the Prophet's Mosque in Medina) is special because it was built by the Pride of Humanity, Muhammad ﷺ. Together with the Companions such as Bilal and Ammar and many others, he also did manual labor: mixed the clay, carried bricks on his back, and broke stones with a hammer. Thus, the base of that Mosque was laid upon goodness. Therefore, a single unit of salah observed therein is deemed to be worthy of hundreds of units of salah to be observed in other places.

5. The time when prayers are responded to on Fridays

Salah is the mast of the ship of religion; it is like a compass showing the way for a believer. In other words, it is a sound rope to let the believer ascend to their *mi'raj*, like a staircase on whose one end is human beings and on the other end is Divine Grace and Mercy.

The quintessence of salah possessing all these qualities is the Friday prayer, which has been an expression of collective enthusiasm of the community. Therefore, it should be observed with a vigilant heart. The Messenger of God ﷺ stated that, فِيهِ سَاعَةٌ، لاَ يُوَافِقُهَا عَبْدٌ مُسْلِمٌ، وَهُوَ قَائِمٌ

---

18   Bukhari, Fadailu's Salat 6; Hajj 26, Sawm 67; Muslim, Haj 288.

يُصَلِّي، يَسْأَلُ اللهَ تَعَالَى شَيْئًا، إِلَّا أَعْطَاهُ إِيَّاهُ "There is such a time within it (Friday) that if a Muslim servant reaches that time while observing salah, God absolutely grants to him whatever he asked from God."[19] Concerning "the hour of response" *(saat al-ijabah)* on Friday, the Companions, the next generation of the Tabiun, and scholars of the following generations stated different opinions. It is my opinion that this special time segment defined as "the hour of response" keeps shifting within Friday, just as the night of Qadr shifts within Ramadan and Ramadan does within the year. Therefore, experiencing those minutes depends on trying to observe the whole of Friday and turning to God with complete devotion.

Therefore, the Messenger of God ﷺ and his Companions would observe this day consciously and fully, as if they were each making their own *mi'raj* every Friday. We hope from the Divine Mercy that as long as we observe Friday with such a manner and spirit, God Almighty will let us find that hour when prayers are answered and will accept our supplications. More often than not, our Prophet ﷺ and other people loved by God, whose prayers proved acceptable, were able to align their supplications with that hour, earnestly praying to God, and God Almighty accepted their prayers.

Here is an example for the Prophet's answered prayers Anas ibn Malik narrates:

> People were suffering from famine. On a Friday, while the Prophet was giving the sermon, a Bedouin stood up and told him that they lost livestock, and their families were starving. He requested the Messenger of God to pray for them. Upon this, the Messenger of God raised his hands. There was not a single cloud in the sky. By God in whose grasp of power my soul is, even before he lowered his hands, clouds like mountains appeared in the sky. Then before he came down from the *minbar*, rain drops began to drip from his beard. That day, it rained until the next day, and the next day, and the next day; it continued to rain until the next Friday. This, to such a degree that the same Bedouin or someone else stood up and said, "O Messenger of God! Our buildings came down, our animals drowned in the water; please pray to God for us (so that the rain stops)." The Prophet raised

---

19 Bukhari, Jumuah 37, Talaq 24, Daawat 61; Muslim, Jumuah 13–15.

his hands and prayed to God to let it rain (to the region) around them but not directly on them. Another narration relates that he prayed to God to let the rain fall not upon them but to mountains, hills, into valleys, and places where trees grow. Then he made a gesture towards the clouds; whichever cloud he pointed at; it was cleared from there. There remained no cloud in the sky. And we came out and walked under the sun.[20]

The Messenger of God raised his hands and God fulfilled his wish. Accordingly, when we too can align our prayers with that "hour of response," God Almighty will fulfill our prayers.

---

20   Bukhari, Istisqa 7; Muslim, Istisqa 1.

Chapter 8

Nafila Prayers

1. The virtue of *nafila* prayers

a. Making up for the obligatory prayers

The *nafila* prayers (also called as *nafl* or *nawafil* in Arabic) are supererogatory salahs, which are voluntary and optional. As with *Sunnah* prayer, they are not considered obligatory but confer extra benefit on the person performing them. They are decreed as being complementary because they will make up for the missing prayers and for any likely flaws that happened during the obligatory prayers. Therefore, our observance of the five daily prayers together with the *mu'akkad* (strong, confirmed) *Sunnah* ones will cure the various diseases that inflict our spiritual life and servitude. They will serve as an atonement for our sins, fill up the gaps caused by the missed obligatory prayers, and become a means for us to earn extra rewards and blessings and thus to enter Paradise. The *hadith* narrated by Hurays ibn Kabisa points to this effect:

> When I came to Medina, I prayed, "O God, let me have a righteous friend please." Later, I sat near Abu Hurairah. I told him, "I prayed to God for letting me have a righteous friend. Tell me a hadith you heard from the Messenger of God, it may be that God Almighty blesses me with benefiting from it!" Upon this he said, "I heard the Messenger of God say":

> "The first thing for which a person will be brought to account on the Day of Judgment will be his salah. If it is complete, then it will be recorded as complete, and if anything is lacking, He (God) will say (to the angels) 'look and see if you can find any voluntary prayers with which to complete what he neglected of his obligatory prayers.' Then the rest of his deeds will be reckoned in a similar manner."[1]

b. A means to gain closeness to God

Another aspect of voluntary prayers is that they serve as a means to acquire closeness to God. Gaining closeness to God means entering the sphere or fold of His Divine Grace and Mercy. The Messenger of God expresses this truth in a hadith that follows:

> Allah said, "whoever shows enmity to a saintly servant of Mine, I declare war against him. Among the acts that let My servant be closer to Me, there is nothing more lovable to Me than his observing the religious duties I have made obligatory upon him. My servant keeps on coming closer to Me through performing *nawafil* (praying or doing extra deeds besides what is obligatory) till I love him. When I love him, [it is as if] I am his hearing with which he hears, his sight with which he sees, his hand with which he grips and his foot with which he walks [I always make him walk to good]. I grant him when he wishes something from Me. Were he to ask something of Me I would surely give it to him and were he to ask Me for refuge, I would surely grant it to him [and protect him]."[2]

A person becomes closer to God by means of the voluntary prayers and thus gains His love. When God Almighty loves a person, He makes others love that person too. In another hadith narrated by Abu Hurairah, the Prophet noted:

> If God has loved a servant (of His), He calls Gabriel and says, "I love such and such therefore love him." Then he [Gabriel] calls out in

---

1 Tirmidhi, Salat 305; Nasai, Salat 9; Ibn Majah, Iqamah 202.

2 Bukhari, Riqaq 38; Ibn Hanbal, *Musnad* 6/256.

heaven saying: "God loves such and such, therefore love him. And the inhabitants of heaven love him." Then acceptance is established for him on earth. And if God has disliked a servant (of His) He calls Gabriel and says I dislike such and such; so, Gabriel dislikes him and calls out to the inhabitants of heaven "God dislikes such and such therefore dislike him." So, they dislike him, and dislike is established for him on earth.³

Whenever such hadiths are mentioned, questions arise as to the current situation of the Muslims in the world, which seems to not be receiving much favor and support from God. One likely answer could be Muslims' failure to gain God's love. It is our shared wish that God honors, with His closeness, who participates in prayer and attends the mosque, engaging in prostration and worship with genuine sincerity.

However, many mosque-going Muslims appear to be physically there, but they are actually in one distant valley while the Qur'an and Mercy of God are in another. As they have failed to meet the Qur'an, they mostly come to the mosque unaware of its meaning. This unawareness is far from being appropriate for the *masjid* or for the Qur'an. Muslims should go there with a vigilant heart which quivers and causes them to weep in due awe of Him. One should not involve other thoughts and intentions in worship of God and the time allocated for Him. Even a moment utilized sincerely for the sake of God is preferable to a thousand years of mundane life devoid of Divine Light.

c. A means to rise spiritually

Since *nafila* acts of worship serve as atonement for certain sins of a person, they make the person rise spiritually. Therefore, every *nafila* has its own special value. For example, one of the optional prayers is the *duha* (forenoon) salah and concerning it the Prophet ﷺ said:

> Charity is required for every part of your body on a daily basis. Every *SubhanAllah* [Glory be to God] is charity, every *Alhamdulillah* [All praise be to God] is charity, every *La ilaha illallah* [There is no deity but God] is charity, every *Allahu Akbar* [The Great is God] is charity,

---

3   Bukhari, Bedu'l Khalq 6, Adab 41, Tawhid 33; Muslim, Birr 157.

every commanding good is charity, and every forbidding evil is charity, and all this is accomplished through two rakahs one can pray in *Duha* [prayer].[4]

The human body contains hundreds of joints, each crucial for enabling smooth movement. This ability to move freely, whether standing up or sitting down, is indeed a blessing. For someone afflicted with discopathy, a spinal condition, or rheumatism, which causes pain in the legs and lower back, this blessing becomes even more apparent. Consider the difficulty they face in performing basic movements. Just imagine if our finger joints were rigid and immovable like bones. The multitude of joints in our body truly underscores the intricate design and functionality of the human form.

We are adorned with blessings from head to toe; we did not gain any of them as our personal right, or they were not given to us by virtue. Therefore, all these blessings require offering thanks. If we attempt to express gratitude, say, solely for the ability to blink our eyes, we would fall short of offering the full measure of thanks owed for a lifetime's worth of blessings. I still cannot help but shiver when I remember the situation of a friend of mine, whose eye nerves had been paralyzed and who was not able to move his eyelids for hours; even being able to open and close our eyelids is such a great blessing. That man told me he could not close them even to sleep; he could only close them with his hands.

What about the other organs of our body! Our eyes are another blessing, our ears another, and our nose another. In order for us to attest to His Knowledge and Power, God Almighty placed these organs to their precise locations; He formed them of flesh and bones, let them carry out vital functions, and adorned them with infinite wisdom. We are supposed to offer thanks every moment in response to His constant blessings. As Saadi al-Sherazi puts it, we need to offer thanks to Him twice for every breath we take,[5] because our breathing constitutes the basis of our life. When we inhale, we take in oxygen, and this allows our

---

4   Muslim, Salatu'l Musafirun 84.

5   al-Sherazi, *Bustan and Gulistan* p. 309.

lungs to be cleansed; when we exhale, we breathe out carbon-dioxide and rid our body of this toxic gas. If we cannot dispose of the harmful gases in our body, we would die from poisoning. Likewise, we will suffocate and die if we do not breathe in or out. Therefore, God Almighty saves our life twice with every breath. Accordingly, should we not offer thanks to God Almighty, who gives us life when we are virtually on the verge of death with every breath? As such, salah, which God formulated and established in a certain form, provides us with such an opportunity to express our gratitude to Him, be it obligatory (*fard*), necessary (*wajib*) or voluntary-optional (*nafila*).

Likewise in one hadith that teaches the importance of the night (*tahajjud*) prayers the Messenger of God states:

> Every night when the last third of the night is due, our Lord descends to the heaven of the world and says: "Whoever is supplicating to Me, let me respond to him. Whoever asks for something from Me, let Me give it. Whoever asks forgiveness from Me, let Me forgive him."[6]

Namely, Divine Mercy descends and is known in our hearts like "hidden treasure" during the night; that is, Manifestations of His Divine Light are hosted in the sanctuary of our inner heart. He grants us a glimpse into our hearts, even though we may not be deserving of it. Our heart is honored by the effusions of His Grace and Mercy despite of us being undeserving. He accepts the prayers and supplications of those who entreat Him; He grants the will of those who ask from Him; and He forgives those who ask for His forgiveness.

Prophet Muhammad ﷺ was a man of his word for a lifetime. He faithfully upheld his lifelong principles, committing himself to lengthy prayers during the night and earnestly seeking guidance from his Lord. Our mother Aisha tells a relevant memory of him as follows:

> One night I missed Allah's Messenger ﷺ from the bed, and when I sought him, my hand touched the soles of his feet while he was in the state of prostration; they (feet) were raised and he was saying:

---

6   Bukhari, Tahajjud 14, Daawat 14, Tawhid 35; Muslim, Salatu'l Musafirin 168–170.

اَللَّهُمَّ أَعُوذُ بِرِضَاكَ مِنْ سَخَطِكَ، وَبِمُعَافَاتِكَ مِنْ عُقُوبَتِكَ، وَأَعُوذُ بِكَ مِنْكَ لَا أُحْصِي ثَنَاءً عَلَيْكَ أَنْتَ كَمَا أَثْنَيْتَ عَلَى نَفْسِكَ

> "O Allah, I seek refuge in Your pleasure from Your anger, and in Your forgiveness from Your punishment, and I seek refuge in You from You (Your anger). I cannot reckon Your praise. You are as You have lauded Yourself."[7]

Based on what our mother Aisha witnessed and stated, the Messenger of God prolonged himself in prostration, observing devotions to his Lord, and kept long vigils until morning. Accordingly—we may inevitably be engaged with worldly things and friends during the daytime—we had better be a guest to God at night, and thus think only of Him, reflect upon and perceive the manifestations of His Names and Attributes, and become enraptured with the reflections of Divine Mercy and Beauty in our inner and outer worlds, in His matchless Divine art of the creation.

By contemplating the creation, a person will grasp human weakness and powerlessness: how feeble we are in the event when even a tiny insect stings us; how we fear, shiver, suffer and even lack willful control in the face of a flash of lighting far in the sky; how air particles help us breathe easily; how droplets of rain form and flow into life-giving streams; how various fruits are offered to us through the wooden hands of trees. If we reckon the things we are in need of, we will see we are not able to provide even a thousandth of them by our own personal will and power. We entrust all of our needs to God, recognizing the boundlessness of human needs contrasted with the limitations of our own power. While human impotence and poverty are infinite, the foes against whom we seek refuge in God are so many. As human beings bear such great burdens, they are supposed to comply with the Divine decree, وَالَّذِينَ يَبِيتُونَ لِرَبِّهِمْ سُجَّدًا وَقِيَامًا "And (those true servants of the All-Merciful are they) who spend (some of) the night (in worship) prostrating before their Lord and standing..." (al-Furqan 25:64).

After contemplation of all this or more, the person will rise out of bed in the night, in hope and reverence; attached to His Grace and Mer-

---

[7] Muslim, Salat 222; Tirmidhi, Daawat 76, 113; Abu Dawud, Salat 340.

cy, they will stand in obedience and humility before the Almighty Creator; as opposed to their own pettiness, they will confess His Greatness and say: "I cannot take if You don't give. I cannot own if You don't bestow. If You do not give Your blessing, I cannot have a voice or Judgment and prevail in this huge universe... All of these are from You. The entire sovereignty belongs to You. Then gratitude is also due to You, my Lord!"

In those instances, the One Whose door you turned to and knocked will admit you in, will meet you like an important guest, and then treat and honor you accordingly. The Messenger of God already gave glad tidings for such instances:

> When the *Qiyamah* starts, people are resurrected and gathered together, and the following address is heard from the heavens: "Where are those whose sides forsook their beds hoping the mercy of their Lord and fearing His punishment [those who sacrificed their comfort for worshipping God; those who rise for the *fajr* prayer at short nights and those who run to the mosque], where are they?" A group of people not many in number gathers in the Divine presence. God commands and they enter Paradise without being questioned. Then the others are called to account.[8]

Devout believers must come to the Divine presence when others, heedless of God, are together with their worldly lovers. Such believers must say, "My God! I ran after other things all day long but now I have come to knock on Your door; most people searched for and after other things, but here I am after You and striving to reach You!" Thus, they should knock at the door of the Infinitely Merciful during dark nights, totally turning to Him, and petition God with the following supplication the Prophet ﷺ did when he got up and prayed for a portion of the night:

اللَّهُمَّ لَكَ الْحَمْدُ، أَنْتَ قَيِّمُ السَّمَوَاتِ وَالْأَرْضِ وَمَنْ فِيهِنَّ وَلَكَ الْحَمْدُ، لَكَ مُلْكُ السَّمَوَاتِ وَالْأَرْضِ وَمَنْ فِيهِنَّ وَلَكَ الْحَمْدُ، أَنْتَ نُورُ السَّمَوَاتِ وَالْأَرْضِ وَمَنْ فِيهِنَّ وَلَكَ الْحَمْدُ، أَنْتَ مَلِكُ السَّمَوَاتِ وَالْأَرْضِ وَلَكَ الْحَمْدُ، أَنْتَ الْحَقُّ وَوَعْدُكَ الْحَقُّ، وَلِقَاؤُكَ حَقٌّ، وَقَوْلُكَ حَقٌّ، وَالْجَنَّةُ حَقٌّ، وَالنَّارُ حَقٌّ، وَالنَّبِيُّونَ حَقٌّ، وَمُحَمَّدٌ صَلَّى اللهُ عَلَيْهِ وَسَلَّمَ حَقٌّ، وَالسَّاعَةُ حَقٌّ، اللَّهُمَّ لَكَ أَسْلَمْتُ، وَبِكَ آمَنْتُ، وَعَلَيْكَ تَوَكَّلْتُ،

---

8   Bayhaqi, Shuabu'l Iman 3/169.

وَإِلَيْكَ أَنَبْتُ، وَبِكَ خَاصَمْتُ، وَإِلَيْكَ حَاكَمْتُ، فَاغْفِرْ لِي مَا قَدَّمْتُ وَمَا أَخَّرْتُ، وَمَا
أَسْرَرْتُ وَمَا أَعْلَنْتُ، أَنْتَ الْمُقَدِّمُ، وَأَنْتَ الْمُؤَخِّرُ، لَا إِلَهَ إِلَّا أَنْتَ

O Allah! To You is due all praise for You are the Sustainer of the heavens and the earth and all that is within them. All praise is Yours, for You are the King of the heavens and the earth and all that is within them. All praise is Yours, for You are the Light of the heavens and the earth and all that is within them. All praise is Yours, for You are the Truth, Your promise is true, the meeting with You is true and Your word is true. Paradise is true, the Hellfire is true, the Prophets are true, Muhammad (peace and blessings be upon him) is true, and the Last Hour is true.

O Allah! To You I have submitted, in You do I believe, in You have I put my trust, and unto You I turn in repentance. For Your sake I have disputed, and from You I seek judgment, so forgive me for what I have done and for what I will do, for what I have concealed and what I have declared, and for that [in me] that You know best about. You are the Hastener and the Postponer, there is no god but You, and there is no strength or power except in Allah.[9]

The Prophet ﷺ did so, for the secret of his unique honorable status was his getting up in the night, standing obediently before the Almighty, opening up to Him with his repeated pleas to Him, and to Him only; no one else.

2. Two important *nafila* prayers: *tahajjud* and *hajah*

a. Tahajjud

Tahajjud is a voluntary salah, which gives life to our nights. (It is observed any time between the *Isha* till the *Fajr*, when a person wakes up after sleeping for some time).

Night is a time when the doors to the spiritual realms are ajar, when some heavenly vistas open and allow the worshiper to behold the realms

---

9   Bukhari, Tahajjud 1, Daawat 10, *Tawhid* 8, 24, 35; Muslim, Salatu'l Musafirin 199.

of beyond. As Said Nursi relates, giving life to the night with *tahajjud* is a like projector that brightens the intermediary *barzakh* realm of the grave.¹⁰

Night worship to some extent holds the meanings of retreat, detachment, turning to God alone, and devotion. In this time, a person cuts relations with all other things and beings other than God and turns to God alone in the solitude and tranquility of the night. The Qur'an points to this with the verse, وَتَبَتَّلْ إِلَيْهِ تَبْتِيلاً "... and devote yourself to Him whole-heartedly" (al Muzzammil 73:8). Devoting oneself to God is detaching oneself from everything but Him, seeking out knowledge and love of Him only, preoccupying oneself with His manifestations only, and experiencing the spiritual delight ensuing from His Grace. This can only be achieved by making an honest effort to wake up and perform such a devotion, willfully forsaking one's sleep and cozy bed for a while and achieving a heightened state of spiritual awareness.

Prior to his mission, the Messenger of God, too, observed retreats within certain measures and always sought ways to become closer to his Creator. Concerning his own inner realm, his already pure feelings and heart were ever open to God. He kept them oriented towards seeking a favorable response from the Divine, as he kept the eyes of his heart searching the horizon. Besides, having access to the depths of the (intermediary) realm of *barzakh* via dreams and engaging profoundly with spiritual reflections, the Prophet ﷺ did, and would, utilize everything that could facilitate his becoming closer to God and that could serve as a means of being showered with Divine effusions, revelations, purest inspirations, and blessed pleasures (*fayd al-aqdas* and *muqaddas*); thus he presented a different map of reasoning.

In the chapter al-Muzzammil of the Qur'an from which we quoted a verse above, there are two evident and important points: the first is that the Prophet ﷺ was inspired to practice retreat. And secondly, he became spiritually prepared for his future mission.

To elucidate a bit further on this, God Almighty inspired every great figure to find the true guidance, the Prophet ﷺ being the prime figure. While this is true for all of the Prophets, it also holds true for all

---

10   See Nursi, *The Words* (Fifth Word, Fourth Point).

asfiya—the pure scholarly saints of insight. For example, Imam Ghazali dedicated himself to Islamic disciplines and then spent his life in schools and centers of learning. In the end, he fulfilled his life journey with *Ihya' 'Ulum al-Din* (Revival of Religious Disciplines), which became a luminous source of knowledge. Likewise, Imam Rabbani (Ahmad al-Sirhindi) traveled through different parts of India; he read, thought, practiced austerity (*riyadat*), and his heart was opened to the realms beyond; he made serious efforts to provide a sound basis for the tenets of belief and founded a brand-new system of thought.

The life of Bediüzzaman is no different from them. He acknowledges in his books the blessings of having spent the early years of his childhood in Islamic schools, too. Then as a phenomenally gifted student, he went through the texts taught in madrasas. He accumulated knowledge in both religious and scientific disciplines and was cultivated with the spirit of mystical orders. As a result, he found himself in a position of serving faith by way of declaring (*bayan*) it with proof (*burhan*) and wisdom (*irfan*). Namely, by blending pieces of knowledge seemingly detached from one another in his time and pairing them with *tafakkur* (systematic reflection), he synthesized them into pure wisdom. Due to World War 1, he had to join the defense of his nation, but even at the battlefront, he did not give up teaching his students. Subsequently, he found himself entangled in court trials and prolonged detentions, yet he remained steadfast in living according to Divine guidance, unwavering in his commitment.

In his preparatory phase—long before the first Revelation and Prophethood, the Messenger of God ﷺ constantly tried to learn the tongue of the otherworldly realms, had dialogue with them, and sought ways to gain insight into the beyond. He practiced *muraqabah* and *muhasabah* by watching over himself and inspecting his inner state, deepening in inner being and meanings, contemplation, self-control, spiritual discipline, and asceticism during the long preparation, after all of which God commissioned him as His Messenger. Considering the gravity and paramount importance of the mission, simply sleeping through the night would not align with his obligations and responsibilities. Rather, he is called upon to awaken during the night and engage in worship, ensuring that his demeanor and devotions are commensurate with his assigned role and duty. In reference to this the Qur'an states:

يَا أَيُّهَا الْمُزَّمِّلُ ۞ قُمِ اللَّيْلَ إِلَّا قَلِيلًا ۞ نِصْفَهُ أَوِ انْقُصْ مِنْهُ قَلِيلًا ۞ أَوْ زِدْ عَلَيْهِ وَرَتِّلِ الْقُرْآنَ تَرْتِيلًا

> Rise to keep vigil at night, except a little; half of it, or lessen it a little, or add to it (a little), and pray and recite the Qur'an calmly and distinctly (with your mind and heart concentrated on it). (al-Muzzammil 73:1–4)

Why? Because such a mission requires extraordinary performance beyond common human norms and the life of such people must always run in excellence.

For common folk like us, a good advice would be to go to bed after having prayed *Isha* with an intention to rise for *Fajr* prayer. With such an intention, even the breath we take in and out during sleep will count as worship.

However, the Qur'anic verse above tells the Prophet ﷺ to rise to keep long vigil at night, because the mission he undertook requires as such. The word نِصْفَهُ in the original verse refers to "half of the night." The verse continues with a command to lessen it a little or to add to it a little. Night is calculated in this manner: for example, if the sun sets at 6 pm and rises at 6 am, then the entire night is 12 hours. Half of it makes six hours. A little less of it means four or five hours and more means at least 6.5 or 7 hours. The Messenger of God kept up this degree of worship from the first day of revelation until his old age and the end of his life. He would observe worship at night until his feet were swollen. If he were unable to fulfill this worship due to a valid excuse, he would compensate by observing additional worship during the daytime.[11]

As for the command to recite the Qur'an "calmly and distinctly" (*tarteel*), it signifies not only articulating each letter with measured rhythm and no haste but also feeling the Qur'an's essence resonating within one's heart and soul. As Nursi articulates in his *al-Mathnawi al-Nuri*, approaching the reading and comprehension of the Qur'an as if receiving it directly from God, listening to it through Archangel Jibril, or as though taking it from the Messenger of God, embodies the manner in

---

11   See Muslim, Salatu'l Musafirin 141; Tirmidhi, Salat 348; Abu Dawud, Tatawwu 26; Nasai, Qibla 13, Qiyamu'l Layl 2, 64.

which the Messenger himself read the Qur'an, or how it is intended for us to engage with it.[12] In essence, *tarteel* entails reciting the Qur'an not merely through one's own cognitive processes of thought and imagination, but rather internalizing its essence within one's conscience, feeling its overarching message and meaning. Through this, one may transcend into a realm of spiritual elevation and otherworldliness. So much so that while articulating each word of a verse, a reciter should feel the same way a thirsty person feels while sipping water. However, this is a matter of personal level and may not be experienced by everyone.

The way many people read or recite the Qur'an nowadays lacks *tarteel*, thus such recitations do not have any impact in one's conscience. They often fail to evoke new inspirations or bring about personal reformation and revitalization in our feelings, thoughts, or actions. To truly honor the Qur'an, we should read it as if it is being revealed directly to us—of course without ascribing to ourselves the status of being a Prophet.

One hadith and incident narrated by Abdullah ibn Umar shed light on this matter. People used to have dreams and then share them with the Prophet ﷺ. Abdullah was wishing for the doors of otherworldly realms to be opened for him, too, so he could see dreams and seek their interpretation from the Prophet ﷺ. Eventually, he had a dream in which two individuals seized him and brought him near a pit of flames, which he understood to be Hell. As they brought him closer, he feared being thrown in and sought refuge in God. One of the individuals assured him that he would not enter the flames. Upon awakening, Abdullah shared his dream with his elder sister Hafsa, who then asked the Prophet ﷺ to interpret it. Upon hearing it, the Messenger of God ﷺ stated: "Abdullah is such a good person, if only he also observed worship (*tahajjud*) at night!"[13]

Here, it becomes evident how to evade the dread of what comes after death: by engaging in worship during the night. Maintaining vigilance in one's heart relies, to a significant extent, on remaining vigilant during the night. Ibrahim Haqqi, who awakened to this truth early on, garnered the attention of almost everyone with his encyclopedic knowledge and held prominence in many disciplines. He expressed profound insights on this matter:

12   Nursi, *The Letters*, 29th Letter, 6th point.

13   Bukhari, Tahajjud 2, 21, Fadailu Ashabinnabi 19, Tabir 35, 36; Muslim, Fadailus Sahaba 139, 140.

O eyes, why sleep? Come on; wake up at nights,

Behold the shooting comets at nights.

Take a look out on this world and watch the wisdoms;

Find the Artist Who made you, and adore Him at nights.

In the hustle of daylight's tasks, you're heedless of Him, lost in myriad affairs;

Cast off this heedlessness, feel shame before the Beloved in the silent embrace of nights!

Eat little, sleep little, attain to the amazement, and be annihilated [in terms of the carnal soul];

Find eternity with Him, and welcome Him to your heart at nights.

How can it be becoming for a lowly servant to sleep heedlessly,

Let the Rahman [All-Merciful] address to the humble servant with compassion at nights.

Do not sleep through the entire night if you do love the Self-Sustainer (Qayyum);

So that you gain life with the Giver of life (Hayy)—O dear soul—at nights.

True lovers don't sleep through the night; you, do not sleep either,

So that the Beloved appears to the eye of the heart at nights.

The heart is the house of God; clear it away from the rest;

So that the King does visit His palace at nights.

Eat little, sleep little, attain the amazement, become annihilated;

Find eternal life with Him; let your heart welcome Him at nights.

While you mix with the people day and night for the sake of God,

O Haqqi, burn with the fire of your hidden love at nights.

Having insight beyond the mundane world into what lies beyond is closely related with providing guidance to humanity. Actually, this can also be taken from the perspective of the *hadith qudsi* stating that if a servant takes one step to God, God responds to that servant by running.[14]

Before delivering his message of salvation to humanity, the Prophet had already committed himself to drawing closer to God through

---

14   Bukhari, Tawhid 15, 50; Muslim, Tawba 1; Dhikr 1, 20–22.

his own volition. Through His immense Divine Grace and Mercy, God Almighty also drew close to him. However, an important aspect to consider here is that the Messenger of God, driven by his constant desire to guide humanity, sought to achieve this by delving into realms beyond the mundane and gaining insight into the spiritual dimensions. This is why he embarked on a unique night journey each night, constantly seeking closeness to God. Just as in all other matters, he fulfilled what was necessary in this regard. Given that his responsibility exceeded that of everyone else, it was fitting for him to experience a distinct journey each night and to recite the Qur'an with deep feeling and reverence.

The Prophet's load was very heavy; the Qur'an continuously reminded that: إِنَّا سَنُلْقِي عَلَيْكَ قَوْلًا ثَقِيلًا "We will surely charge you with a weighty Word" (al-Muzzammil 73:5). What is meant by weight here, no doubt, is the mission of Prophethood. No matter whether those whom he addressed treasured it or not, no matter whether they did not want to understand the Qur'an, God always told him to convey His Message. Being effective at serving God in imparting the Message has always depended on having a sound relationship with God.

With regard to the wisdom of rising for worship at night, the Qur'an states,

إِنَّ نَاشِئَةَ اللَّيْلِ هِيَ أَشَدُّ وَطْئًا وَأَقْوَمُ قِيلًا ۞ إِنَّ لَكَ فِي النَّهَارِ سَبْحًا طَوِيلًا

> Rising and praying at night impresses [mind and heart] most strongly and (makes) recitation more certain and upright. For by day, you do have extended preoccupations. (al-Muzzammil 73:6, 7)

With their fascinating profundities, nights are an important ground for us to have certainty in faith, to hear what we really mean before God, and to feel deeply what we are practicing. Nights are like a bay of retreat where hearts can open to God and most definitely should be utilized for that purpose. We ordinary people are fully preoccupied or engaged with different pursuits during the day, keep wandering about the mundane world of outward feelings, and live on under their influence. Although this was never the case for the Messenger of God, it can always be the case for ordinary people like us.

Accordingly, the verse above may be interpreted as follows: Through His Messenger, God is indicating to us that during the day, we are preoccupied with various worldly matters, living heedlessly and failing to delve into our inner selves or establish a connection with the spiritual realms. Therefore, the opportunity to establish this connection arises during the night. Nights are crucial for journeying to God as they provide the ideal environment when distractions are minimal. It is during this auspicious time that believers turn to God, earnestly beseeching Him and even shedding tears in awe during prostration. While opening yourself to God during the night, you will know that it is He alone Who knows, sees, hears and responds to you—and you will act accordingly.

The night vigils of the "inheritors of the Prophetic mission"

Prophet Muhammad ﷺ is the last Prophet, and his arrival sealed Prophethood (al-Ahzab 33:40). However, his mission will continue forever. With whom? With the inheritors of the Prophetic cause.

To fulfill the duty entrusted to them by the Prophets, it is essential for their successors to travel on the same bridge that the Prophets themselves walked. This is a fundamental requirement. Thus, it is imperative to observe night vigils and strive to unlock the doors to the realms that lie beyond the material world, ensuring the proper carrying of this weighty responsibility mentioned in the verse (al-Muzzammil 73:5). Those standing on precarious and unstable ground, swayed by negative human impulses like greed, caprice, hatred, and grudge, must first purge themselves of these traits. Only then can they effectively confront the formidable challenges posed by various predicaments. Otherwise, even though they may be on the path to victory, they are destined to become losers.

God has always entrusted this noble cause or service, which was once carried out by the blessed Prophets, to be championed by individuals who achieved to remain vibrant and fresh, rather than those with apathetic and lifeless souls. In other words, not by individuals who merely appear to be there, but not really there. There is a significant distinction between "being" and "merely appearing." God appoints not those who "appear" to be doing something, but not really doing anything other than showing some reaction to events, and taking no positive action to change things, to fulfill this service. He entrusts it to the heroes of spirituality and the heart.

Alternatively, if this cause falls into the hands of individuals lacking genuine sincerity and spirit, as mentioned in the Qur'an, God substitutes them with others who remain vibrant, who have devoted their lives to this cause day and night, and who are dedicated to guiding humanity at every moment. God willing, there are thousands, maybe millions, who are committed to this cause. Here are two relevant verses:

مَنْ يَرْتَدَّ مِنْكُمْ عَنْ دِينِهِ فَسَوْفَ يَأْتِي اللّٰهُ بِقَوْمٍ يُحِبُّهُمْ وَيُحِبُّونَهُ

O you who believe! Whoever of you turns away from his Religion, (know that) in time, God will raise up a people whom He loves, and who love Him…(al-Maidah 5:54)

اِنْ يَشَأْ يُذْهِبْكُمْ وَيَأْتِ بِخَلْقٍ جَدِيدٍ

He can put you away and bring a new generation (in your place). (al-Fatir 35:16)

Therefore, the inheritors of the cause of the Prophet ﷺ must observe night worship like their perfect guide Muhammad ﷺ did. Almost as a spokesperson for the conscience of those who keep vigils during the night, Ibrahim Haqqi says:

> *In the hustle of daylight's tasks,*
>
> *you're heedless of Him, lost in myriad affairs;*
>
> *Cast off this heedlessness,*
>
> *feel shame before the Beloved in the silent embrace of nights!*

Any night without worship is a wasted night. When we neglect one night observing no *tahajjud*, we must recognize it as an error, feeling its weight with embarrassment. With such an error, we must lower our gaze and earnestly seek forgiveness, saying, "I failed to rise for You or keep vigil last night. Yet here I stand, burdened by the weight of a wasted night, seeking Your Mercy." This is how those who claim to be "servants of the Qur'an" must feel in this matter.

When we visited the house where Bediüzzaman Said Nursi once resided in Barla, the elderly landlady spoke about how Nursi would spend the night on a wooden platform on a treetop: "Until morning, the teacher Bediüzzaman would hum like a bee on top of that old tree. We did not witness him sleep until morning."

One last point to consider about night vigil is a fact that has stood the test of time many times: those who illuminate their night with worship also fulfill their day work at the maximum and serve tirelessly for the sake of God. I have encountered numerous individuals who steadfastly follow this path of devotion: they have never faltered in their commitment to prostrate before God and uphold their nightly vigils, nor have they lagged in their service for society.

On the contrary, individuals who demonstrate fluctuations in their nightly worship often show similar inconsistencies in their daytime service. Despite appearing to take the lead, they retreat when confronted with difficulties, lacking endurance even in the face of minor challenges. By contrast, as mentioned above, I've observed that those who maintain night vigils are also dedicated to serving humanity during the day and aspire towards the Heavenly realms with a generous spirit at night.

b. The salah of hajah (need) and its supplication

The *hajah* (need) salah and supplication are among the established acts of worship in the authenticated *Sunnah*. When someone is in need, they perform two *rak'ahs* of salah, recite specific supplications taught by the Prophet, and then beseech God for their needs. There are two different narrations for the supplication of *hajah* to be recited in time of need. Since both of them are from the Messenger of God, we usually read them both, in order not to be devoid of the blessings to be received by means of them. According to a hadith narrated by Tirmidhi concerning times of need or affliction, the individual prays two *rak'ahs*, praises Allah, invokes blessings upon the Prophet ﷺ, and then reads the following supplication:

لَا إِلَهَ إِلَّا اللهُ الحَلِيمُ الكَرِيمُ، سُبْحَانَ اللهِ رَبِّ العَرْشِ العَظِيمِ، الحَمْدُ لِلَّهِ رَبِّ العَالَمِينَ، أَسْأَلُكَ مُوجِبَاتِ رَحْمَتِكَ، وَعَزَائِمَ مَغْفِرَتِكَ، وَالغَنِيمَةَ مِنْ كُلِّ بِرٍّ، وَالسَّلَامَةَ مِنْ كُلِّ إِثْمٍ، لَا تَدَعْ لِي ذَنْبًا إِلَّا غَفَرْتَهُ، وَلَا هَمًّا إِلَّا فَرَّجْتَهُ، وَلَا حَاجَةً هِيَ لَكَ رِضًا إِلَّا قَضَيْتَهَا يَا أَرْحَمَ الرَّاحِمِينَ

> There is no god but Allah, the All-Clement, the All-Generous. Glory be to Allah, the Lord of the Supreme Throne! All praise is due to Allah, Lord of the worlds. I ask You for the means of deserving Your mercy, the means of ascertaining Your forgiveness, protection from every sin, the benefit of every virtue, and freedom from every error.

Leave me not with a sin without Your having forgiven it, a worry without Your having relieved it, or a need which has Your approval, without Your having fulfilled it, O Most Merciful of the merciful![15]

Likewise, according to another hadith related by many sources, a person who was visually impaired came to the Prophet and asked him to pray to God for the restoration of his eyesight. The Messenger of God said if the man wished he would pray for him, or if he wished he could be patient and that would be better for him. When the man asked the Prophet to pray for him, the Prophet instructed him to perform ablution properly, offer two *rak'ah*s of salah, and then supplicate to God in the following manner:

اللَّهُمَّ إِنِي أَسْأَلُكَ وَأَتَوَجَّهُ إِلَيْكَ بِنَبِيِّكَ مُحَمَّدٍ نَبِيِّ الرَّحْمَةِ، يَا مُحَمَّدُ إِنِّي تَوَجَّهْتُ بِكَ إِلَى رَبِّي فِي حَاجَتِي هَذِهِ لِتُقْضَى لِي، اَللَّهُمَّ فَشَفِّعْهُ فِيَّ

O Allah! Verily I ask You, and turn to You, for the sake of Your Prophet Muhammad, the Prophet of mercy. O Muhammad, I turn to my Lord through you, with my need, so that it may be fulfilled for me. O Allah, grant him (the Prophet, peace and blessings be upon him) intercession for me![16]

The matters deemed as needs by individuals can vary greatly, depending on their values, the true significance of their desires, and the scope of their knowledge, understanding, aspirations, ideals or benevolence. However, there are no restrictions on what can be asked for in the prayer of need. For instance, someone may consider a bountiful harvest from their field as their need and pray solely for that. Instead of praying for the general welfare of people, an individual may pray for rain specifically for their own crops. This is distinct from the collective prayer for rain (*istisqa*), which is observed for the common good of the community. Similarly, one may pray specifically for their children to be righteous and virtuous, imploring God to safeguard them from corruption. These desires reflect individuals' personal perspectives and benevolent intentions. We should not underestimate the significance of these prayers.

15 Tirmidhi, Witr 348; Ibn Majah, Iqamah 189.

16 Tirmidhi, Daawat 119; Ibn Majah, Iqamahtu's Salat 189.

Wishing for a good spouse or children, or desiring a bright future for one's child, is considered commendable in accordance with how big or small a person's scope of aspirations and benevolence are. The Companions asked everything from God. "Let one of you ask his Lord for his needs, all of them, even for a shoelace when his breaks."[17] So, it is entirely normal to seek even the smallest of blessings from God. In essence, we turn to God for everything, from the most trivial to the most significant matters.

The scope of the Prophets' benevolence is remarkably larger than anybody else's. For instance, when they raise their hands in supplication to God, they implore, "O God, please soften the hearts of people to belief!" Although the exact wording of that supplication is not from the Prophet, there are similar, yet much deeper expressions in his supplications. Everybody petitions to God about a matter according to the level of their aspirations, ideals or benevolence. Some people dedicate their entire lives to the dissemination and supremacy of His love and Message all over. Until then, each day is like a day of mourning for them. They eat to sustain themselves and maintain familial relationships, yet their gaze is always fixed on His Grace and Mercy.

To elaborate further, some people observe the prayer of need to attain a petty need in this world. Some people observe it for the matters that concern the entire humanity. Some petition God for faith to spread on earth. Some ask God to soften the hearts of unbelievers and sinners and to ease down the hearts of the most sinful and evil so that they become receptive towards His Message. In short, people who have a certain consciousness about God and who know the Prophet ﷺ and the Qur'an at least to a certain degree should not be after simple and petty things. They should always cherish lofty ideals. In a position where one can ask for gold and gems, it will be mistaken to ask for tinware and trinkets.

It is possible to observe prayer of need to ask for having a sound faith and saving heart from misguidance; because these are essential to cherish lofty ideals. If we do not have sound faith or if our heart is inconsistent, unstable, and faltering, how can we cherish loftier aspirations for humanity? One needs to have a very broad horizon of Divine knowledge

---

17   Tirmidhi 3973.

(*marifa*), a serious degree of love and eagerness for God, along with a deep sense of awe for God. These should be what a person should ask for as he or she observes the prayer of need.

How to observe the prayer of need (hajah)

The prayer of need is described in hadith as a salah of 2 or 4 *rak'ahs*.[18] There is no explicit specification about which surahs are to be recited in this salah. Some scholars stated that surahs recited in *salatu'l hifdh*[19] such as as-Sajdah, al-Dahr (aka al-Insan), and Ya-Sin, can be recited; however, this is not substantiated with strong reports. One may rather recite verses that remind them of the immense mercy of God Almighty, such as the following:

الَّذِينَ يَحْمِلُونَ الْعَرْشَ وَمَنْ حَوْلَهُ يُسَبِّحُونَ بِحَمْدِ رَبِّهِمْ وَيُؤْمِنُونَ بِهِ وَيَسْتَغْفِرُونَ لِلَّذِينَ آمَنُوا رَبَّنَا وَسِعْتَ كُلَّ شَيْءٍ رَحْمَةً وَعِلْماً فَاغْفِرْ لِلَّذِينَ تَابُوا وَاتَّبَعُوا سَبِيلَكَ وَقِهِمْ عَذَابَ الْجَحِيمِ

> Those (angels) who bear the Supreme Throne (of God), and the others around it glorify their Lord with His praise; and they believe in Him [as the Unique Deity, Lord, and Sovereign of all creation], and ask for His forgiveness for those (among His creation) who believe, saying: "Our Lord! You embrace all things with mercy and knowledge [having perfect knowledge of every creature's need, and answering that need with mercy], so forgive those who repent (of their sins) and follow Your way, and protect them from the punishment of the Blazing Flame!" (al-Mu'min 40:7)

لَقَدْ جَاءَكُمْ رَسُولٌ مِنْ أَنْفُسِكُمْ عَزِيزٌ عَلَيْهِ مَا عَنِتُّمْ حَرِيصٌ عَلَيْكُمْ بِالْمُؤْمِنِينَ رَءُوفٌ رَحِيمٌ ۞ فَإِنْ تَوَلَّوْا فَقُلْ حَسْبِيَ اللهُ لَا إِلَهَ إِلَّا هُوَ عَلَيْهِ تَوَكَّلْتُ وَهُوَ رَبُّ الْعَرْشِ الْعَظِيمِ

> There has come to you (O people) a Messenger from among yourselves; extremely grievous to him is your suffering, full of concern for you is he, and for the believers full of pity and compassion. Still,

---

18   Ibn Hanbal, *Musnad* 6/450.

19   Prayer and its supplications done to memorize the Qur'an and sharpen the memory.

if they turn away from you (O Messenger), say: "God is sufficient for me; there is no deity but He. In Him have I put my trust, and He is the Lord of the Supreme Throne [as the absolute Ruler and Sustainer of the universe and all creation, Who maintains and protects it]." (at-Tawbah 9:128-129)

لَا يُكَلِّفُ اللهُ نَفْسًا إِلَّا وُسْعَهَا لَهَا مَا كَسَبَتْ وَعَلَيْهَا مَا اكْتَسَبَتْ رَبَّنَا لَا تُؤَاخِذْنَا إِنْ نَسِينَا أَوْ أَخْطَأْنَا رَبَّنَا وَلَا تَحْمِلْ عَلَيْنَا إِصْرًا كَمَا حَمَلْتَهُ عَلَى الَّذِينَ مِنْ قَبْلِنَا رَبَّنَا وَلَا تُحَمِّلْنَا مَا لَا طَاقَةَ لَنَا بِهِ وَاعْفُ عَنَّا وَاغْفِرْ لَنَا وَارْحَمْنَا أَنْتَ مَوْلٰينَا فَانْصُرْنَا عَلَى الْقَوْمِ الْكَافِرِينَ

God burdens no soul except within its capacity: in its favor is whatever (good) it earns, and against it whatever (evil) it merits. [So, pray thus to your Lord:] "Our Lord, take us not to task if we forget or make mistakes. Our Lord, lay not on us a burden such as You laid on those gone before us. Our Lord, impose not on us what we do not have the power to bear. And overlook our faults, and forgive us, and have mercy upon us. You are our Guardian and Owner [to Whom We entrust our affairs and on Whom we rely], so help us and grant us victory against the disbelieving people!" (al-Baqarah 2:286)

While these verses remind us of the immense mercy of God Almighty, they also help a person's heart soften and maintain concentration. After observing the salah, one needs to glorify God Almighty as follows:

اَللهُ أَكْبَرُ كَبِيرًا، وَالْحَمْدُ لِلّهِ كَثِيرًا، وَسُبْحَانَ اللهِ بُكْرَةً وَأَصِيلًا ۝ لَا إِلَهَ إِلَّا اللهُ وَحْدَهُ، نَصَرَ عَبْدَهُ، أَعَزَّ جُنْدَهُ، وَهَزَمَ الْأَحْزَابَ وَحْدَهُ، لَا شَرِيكَ لَهُ ۝ اَللّٰهُمَّ لَا مَانِعَ لِمَا أَعْطَيْتَ، وَلَا مُعْطِيَ لِمَا مَنَعْتَ، وَلَا مُبَدِّلَ لِمَا حَكَمْتَ، وَلَا يَنْفَعُ ذَا الْجَدِّ مِنْكَ الْجَدُّ

Allah is great. Every kind of praise is due for the Most Exalted and He is the sole one deserving of being remembered with glorification day and night. There is no deity except for God, the One. He is the One Who helped His servant, made His army victorious and routed the enemies on His own. He has no partners. My God! Nobody can hold back what You give, and nobody can give what You hold back. There is nobody to revert what You willed to occur; nobody can change Your decree. Richness, glory, esteem, and power have no benefit to their owners against You.

One should say these as a tribute to the greatness of God Almighty. However, the Prophet ﷺ left this unspecified. So, you can, for instance, even recite just the first three verses of al-Fatiha, if you wish. One should begin by declaring His greatness, praising Him, and glorifying Him in the most fitting manner. With reverence for God, one begins by invoking a comprehensive *salawat* on the Messenger of God ﷺ. Additional names may also be included in the *salawat*. Following this, the names of the Rightly Guided Caliphs are mentioned separately, followed by the names of the *Ahl al-Bayt* (Prophet's household). Then, the names of the Prophets are recited one by one, followed by the names of the angels closest to God. Subsequently, one may mention the names of the greatest saintly figures and include them in the supplication.

After reciting this comprehensive *salawat* and peace greetings, one may pray, "بِعَدَدِ ذَرَّاتِ الْكَائِنَاتِ وَمُرَكَّبَاتِهَا "May this prayer fill the heavens and earth," or مِلْءَ السَّمَوَاتِ وَمِلْءَ الْأَرْضِ وَمِلْءَ مَا بَيْنَهُمَا وَمِلْءَ مَا شِئْتَ مِنْ شَيْءٍ بَعْدُ "encompassing the atoms of existence and all that lies between them, and extending to whatever You will, O God!" However, all these expressions convey finite numbers. To express the infinite with infinity, one may say, بِعَدَدِ عِلْمِكَ وَبِعَدَدِ مَعْلُومَاتِكَ "O God, may salat and salam be upon them to the extent of Your knowledge."

After having done these, one prays for believers in general saying, رَبَّنَا اغْفِرْ لِي وَلِوَالِدَيَّ وَلِلْمُؤْمِنِينَ يَوْمَ يَقُومُ الْحِسَابُ "O our Lord; forgive me, my parents, and all believers on the Day of Reckoning" (Ibrahim 14:41). Another prayer that saintly servants of God like *abdals*[20] prefer to recite day and night can be added: اَللَّهُمَّ ارْحَمْ أُمَّةَ مُحَمَّدٍ، اَللَّهُمَّ اغْفِرْ لِأُمَّةِ مُحَمَّدٍ "O God, have mercy on the *ummah* of Muhammad. O God, please forgive the ummah of Muhammad!" These are the things to be done before beginning supplication to God. After having done these, the supplication of need is recited:

---

20   The word "*abdal*" is the plural form of "*badil*." It is a term used for defining pure and dervish spirited people from among the saintly servants of God; they are assigned to attend to people and their needs, serving in the name of God and serve as apparent causes to God's works, and who are in a way like applauders of the operation of Divine power (Gülen, "Wali and Awliyaullah" (Saintly Servants of God), *Emerald Hills of the Heart Vol. 3*), p. 75.

Nafila Prayers

لَا إِلَهَ إِلَّا اللهُ الْحَلِيمُ الْكَرِيمُ ۞ سُبْحَانَ اللهِ رَبِّ الْعَرْشِ الْعَظِيمِ ۞ الْحَمْدُ لِلهِ رَبِّ الْعَالَمِينَ ۞ أَسْأَلُكَ مُوجِبَاتِ رَحْمَتِكَ وَعَزَائِمَ مَغْفِرَتِكَ وَالْعِصْمَةَ مِنْ كُلِّ ذَنْبٍ وَالْغَنِيمَةَ مِنْ كُلِّ بِرٍّ وَالسَّلَامَةَ مِنْ كُلِّ اثْمٍ، لَا تَدَعْ لَنَا ذَنْبًا إِلَّا غَفَرْتَهُ وَلَا هَمًّا إِلَّا فَرَّجْتَهُ وَلَا حَاجَةً هِيَ لَكَ رِضًى إِلَّا قَضَيْتَهَا يَا أَرْحَمَ الرَّاحِمِينَ ۞ اَللَّهُمَّ أَنْتَ تَحْكُمُ بَيْنَ عِبَادِكَ فِيمَا كَانُوا فِيهِ يَخْتَلِفُونَ ۞ لَا إِلَهَ إِلَّا اللهُ الْعَلِيُّ الْعَظِيمُ ۞ لَا إِلَهَ إِلَّا اللهُ الْحَلِيمُ الْكَرِيمُ ۞ سُبْحَانَ رَبِّ السَّمَوَاتِ السَّبْعِ وَرَبِّ الْعَرْشِ الْعَظِيمِ ۞ اَلْحَمْدُ لله رَبِّ الْعَالَمِينَ ۞ اَللَّهُمَّ مُفَرِّجَ الْهَمِّ كَاشِفَ الْغَمِّ مُجِيبَ دَعْوَةِ الْمُضْطَرِّينَ إِذَا دَعَوْكَ، رَحْمَانَ الدُّنْيَا وَالْآخِرَةِ وَرَحِيمَهُمَا، فَارْحَمْنَا فِي حَاجَتِنَا هَذِهِ بِقَضَائِهَا وَنَجَاحِهَا رَحْمَةً تُغْنِينَا بِهَا عَنْ رَحْمَةِ مَنْ سِوَاكَ

There is no god but Allah, the All-Clement, the All-Generous. Glory be to Allah, the Lord of the Supreme Throne! All praise is due to Allah, Lord of the worlds. I ask You for the means of deserving Your mercy, the means of ascertaining Your forgiveness, protection from every sin, the benefit of every virtue, and freedom from every error. Leave me not with a sin without Your having forgiven it, a worry without Your having relieved it, or a need which has Your approval, without Your having fulfilled it, O Most Merciful of the merciful!

O Allah! You are the One who judges Your servants concerning their disagreements. There is no god but Allah, the Exalted, the All-Mighty. There is no god but Allah, the All-Clement, the All-Generous. Glory be to the Lord of the seven heavens and the Lord of the Supreme Throne. Praise be to Allah, the Lord of the worlds. O Allah, Alleviator of distress, Reliever of worry, and the One who responds to the prayer of those in dire need if they call on You! O, All-Merciful in this life and the Hereafter, and Beneficent in both! Have mercy on me in this need of mine, by fulfilling it, with a successful outcome, such that I dispense with the mercy of all other than You.

After that, the person should say whatever they wish from God. Those with great *himmah* of benevolence and aspirations can say the following as a need:

اللَّهُمَّ أَعْلِ كَلِمَةَ اللهِ وَكَلِمَةَ الْحَقِّ وَدِينَ الْإِسْلَامِ فِي كُلِّ أَنْحَاءِ الْعَالَمِ ۞ وَاشْرَحْ صُدُورَنَا وَصُدُورَ عِبَادِكَ فِي كُلِّ أَنْحَاءِ الْعَالَمِ إِلَى الْإِيمَانِ وَالْإِسْلَامِ وَالْإِحْسَانِ وَالْقُرْآنِ وَإِلَى خِدْمَتِنَا

O God, let Your exalted name, the truth, and religion of Islam be exalted everywhere. Open our hearts and the hearts of all Your other servants to belief (*iman*), to Islam, to the excellence of God consciousness (*ihsan*), to the Qur'an and to the services for it!

One hadith states that when God Almighty favors a servant, acceptance is decreed for them both on earth and in the heavens.[21] In light of this, one can pray as follows: وَضَعْ لَنَا الْوُدَّ بَيْنَ عِبَادِكَ فِي السَّمَاءِ وَالْأَرْضِ "O God, please instill love for us in the hearts of Your servants in both the heavens and the earth!" With these words, we ask to be welcomed in society, the opening of hearts towards us, and the ability to serve with sincerity for the sake of faith.

One thing believers should consider while offering their supplications is to include others in their prayers, especially the fellow followers of the Prophet, peace be upon him. For, such an inclusion resonates with Divine Mercy. In doing so, God Almighty may regard you as "My servant who cares about my other servants," which holds significant importance.

---

21   Bukhari, Badu'l Khalq 6; Adab 41; Tawhid 33; Muslim, Birr 157.

Chapter 9

Some Supplications to Be Offered During Salah

Here are some supplications reported from the Messenger of God ﷺ to be offered at different stages of the salah:

1. Supplications during *ruku'* (bowing)

سُبْحَانَ رَبِّيَ الْعَظِيمِ

Glory be to my Lord, the Most High.[1]

سُبْحَانَ ذِى الْجَبَرُوتِ وَالْمَلَكُوتِ وَالْكِبْرِيَاءِ وَالْعَظَمَةِ

Glory be to the Owner of the world of Names and Attributes (*jabarut*, or the intermediary world) and heavenly kingdom (*malakut*; the realm of spirits, the veiled reality beyond), Possessor of Greatness and Absolute Might.[2]

سُبْحَانَكَ اللَّهُمَّ رَبَّنَا وَبِحَمْدِكَ اللَّهُمَّ اغْفِرْ لِي

Glory be to You O Allah, our Lord! And to You is all praise. O Allah, forgive me![3]

---

1   Muslim, Salatu'l musafirin, 203; Tirmidhi, Salat 194; Nasai, Iftitah 77, 78, Tatbik 9, 26, 77, 86; Ibn Majah, Iqamah 20, 179.

2   Abu Dawud, Salat 147, 147; Nasai, Tatbik 12.

3   Bukhari, Adhan 123, 139, Maghazi 51, Tafsiru sura (110) 1; Muslim, Salat 217.

سُبُّوحٌ قُدُّوسٌ رَبُّ الْمَلاَئِكَةِ وَالرُّوحِ

Transcendent and Holy is You, the Lord of the angels and the Spirit.[4]

اللَّهُمَّ لَكَ رَكَعْتُ وَبِكَ آمَنْتُ وَلَكَ أَسْلَمْتُ أَنْتَ رَبِّي خَشَعَ سَمْعِي وَبَصَرِي وَمُخِّي وَعَظْمِي وَعَصَبِي وَمَااسْتَقَلَّتْ بِهِ قَدَمِي لِلَّهِ رَبِّ الْعَالَمِينَ

O Allah! To You I bow, in You I believe, and to You I submit. Humbled before You are my hearing, my sight, my brain, my bones, my nerves and what is borne on my two feet for the sake of Allah, the Lord of the worlds.[5]

2. While rising from *ruku'*

رَبَّنَا وَلَكَ الْحَمْدُ

Our Lord all praise is due for You.[6]

حَمْدًا كَثِيرًا طَيِّبًا مُبَارَكًا فِيهِ رَبَّنَا وَلَكَ الْحَمْدُ

O Allah, our Lord! To You belongs all praise, praise manifold, pure and blessed.[7]

رَبَّنَا لَكَ الْحَمْدُ مِلْءَ السَّمَوَاتِ وَالْأَرْضِ، وَمِلْءَ مَا بَيْنَهُمَا وَمِلْءَ مَا شِئْتَ مِنْ شَيْءٍ بَعْدُ

O Allah! To You belongs praise that fills the heavens, the earth, that which is between them, and fills whatever You wish beyond that.[8]

---

4   Muslim, Salat 223; Abu Dawud, Salat 147; Nasai, Tatbik 11.

5   Nasash, Iftitah 104; Ibn Hanbal, *al-Musnad* 2/268.

6   Bukhari, Adhan 51; Muslim, Salat 28.

7   Bukhari, Adhan 126; Muslim, Masajid, 149.

8   Muslim, Salatu'l-musafirin 201; Tirmidhi, Daavat 32; Abu Dawud, Salat 118.

أَهْلَ الثَّنَاءِ وَالْمَجْدِ أَحَقُّ مَا قَالَ الْعَبْدُ وَكُلُّنَا لَكَ عَبْدٌ لَا مَانِعَ لِمَا أَعْطَيْتَ وَلَا مُعْطِيَ لِمَا مَنَعْتَ وَلَا يَنْفَعُ ذَا الْجَدِّ مِنْكَ الْجَدُّ

> O Owner of glory and praise! The most truthful words spoken by a servant—and all of us are Your servants—are: "No one can deny the one to whom You have given, no one can give to the one whom You have denied, and the possessor of fortune is not availed against You by his fortune."[9]

اللَّهُمَّ طَهِّرْنِي بِالثَّلْجِ وَالْبَرَدِ وَالْمَاءِ الْبَارِدِ اللَّهُمَّ طَهِّرْنِي مِنَ الذُّنُوبِ وَالْخَطَايَا كَمَا يُنَقَّى الثَّوْبُ الْأَبْيَضُ مِنَ الدَّنَسِ

> O Allah! Purify me with snow, hail, and cold water! O Allah! Purify me from sin and error as the white garment is cleansed from filth.[10]

3. During *sajdah* (prostration)

سُبْحَانَ رَبِّيَ الْأَعْلَى

> Glory be to my Lord, Most High![11]

سُبْحَانَكَ اللَّهُمَّ رَبَّنَا وَبِحَمْدِكَ اللَّهُمَّ اغْفِرْ لِي

> Glory be to You, O Allah, our Lord, and to You be all praise! O Allah, forgive me![12]

---

9   Muslim, Salat 205; Abu Dawud, Tahara, 143.

10   Bukhari, Daavat 44; Muslim, Masajid 129.

11   Muslim, Salatu'l-musafirin 203; Tirmidhi, Salat 79; Abu Dawud, Salat 150, 153.

12   Bukhari, Adhan 123, 139, Tafsiru sura (1) 2; Muslim, Salat 217.

اللَّهُمَّ إِنِّى أَعُوذُ بِرِضَاكَ مِنْ سَخَطِكَ، وَبِمُعَافَاتِكَ مِنْ عُقُوبَتِكَ، وَأَعُوذُ بِكَ مِنْكَ، لاَ أُحْصِى ثَنَاءً عَلَيْكَ أَنْتَ كَمَا أَثْنَيْتَ عَلَى نَفْسِكَ

O Allah, truly I seek refuge in Your good pleasure from Your anger, in Your exemption from Your punishment, and I seek refuge in You from You. I admit that I am unable to praise You as You have praised Yourself.[13]

اللَّهُمَّ لَكَ سَجَدْتُ، وَبِكَ آمَنْتُ، وَلَكَ أَسْلَمْتُ، سَجَدَ وَجْهِىَ لِلَّذِى خَلَقَهُ فَصَوَّرَهُ، فَشَقَّ سَمْعَهُ وَبَصَرَهُ، تَبَارَكَ اللهُ أَحْسَنُ الْخَالِقِينَ، خَشَعَ سَمْعِي وَبَصَرِي وَدَمِي وَلَحْمِي وَعَظْمِي وَعَصَبِي وَمَا اسْتَقَلَّتْ بِهِ قَدَمَيَّ لِلهِ رَبِّ الْعَالَمِينَ

O Allah! To You I prostrate myself, in You I believe, and in You have I placed my trust. My face is prostrated to the One Who created and formed it, and gave it openings for hearing and sight; blessed is Allah the Best of creators! Humbled before You are my hearing, my sight, my blood, my flesh, my bones, my nerves and what is borne on my two feet for the sake of Allah, the Lord of the worlds.[14]

سُبُّوحٌ قُدُّوسٌ رَبُّ الْمَلاَئِكَةِ وَالرُّوحِ

Transcendent and Holy is the Lord of the angels and the Spirit.[15]

اللَّهُمَّ اغْفِرْ لِي ذَنْبِي كُلَّهُ، دِقَّهُ، وَجِلَّهُ، أَوَّلَهُ وَآخِرَهُ، سِرَّهُ وَعَلاَنِيَتَهُ، سُبْحَانَ ذِى الْجَبَرُوتِ وَالْمَلَكُوتِ وَالْكِبْرِيَاءِ وَالْعَظَمَةِ

O Allah! Forgive me for all my sins, the greater and the minor, the

---

13 Muslim, Salat 222; Tirmidhi, Daavat 76, 113; Abu Dawud, Salat 340.

14 Muslim, Salat 216; Abu Dawud, Salat 147.

15 Muslim, Salat 223; Abu Dawud, Salat 147; Nasai, Tatbik 11.

first and the last, and the openly known and those kept secret! Glory be to the Owner of the world of Names and Attributes (*jabarut*) and heavenly kingdom (*malakut*), Possessor of Greatness and Absolute Might.[16]

4. When sitting between two prostrations

اللَّهُمَّ اغْفِرْ لِي وَارْحَمْنِي وَعَافِنِي وَاجْبُرْنِي وَاهْدِنِي وَارْزُقْنِي، وَارْفَعْنِي

O Allah! Forgive me, have mercy on me, grant me health, guide me, provide for me, restore me, and raise me up![17]

اللَّهُمَّ هَبْ لِي قَلْبًا تَقِيًّا نَقِيًّا مِنَ الشِّرِّ بَرِيًّا لَا كَافِرًا وَلَا شَقِيًّا

O Lord! Grant me a pious heart, clean from association (*shirk*), and righteous, not disbelieving nor wretched![18]

رَبِّ اغْفِرْ وَارْحَمْ وَتَجَاوَزْ عَمَّا تَعْلَمُ، إِنَّكَ أَنْتَ الْأَعَزُّ الْأَكْرَمُ

O Lord, forgive and show mercy, and overlook what You know best about, for truly You are the Honorable with irresistible Might, the All-Generous.[19]

5. During sitting (*tashahhud*)

اللَّهُمَّ إِنِّي ظَلَمْتُ نَفْسِي ظُلْمًا كَثِيرًا، وَلاَ يَغْفِرُ الذُّنُوبَ إِلاَّ أَنْتَ، فَاغْفِرْ لِي مَغْفِرَةً مِنْ عِنْدِكَ، وَارْحَمْنِي إِنَّكَ أَنْتَ الْغَفُورُ الرَّحِيمُ

---

16   Muslim, Salatu'l-musafirin 201; Abu Dawud, Salat 118; Tirmidhi, Daawat 32.

17   Tirmidhi, Salat 211; Ibn Majah, iqamah 23.

18   al-Bayhaqi, *Fadailu'l-awqat*, p. 27.

19   Ibn Abi Shayba, *al-Musannaf* 3/420.

O Allah! Truly I have greatly wronged my soul, and no one forgives sins except You, so forgive me with Your forgiveness, and have mercy on me, for You are the All-Forgiving, the All-Compassionate.[20]

اَللَّهُمَّ اغْفِرْ لِي مَا قَدَّمْتُ وَمَا أَخَّرْتُ، وَمَا أَسْرَرْتُ وَمَا أَعْلَنْتُ، وَمَا أَسْرَفْتُ وَمَا أَنْتَ أَعْلَمُ بِهِ مِنِّي، أَنْتَ الْمُقَدِّمُ وَأَنْتَ الْمُؤَخِّرُ لاَ إِلَهَ إِلاَّ أَنْتَ

O Allah! Forgive me for what I have done and for what I will do, for what I have concealed, and what I have declared, and what I committed excess in, and for what You know best about from me. You are the Hastener, You are the Postponer, and there is no god but You.[21]

اَللَّهُمَّ إِنِّي أَعُوذُ بِكَ مِنْ عَذَابِ الْقَبْرِ، وَأَعُوذُ بِكَ مِنْ فِتْنَةِ الْمَسِيحِ الدَّجَّالِ، وَأَعُوذُ بِكَ مِنْ فِتْنَةِ الْمَحْيَا وَالْمَمَاتِ

O Allah! I take refuge in You from the punishment of the grave. I take refuge in You from the trial of the Antichrist (Al Dajjal), and I take refuge in You from the trial of life and death.[22]

اللَّهُمَّ إِنِّي أَعُوذُ بِكَ مِنْ عَذَابِ جَهَنَّمَ وَأَعُوذُ بِكَ مِنْ عَذَابِ الْقَبْرِ، وَأَعُوذُ بِكَ مِنْ فِتْنَةِ الْمَسِيحِ الدَّجَّالِ، وَأَعُوذُ بِكَ مِنْ فِتْنَةِ الْمَحْيَا، وَفِتْنَةِ الْمَمَاتِ، اللَّهُمَّ إِنِّي أَعُوذُ بِكَ مِنَ الْمَأْثَمِ وَالْمَغْرَمِ

O Allah! Truly I take refuge in You from the punishment of Hell, from the punishment of the grave, from the trial of life and death, and from the trial of the Antichrist.[23]

20   Bukhari, Adhan 149; Tawhid 9; Daavat 16; Muslim, Dhikr 47, 48.

21   Muslim, Salatu'l-musafirin 201, Dhikr 70; Tirmidhi, Daawat 32; Abu Dawud, Salat 121, Fadail 358.

22   Bukhari, Janaiz 86; Muslim, Masajid 129.

23   Bukhari, Adhan 149; Muslim, Masajid 129, 134.

6. Verses of the Qur'an which can be recited as supplication at any phase of salah:

Supplication of Prophet Adam:

رَبَّنَا ظَلَمْنَا أَنْفُسَنَا وَإِنْ لَمْ تَغْفِرْ لَنَا وَتَرْحَمْنَا لَنَكُونَنَّ مِنَ الْخَاسِرِينَ

"Our Lord! We have wronged ourselves, and if You do not forgive us and do not have mercy on us, we will surely be among those who have lost!" (al-A'raf 7:23)

Supplication of Prophet Yunus:

لَا إِلَهَ إِلَّا أَنْتَ سُبْحَانَكَ إِنِّي كُنْتُ مِنَ الظَّالِمِينَ

"There is no deity but You, All-Glorified are You (in that You are absolutely above having any defect). Surely I have been one of the wrongdoers (who have wronged themselves)." (al-Anbiya 21:87).

Supplication of Prophet Ayyub:

أَنِّي مَسَّنِيَ الضُّرُّ وَأَنْتَ أَرْحَمُ الرَّاحِمِينَ

"Truly, affliction has visited me (so that I can no longer worship You as I must); and You are the Most Merciful of the merciful." (al-Anbiya 21:83)

Supplication of Prophet Moses:

رَبِّ إِنِّي ظَلَمْتُ نَفْسِي فَاغْفِرْ لِي

"My Lord! Indeed I have wronged myself, so forgive me." (al-Qasas 28:16)

Supplication of dedicated servants striving on the way of God:

رَبَّنَا اغْفِرْ لَنَا ذُنُوبَنَا وَإِسْرَافَنَا فِي أَمْرِنَا وَثَبِّتْ أَقْدَامَنَا وَانْصُرْنَا عَلَى الْقَوْمِ الْكَافِرِينَ

"Our Lord! Forgive us our sins and any wasteful act we may have done in our duty, and set our feet firm, and help us to victory over the disbelieving people!" (Al Imran 3:147)

Supplication of the God-revering (*muttaqi*) ones:

رَبَّنَا إِنَّنَا آمَنَّا فَاغْفِرْ لَنَا ذُنُوبَنَا وَقِنَا عَذَابَ النَّارِ

"Our Lord, we do indeed believe, so forgive us our sins and guard us against the punishment of the Fire." (Al Imran 3:16)

Supplication of Ashab al-Kahf:

رَبَّنَا آتِنَا مِنْ لَدُنْكَ رَحْمَةً وَهَيِّئْ لَنَا مِنْ أَمْرِنَا رَشَدًا

"Our Lord! Grant us mercy from Your Presence and arrange for us in our affair what is right and good!" (al-Kahf 18:10)

For rectitude of the heart:

رَبَّنَا لَا تُزِغْ قُلُوبَنَا بَعْدَ إِذْ هَدَيْتَنَا وَهَبْ لَنَا مِنْ لَدُنْكَ رَحْمَةً إِنَّكَ أَنْتَ الْوَهَّابُ

"'Our Lord, do not let our hearts swerve after You have guided us, and bestow upon us mercy from Your Presence. Surely You are the All-Bestowing." (Al Imran 3:8)

7. Some prayers from the Prophet ﷺ

يَا حَيُّ يَا قَيُّومُ، بِرَحْمَتِكَ أَسْتَغِيثُ، أَصْلِحْ لِي شَأْنِي كُلَّهُ وَلاَ تَكِلْنِي إِلَى نَفْسِي طَرْفَةَ عَيْنٍ

"Ya Hayyu Ya Qayyum (O All-Living, Self-Subsistent [Lord]!)! For the sake of Your Mercy I beg for help. Rectify for all my states and leave me not to myself even for the blinking of an eye!"[24]

اللَّهُمَّ حَبِّبْ إِلَيْنَا الْإِيمَانَ وَزَيِّنْهُ فِي قُلُوبِنَا، وَكَرِّهْ إِلَيْنَا الْكُفْرَ وَالْفُسُوقَ وَالْعِصْيَانَ وَاجْعَلْنَا مِنَ الرَّاشِدِينَ

"O Allah! Make faith beloved to us, endearing it to our hearts, and make unbelief, impiety and disobedience hateful to us, and make us among the rightly guided."[25]

اللَّهُمَّ أَحْسِنْ عَاقِبَتَنَا فِي الْأُمُورِ كُلِّهَا، وَأَجِرْنَا مِنْ خِزْيِ الدُّنْيَا وَعَذَابِ الْآخِرَةِ

"O Allah! Grant us a good outcome in all of our affairs, and save us from disgrace in this life and punishment in the Hereafter!"[26]

24 An-Nasai, *as-Sunanu'l kubra* 6/147; al-Bazzar, *al-Musnad* 13/49.

25 Ibn Hanbal, *al-Musnad* 3/424; an-Nasai, *as-Sunanu'l kubra*, 6/156.

26 Ibn Hanbal, *al-Musnad* 4/181; Tabarani, *al-Mu'jamu'l-kabir* 2/33.

لَا إِلَهَ إِلَّا أَنْتَ، سُبْحَانَكَ اللَّهُمَّ أَسْتَغْفِرُكَ لِذَنْبِي وَأَسْأَلُكَ رَحْمَتَكَ اَللَّهُمَّ زِدْنِي عِلْماً وَلاَ تُزِغْ قَلْبِي بَعْدَ إِذْ هَدَيْتَنِي وَهَبْ لِي مِنْ لَدُنْكَ رَحْمَةً إِنَّكَ أَنْتَ الْوَهَّابُ

"Glorified are You, O Allah! I seek Your forgiveness for my sins, and I ask You for Your mercy. O Allah! Increase my knowledge, and let not my heart stray after You have guided me, and grant me Your mercy, for truly You are the One Who bestows."[27]

---

27   Abu Dawud, Adab 99; Nasai, *Sunanu'l kubra*, 6/216; Hakim, *Al-Mustadrak*, 1/724

Chapter 10

Reflections on Salah

Salah is the *mi'raj* (ascension) of a believer; it is their light—the steed they ride on the way to ascension; the vehicle for believers journeying to God. For those journeying toward closeness to and reunion with God, Salah is the nearest station to the realms beyond. Salah is one of the greatest means of this ascension—a means bordering on the purpose.

To rise on the Day of Judgment with a pure face, bright looks, signs of purifications on our body, and a conscience as clear as the dwellers of the heavens is dependent on our salah and on our preparations prior to it. Salah is another title for being close to God and carries profound meanings. It can also be referred to as "*ribat*," symbolizing a steadfast commitment to servanthood and a life spent in awe of God.

Ablution—while deserving a separate essay—is the first step and essential preparation for salah. Similarly, the *adhan* (call to prayer), which also merits separate attention, serves as a second reminder, fostering metaphysical alertness. Through the *adhan*, a person purified of bodily impurities and other unseen negativities begins to listen to their conscience and imagination. With the *nafila* (voluntary) salah, they seek to connect with the inner voice calling out to them. Finally, they prepare themselves to participate in the grand salah (the obligatory prayer), ideally performed in congregation.

Salah is a blessed act of worship, imbued with the depth of *mi'raj*, resembling a spiraling staircase that ascends ever higher. It allows a person to traverse the skies of infinity and reach the realm of angels. Like a river, salah immerses and purifies us five times a day. Each time we plunge into it, it cleanses us of our wrongs, carrying us toward the vast ocean of the Divine. This continuous cycle takes us on a journey between the beginning and the end, serving as an exercise in transcending our earthly dimensions and embracing the eternal.

With salah, our nights and days are subjected to a mysterious division. Our daily lives are designed based on a perception of time which has "worship" in its very center. This design cultivates an awareness of being under God's supervision, transforming all we do into worship. As a result, our mortal life on earth begins to reflect the colors and essence of the heavenly realm.

Time and space take on a new form as salah approaches, heralded by the *adhan* piercing through the clamor or stillness of the world. As the clock ticks forward and the sun continues its course, crowds gather around the mosque, preparing for the salah. The *muadhin* turns the loudspeakers on and clears his throat, igniting an excitement for eternity. Within hearts, quiet conversations begin, while some murmur in the confusion of those who have just woken up—others hear echoes of words from beyond our dimensions, as if we are in an intermediate realm between this world and the next.

Even before salah begins, the very thought of being on its path stirs countless emotions. People mumble invocations, seeking metaphysical dynamism and focus, striving to maintain the right mode with all their spiritual faculties, preparing themselves for the worship soon to be observed.

Everything done on the way to salah is part of the spiritual preparation: walking to the mosque, contemplating at each step, and performing ablution. The *adhan* is virtually an invitation to the special chamber; a heavenly voice that helps our concentration by resonating in the depths of our soul, like a plectrum striking the chords of our emotions. Although our ears are familiar to hearing it, and flat logic may tend to feel disregard for it, the *adhan* often surprises us, like the sudden appearance of the moon from behind distant hills that separate us from the realms beyond. It flashes like lightning and thunders like a storm, instantly turning our gaze from the earthly to the heavenly.

And then a new God-oriented phase begins; one that streams gently like fountains and floods magnificently like waterfalls. And as soon as it begins, it pours into our souls the most delightful, striking, and invigorating tune in the world. It doesn't stop there but draws us into a satin clime of reflections and connections, whispering into our hearts the charms of bright eras. It kindles our dreams, which are open to being time-transcendent, helping us rediscover what was lost at different turning points in history and returning them to us. Each time, it offers us a very fresh bouquet of sounds, poetry, and harmony.

We always feel the *adhan* with our entire being, as if bathing in music, and every time we hear it, we awaken to a new charm, taste, grace, and delight. This sensation often evokes in us a feeling of rising to the skies through a magical helix or soaring at great heights with a balloon. This is especially true when the *adhan* is rendered in proper fashion, with sincerity as the voice of the caller's conscience.

The moments when the *adhan* is called are truly blessed and emotive, filling the skies with its light, spreading the comforting spirit of the noble Prophet, and resonating through the heavens and the earth. When a person delves into the depths of their spirit and truly listens to their conscience, they will uncover hidden meanings flowing into their soul and feel profound connections boiling within!

With every *adhan*, those with awakened consciences, who continually renew themselves and remain vibrant in their hearts and spiritual lives, feel the sweetness and freshness of the era when the *adhan* was first revealed. In the voices rising from the minarets, they hear the call of the Prophets. Within their hearts, they join the angels' chorus of glorification and testimony, as if they can sense the life-giving breaths of Jibril and Israfil.

When the spiritual preparation and fulfillment outside salah is completed with the *adhan*, and before stepping into the vast immensities of closeness to God through the obligatory prayer, souls are once again embraced by the gentle breezes of Divine Mercy through the first *nafila* salah, followed by the *iqamah*. This step-by-step deepening of concentration allows for a final check of one's focus and self-possession, ensuring the readiness required to appear in the Divine presence. At this moment, the worshipper walks toward salah as if ascending on a *mi'raj*.

The sounds, words, and actions that have touched the heart and awakened the soul thus far act as a fine-tuning process, harmonizing the strings of the conscience to produce the true melodies of the heart. As for the highest note of this ensemble, it begins with the collective behaviors of the congregation, united in feelings and thought before the only sanctuary they all turn to. Standing obediently in Divine presence behind an imam, they express their reverence by bowing, show their obedience to God, and walk toward Him by prostrating, humbly bringing their heads to the same level as their feet. The extent to which we are aware of our collectivity determines how deeply we can experience the beauty and festivity reminiscent of the times of the Prophets during salah.

For those who have become unified with the harmony of salah in the heavens, every act and word behind the imam echoes humanity's homesick yearning for the lost Paradise, misted with feelings of hope and reunion. For almost all those who surrender themselves to the Ascension-like atmosphere of Salah, it is as though the hills of heavenly gardens come into view at dawn. To the extent of our emotional depth, every time we start observing salah, we sip and savor the purity and serenity of a band of light, stretching from the beauties of Paradise to the golden age of Muslims, and we rise with joy. This way, our minds, disoriented with many worldly concerns, are restored... our spirits are freed from the gloomy atmosphere of the mundane world, and the world of our hearts overflow once more with the joy of reunion.

While this may not happen during every prayer and observance of the *fard* for everyone, heroes of spirit and heart experience eternity several times a day. They frequently sieve both the past and future with their thoughts. And they deem the golden segments of time, which seem to have been left behind, along with the verdant green emerald hills of the future, misted with hopes. They simultaneously traverse their own lifespan and that of others, uncovering memories of boundless joy and bliss, like drinking from the *Kawthar*, the fountain of Paradise. They cover distances just as it happens in dreams, traveling through realms that transcend time. They revel in extraordinary delights, flowing seamlessly from one feeling to another and one thought to the next, living each moment in a fresh influx of Divine knowledge (*marifa*), love, and delight. These reflections are for those whose spiritual knowledge (*irfan*) has reached such profound horizons.

Once the spirit and heart enter the mode of salah, this brightened state takes over, establishing its own harmony, poetry, and heavenliness, replacing the routine of our usual deeds.

A few times a day, the mysterious and magical moves of salah nourish our thoughts and dreams, opening a vista to the realms beyond and giving voice to our hearts:

> *My place has become no-place*
>
> *This body of mine is now pure spirit;*
>
> *All manifest, God's gaze.*
>
> *By reunion, I am intoxicated.*
>
> Nesimi

Through worship, the eternal beauty hidden as a treasure in the heart is unearthed once more, revealing a source of blessings with depths beyond dimensions. For this reason, salah is not limited to its outwardly visible aspects; it evokes a storm of senses and a whirlpool of feelings that transcend quantity and quality. During salah, unspeakable truths envelop the horizons of our speech; while indescribable emotions whisper a strange melody to our soul. Profound sensations and thoughts beyond the scope of everyday language fill our being.

A transcendent intelligence or foresightedness (*fatanah*), bordering realms beyond the reach of human logic, opens doors to otherworldly contemplation in the footsteps of the Prophet. In this respect, we can say that for a servant, there is no greater form of worship than salah, nor is there a more profound or immense state than the imagination and insights it awakens within.

Through salah, the human soul perceives and feels what lies beyond the visible world and physical existence. It speaks of the longings, grief, and homesickness that many others feel when they pray. Salah conveys the contentment of the heart, the flourishing and comfort of human emotions, the eternal saga of existence, the stars' gaze upon the earth, the secrets of the skies, the lights of the next world, the slopes of Paradise, the swaying trees, and the ever-flowing rivers beneath them. Salah achieves this through its pillars, Qur'anic verses, and supplications. In doing so, the horizons of Salah reiterate these truths in a fresh style, allowing our souls to sip from the *Kawthar* of Paradise.

After completing the standing portion of the salah, these loyal devotees of worship bow down to *ruku'*, eager to express the excitements of their pure souls and upright thoughts once more. With an aura of awe, they bend like a branch, carrying the weight of grandeur and majesty on one side and mercy and grace on the other.

Bowing with a deep consciousness of servitude that permeates their entire being, they whisper of Divine Grandeur. Through this bowing—a gesture akin to the angelic mode of turning to God—they seek to open the door to the special chamber of the Divine (*Haziratu'l Quds*). To the extent that these doors are opened, they glimpse the profound depths of their own spiritual world.

Much like pilgrims chanting glorifications and testifying to faith as they journey through hills and plains during Hajj, worshippers move from one act of salah to another in a heavenly journey, infused with blessed feelings, thoughts, and phrases. With praises, thanks, and glorifications, expressed at almost every phase in order to express reverence for God in the best way, worshippers knock the door of the Divine Court. Then, with attention, vigilance, and caution, they wait to make the most of this sacred moment. Like a cat intently watching its prey or a spider patiently waiting in its web, they seek Divine gifts and manifestations with unwavering attention and patience.

The *ruku'* of salah brings its gentle breezes upon us, following the standing, and whispers to our souls of a dream more beautiful than this life, more delightful than material pleasures, and beyond the confines of this restricted mundane world—a dream that transcends our imagination. It promises our hearts emerald days, hours, and minutes beyond our expectations. After all, are we not, to some extent, the children of our hopes, ideals, and dreams? When roughed up by the adversities of today and awakened to the future, almost all of us transcend the present moment, gazing toward the future with the hope of the life and happiness we will attain; we behold the slopes of Paradise with smiles.

In the act of modestly bowing before the Divine, *ruku'* carries profound meaning for all those who perform it. At times they petition their Lord with words like أَنِّي مَسَّنِيَ الضُّرُّ "Truly, affliction has visited me..."

(al-Anbiya 21:83) and sometimes with اِنَّمَا اَشْكُوا بَثِّي وَحُزْنِي اِلَى اللّٰهِ "I only disclose my anguish and sorrow to God..." (Yusuf 12:86), letting us feel the outpouring from the river of life and the scent on a shirt from the land of Yusuf... Through such moments, they awaken within us the excitement of wonders yet to unfold and truths beyond our grasp, allowing us to rise with a surge of praise and glorification for God. With this, we offer our gratitude to Him in an additional session.

This brief act of standing differs from the first; it is a steppingstone on the path to God. In this radiant pause, we let the standing, recitation, and glorification of *ruku'* flow from the depths of our hearts. We try to sense the boundlessness of our feelings and the infinity of our dreams within this short moment. Gathering the full strength of our emotions, we seek out inspirational blessings. With the rays of hidden treasures we catch, we immerse ourselves in a waterfall of new feelings, imbued with the hue of nearness to God. It is difficult to fathom the pleasure and delight experienced by those who truly feel the salah in *ruku'*, how they are overcome with reverence, awakened with hope, and how they tremble with awe. This awareness is the first of the most serious steps toward reunion, with prostration as the second.

Prostration is a ground for offering gratitude for the blessings within Salah, a vessel of awe where melted hearts are poured into the proper form of servitude. It is the straight-line connecting supplications to God's acceptance, a haven of reunion, and a meeting place for the feelings cherished for God Himself. When we experience prostration in its true essence, we feel a quintessence distilled from *iman* (faith), *Islam* (submission), and *ihsan* (excellence) flowing into the emerald hills of our hearts, passing through the standing, bowing, and *qawma* (straightening) of salah.

In prostration, we humble ourselves by bringing our feet and head to the same level, becoming rounded like a bow and transforming into an imploring voice or sigh. In this state, we unify our faith with the vastness of our hopes—hopes that far surpass our deeds and encompass everything. We also embrace the precedence of Divine Mercy, which overrules all. By passing beneath this colorful belt, resembling a rainbow stretched between this world and the next, we strive to alter our fortune.

At the point where the sensations and feelings of prostration elevate a person, one can gaze from the peak of their fortune and behold reality. Through the tongue of the heart, by pouring out the words of one's deepest feelings, channeling the world toward the Afterlife, and allowing the realms beyond to reflect within, one can sense and experience a Divine bestowal—as if witnessing the epic of their servitude. When their supplications, stirred by a consciousness of servitude, meet and blend with the floods of Divine mercy and grace, the union of prayer and response creates a stream of feelings as beautiful as life in Paradise and as immense as reunion. For those who understand, the taste of these blessings is so exquisite and their essence so captivating that those who experience it even once are left unable to express adequate gratitude for these blessings to their Giver.

A hero of closeness to God, with their head humbly lowered to the ground, ascends the most insurmountable peaks through a staircase of light, deepening their closeness to God with a heavenly journey. With the feeling, consciousness, and rapture of having reached the holy chamber of the Divine, they offer reverence and veneration, adding new dimensions to their reunion. Respectfully, they rise back to a sitting position. In the proper manner of being in the Divine presence, they recite, "*at-tahiyyatu...*" and are overcome with ecstasy, as if no longer an earthly being. At this point, they attain a supernatural state, meaning, and charm.

The hero of salah, uplifted by these immense delights, sets about expressing gratitude to God for wealth, life, and all Divine bestowals. With an insatiable feeling, they deepen their gratitude into infinity through intention, transcending the bounds of quality and quantity. They remember God with full receptiveness of their heart, sighing with devotion. They recall the noble Prophet, finding solace, and think of others sharing the same happiness, resonating with prayers of goodness. The worshipper's journey of *mi'raj*, which began with *takbir*s, reaches its conclusion with the *shahadah*s, the essence of religion.

Those who are accustomed to observing salah and are nourished by it will never have enough of it. Let alone having enough of it, they yearn for more at the conclusion of each prayer, running from one voluntary prayer to the next; they rise like the sun with *duha*, touch the doorknob of closeness to God with *awwabin*, and, through *tahajjud*, send light to illuminate the darkness of the grave (*barzakh*). They try to weave their lives like delicate lacework with threads of worship, never wishing to be separated from the light in which they dwell or the meanings that envelop their souls. Always, they rush toward the bounties that worship promises.

***

This essay by M. Fethullah Gülen was originally published in Sızıntı *magazine, July 1994.*

Index

A

Abbad ibn Bishr 78
Abbasid state 80
abd al-jannah 177
*abdal*s 270
Abdullah ibn Umar 69, 95, 260
Abu Bakr, the Caliph 146, 228
Abu Dharr 5, 98
Abu Hanifa 80
Abu Hurairah 22, 134, 174, 228, 240, 249, 250
Abu Mahzura 146
Abu Musa al-Ashari 190
Abu Said al-Khudri 136
Abu Talib 68, 69, 87
Abu Ubayda al-Basri 80
Abu Uthman al-Nahdi 80
Adam, Prophet 4, 10, 11, 15, 16, 26, 83, 101, 103, 153, 154, 164, 197, 220, 223, 231, 240, 279
Adha, the Day of 231
adhan x, 27, 59, 67, 69, 72-74, 101, 143-146, 148, 149, 198, 200, 207, 214-216, 219, 226, 233-235, 242, 243, 283-285
adhkar 77
Afterlife 17, 44, 53, 61, 96, 105, 111, 120, 131, 199, 210, 290
Age of Bliss 7, 74, 80, 198, 199
ahadiyyah 87
Ahl al-Bayt 270
Ahmad al-Sirhindi. See Imam Rabbani

Ahmad ibn Hanbal 75, 179, 180
ahsan al-taqwim 162
Aisha 30, 33, 61, 97-100, 103, 203, 253, 254
ajz and *faqr* 220
ala al-makarih 132
a'la-i illiyyin 213
alam al-barzakh 64
alam al-mithal 64, 83, 104
Ali, the Caliph 68, 69, 78, 122, 208
Ali al-Qari 13, 94
alms 3
Al-Samarqandi 53
Alvarlı Efe 66. See also Muhammed Lutfi
amanah 103
Ammar ibn Yasir 78
Arafat 4, 16, 34
arkan x, xv, 59, 82, 103, 174, 175, 219
Arsh xiv, 20, 67, 72
Asad ibn Zurara 243, 244
asfal al-safilin 213
Ata ibn Rabah 79
awrad 77
awwabin 95, 148, 290

B

Badr 7
baqa billah 157
Baqi cemetery 134
barakah 72, 91
Barzakh 94, 160
batini 59

bayan 258
Bayt al-Atiq 154
Beautiful Names of God 159
Bediüzzaman. See Nursi
Bilal al-Habashi 99, 110, 143, 146, 191, 207, 236, 245
Bishr ibn al-Mufaddal 80
Blessed Months 23. See also Sacred Months
Blue Mosque 119
Bridge of Sirat 41, 70, 132, 141, 209
burhan 258

C

Celal Efendi 111
circumambulation. See *tawaf*

D

Destiny 2, 105
Dhat al-Riqa 78
dhikr 6, 50, 88, 89, 233
Dhul Yadain 229
Divine Names 13, 19, 39, 157, 163, 192, 207, 239
Doomsday 2
dua 77
duha 60, 95, 148, 251, 290

E

Era of Ignorance 12, 119. See also *Jahiliyya*

F

fana fillah 157
fard al-ayn 180
fard al-kifayah 180
Farewell Sermon 194, 195
fatanah 287
Fath-u Bab al-Inayah 94
fayd 72; *al-aqdas* 232, 257
fiqh xv, 35, 59, 71, 93, 128, 130, 161, 174, 175
Fitr, Day of 231
five pillars of Islam xiii, 2
fuqaha 161

G

Gabriel. See Jibril
ghaflah 88, 188
ghayb 207
ghusl 123, 139, 152, 242, 243

H

hadath x, 123, 140, 152
hadith qudsi 73, 88, 165, 216, 261
hafadha 125
hajah xii, 148, 256, 265, 268
Hajj 3, 4, 16, 30, 34, 44, 45, 56, 86, 89, 181, 194, 219, 245, 288. See also pilgrimage
hamd 163
Hanafi school 14, 93, 146, 174, 175
hanif 12
Harun Rashid 80
hashyat viii, 66
hawas 157
Haziratu'l Quds 288
Heraclius 11
hidden treasure 207, 253
himmah 271
hudhur al-qalb 209, 210
Hurays ibn Kabisa 249
hypocrites xvi, 30, 41, 49, 50, 57, 179, 193

I

ibadah 3
Ibn Abbas 153, 187, 189, 235
Ibn Hajar 244
Ibn Masud 98, 99, 236
Ibn Ummi Maktum 146
Ibrahim, Prophet 10, 11, 12, 14, 15,

21, 79, 83, 107, 154, 162, 200, 220, 260, 264, 270
Ibrahim Haqqi 107, 260, 264
Idris, Prophet 83
iftitah 82
ihram 34, 82
ihsan xiv, 2, 61, 91, 176, 272, 289
Ihya' 'Ulum al-Din 258
ijma 234
Imam Abu Yusuf 174
Imam Ahmad Ibn Hanbal 179
Imam A'mash 179
Imam Busiri 203
Imam Ghazali 117, 138, 258
Imam of Alvar 79. See also Muhammed Lutfi
Imam Rabbani 72, 156, 258. See also Ahmad al-Sirhindi
iman viii, 2, 17, 32, 104, 219, 272, 289
imkan 100, 172, 230
insan al-kamil xvi, 39
intercalation 194
irfan 258, 286
Isa, Prophet 16, 83, 113. See also Jesus
Ishaq, Prophet 10
ishtirak amal uhrawiyyah 181
Ismail, Prophet 10, 154
Israfil 200, 285
istibra 37, 136, 137
istikhara 148
istisqa 148, 266
i'tikaf 100, 136
itiqad 3

J

Jahiliyya 6. See also Era of Ignorance
Jalal (attribute of God) 47, 189
Jamal (attribute of God) 115, 189
Jamalullah 41

jazba 54, 72
Jesus, Prophet 4, 16, 83, 113, 220
Jibril xiv, 1, 2, 15, 129, 173, 189, 190, 224, 244, 250, 251, 259, 285; hadith xiv, 1
John the Baptist 83
Judgment Day xvi, 2, 22, 30, 31, 44, 83, 94, 105, 106, 132, 155, 162, 163, 165, 217, 221, 250, 283
Junayd al-Baghdadi 80, 160
juz 77

K

Ka'ba 29, 39, 56, 69, 70, 123, 153, 154, 155, 219
Ka'b ibn Malik 243
kalima tayyiba 86
kanz-i makhfi 207
karamat 48
Kawthar 131, 135, 286, 288
Khadijah 87
khilafah 46
khudu 175
khushu 25, 70, 71, 109, 175, 209
khusuf 148
khutbah 233, 234, 239, 241
Kırkıncı, Mehmet 111

L

lataif al-rabbaniyya 20
Laylat Al-Qadr 136, 222
Liwa ul-Hamd 145, 178, 198
lunar calendar 194

M

Ma'bud-u Mutlaq 114
makruh 79, 128
Mala' al-A'la 38, 53, 125
Maliki school 180
mandub 123

maqam al-mahmud 145, 203
ma'rifa 48
marifatullah 158
Mary, mother of Jesus 220
Masjid al-Aqsa 245
Masjid al-Haram 155, 245
Masjid al-Nabawi 245
Mawlana Abd al-Rahman Jami 159
Mecca 3, 7-10, 87, 134, 154, 155, 243, 244, 245
Medina 7, 8, 39, 111, 118, 121, 122, 207, 226, 236, 243-245, 249
middle prayer 187, 188
mihrab 108
minbar 233, 236, 241, 242, 246
mindfulness 2, 19, 63, 110
mi'raj xiv, 30-32, 43, 66, 68, 75, 76, 82, 83, 86, 87, 102, 103, 158, 159, 170, 172, 189, 193, 215, 218, 225, 231, 232, 245, 246, 283, 285, 290
miswak 129, 130, 241
Mount Sinai 220
muadhin 26, 27, 73, 143, 148, 191, 199, 207, 208, 233, 284
muamalat 3, 46
Muhajirun 241, 243
Muhammed Lutfi 48, 91, 159. See also Imam of Alvar
muhaqqiqin al-ulama 170
muhasabah 258
munafiqun xvi
Munkar and *Nakir* 201
muraqabah 258
Musa, the Prophet 16, 83, 190
Mus'ab ibn Umayr 243, 244
mushaf 123

N

nafs 17, 36, 62
najasah x, 140, 153
nasi' 194

nawafil 3, 32, 41, 73, 77, 80, 92, 249, 250
Nesimi 287
nifaq a'mali 30
Night of Qadr 136, 222
Nuh, the Prophet 10, 11, 15
Nursi, Bediüzzaman Said 17, 46, 47, 53, 54, 61, 81, 82, 89, 90, 117, 157, 158, 196, 218, 257-260, 264

P

penal code 3
pilgrimage 1, 194. See also Hajj
profession of faith 4

Q

qabd 176, 177
Qasida al-Burda 203
qawmah 66
qiblah x, 10, 154, 155, 219
qiyam xv, 78, 162
Quba 122, 244
qunut 14
Quraysh 7, 8, 87

R

Rabia al Adawiyya 141
Ramadan 1, 3, 33, 100, 119, 136, 233, 246
Rawda al-Tahira 245
Realm of Ideal Forms 104
Reckoning 30, 42, 44, 105, 163, 200, 210, 221, 270
Resurrection 30, 70, 105, 117, 134, 145, 198, 200, 210
ribat 132, 283
Righteous Predecessors 81, 116, 117, 131, 136
Risale-i Nur 117

riya viii, 49, 51, 52, 53, 54
riyadat 258
rububiyya 11
rukn xv
ruku xii, xiv, xv, 36, 40, 58, 59, 65, 66, 77, 80, 100, 165, 166, 168, 171, 174, 188, 197, 209, 211, 228, 273, 274, 288, 289
Rumi 117, 171

S

Saadi al-Sherazi 252
saat al-ijabah 246
sacred months 195. See also Blessed Months
Safwan ibn Umayya 7, 8, 9
Sahw 57, 97, 102, 183, 229
Sa'id ibn al-Musayyib 80, 179
Said ibn Jubayr 237
Said ibn Mansur 94
sakina 36
salaf al-salihin. See Righteous Predecessors
salat al-khawf 28, 112
salatu'l hifdh 268
salawat 172, 187, 270
Salim ibn Awf 244
Salman al-Farisi 236
Satan ix, 49, 51, 77, 89, 101, 102, 103, 131, 143, 163, 217, 218, 223, 224
satr al-awrah x, 153
sawm 3, 44
sayr fi'llah 19
sayr ila'llah 19
sayr min Allah 19
Shafa'at-i Uzma 104
shahadah viii, 3, 4, 9
shirk viii, 50, 51, 52, 53, 54, 277
Shu'ba bin al-Hajjaj 79
shukr 131, 163
Sidratul Muntaha 154
sirat al-mustaqim 13, 147
sirr 44, 97, 122
siwak 130
Sublime Throne 20, 67, 72, 132, 176
Subuhat al-Wajh 157
sujud xiv, xv, 137
Sulayman ibn Mihran 179
Süleyman Çelebi 159
Sultan Ahmed I 119
sum'a 49, 53
sunnah mu'akkadah 180
Sur 200

T

ta'abbudi 44, 45, 46, 47, 123
Taba al-Tabiun 79, 179
tabattal 21
ta'dil al-arkan x, 174
tafakkur 63, 84, 85, 258
tahajjud xi, xii, 33, 94, 95, 98, 107, 113, 148, 202, 253, 256, 257, 260, 264, 290
tahiyyat x, 60, 61, 86, 171-173, 211
tahiyyatu'l masjid 148
tahlil 162
tahmid 83, 84, 86
tahrim 82, 162
tajalli 63, 90, 151
takalluf 160
takbir x, 70, 80, 82-85, 90, 91, 143, 155, 157, 161-163, 174, 179, 188, 207, 219
taklif 160
Talha ibn Ubaydullah 3
tanzih 90, 189
tarawikh 148
tarteel 259, 260
tasbih 83, 84, 86, 148, 166, 188
tashahhud x, xii, 60, 171, 172, 220, 277
taslim 162
tawaf 123, 153-155

tawajjuh 93
tawbah ix, xv, 88-91, 222
tawhid 32, 47, 88, 189, 192, 224, 240, 251, 253, 256, 261, 272, 278
Tawus ibn Kaysan 80
tayammum 124, 139, 152
tayyibat 172
tilawah 123
Trench, the Battle of 68, 187

U

ubudiyyah 47
uluhiyya 11
Umar, the Caliph 1, 2, 7, 8, 12, 16, 28, 69, 78, 95, 146, 208, 241-243, 260
Umayr ibn Wahb 7-9, 244
ummah xiv, 81, 134, 135, 159, 190, 198, 206, 270
uqubat 3
uqulu ashara 13
Uthman, the Caliph 80, 146, 233

V

voluntary prayers 3, 32, 73, 77, 146, 250

W

Wahb ibn Munabbih 80
wahidiyyah 87
wajib 41, 59, 123, 146, 175, 180, 241, 253
Waraqa ibn Nawfal 12
waridat 26
wudu ix, 26, 27, 121, 123, 127, 128, 130, 132, 152, 242
wujub 100, 172, 230

Y

Yahya, the Prophet 83. See also John the Baptist
Ya'kub, the Prophet 10
yaqin 108
Year of Sorrow 87
Yunus Emre 125, 206
Yusuf, the Prophet 10, 11, 83, 159, 174, 289

Z

zahiri 59
zakat 1, 3, 30, 33, 35, 45, 86, 227, 230
zawal 240